IN SEARCH OF REALITY

IN SEARCH OF REALITY

VISCOUNT SAMUEL
(Herbert Louis Samuel)

Essay Index

Essay Index Reprint Series

BOOKS FOR LIBRARIES PRESS
FREEPORT, NEW YORK

INTERNATIONAL STANDARD BOOK NUMBER:
0-8369-2426-6

LIBRARY OF CONGRESS CATALOG CARD NUMBER:
76-128310

PRINTED IN THE UNITED STATES OF AMERICA
BY
NEW WORLD BOOK MANUFACTURING CO., INC.
HALLANDALE, FLORIDA 33009

CONTENTS

PREFACE

WE live in a civilization that is ill at ease. Old problems have become more urgent, new problems crowd upon us. In international affairs, social relations, family life, individual conduct, we find widespread confusion and often failure. Looking for the root causes, it is easy to see that this is due to doubts and uncertainties as to first principles. The discoveries of science have shaken faith in many of the doctrines of the ancient theologies. The discoveries have been wonderful, but science itself is unable to give any answers to the next range of questions that reveal themselves, as to the basic nature of the material universe. During the first half of the present century there was what was called 'the retreat from Reason'. Men were pursuing myths, fictional abstractions in philosophy, irrational intuitions in personal conduct. It is time for a return to realities.

Realism is not to be identified with materialism. The real universe includes matter; but it includes much else as well. It includes life; and it includes mind; Deity also. With mind, it includes human ideas, and institutions — ethics, politics and all the practical affairs of the world in which we live.

This book is a search for reality. It originated with a comparatively limited aim, to discuss some basic differences that had arisen in recent years between theoretical physics and philosophy. But having started without preconceived opinions — and 'whither the argument may blow, thither we go' — it has taken a much wider scope.

The book is addressed to the ordinary reader, and I have tried to avoid technicalities. But any specialist who might read it would be dissatisfied if no attempt were made to meet doubts and difficulties that would be sure to occur to him. Answers may be offered to some of these; but they often involve the use of language that may be unfamiliar to many readers. I have therefore relegated such matters to appendices, which the reader may omit, if he will, without losing the thread.

In the writing of the book, however, the help of the specialists has been indispensable. Several friends among the physicists, and others as well, have most kindly read the earlier drafts, either of the whole book or of particular chapters, and have made many valuable comments, and corrections. I would specially record my thanks to the late Sir Edmund Whittaker, and to Dr. Herbert Dingle, Dr. E. N. da C. Andrade, Dr. G. J. Whitrow, Sir John Cockcroft and Sir Russell Brain. Mr. C. B. Spurgin, teacher of Physics at the Edinburgh Academy, has scrutinized the earlier chapters in detail and made a number of useful suggestions. I am specially indebted to Sir Richard Livingstone, whose cogent criticisms, particularly of the final chapter in its earlier stages, have been most helpful. Mr. Maxwell Fry also has been good enough to advise on the later chapters. And, above all, I must again acknowledge, as in my previous book, *Essay in Physics*, the encouragement I had had from Albert Einstein's interest and constructive criticisms.

To all of these I am very grateful. They are not, of course, in any degree sponsors of the book, or of any parts of it, but without the prospect of such help the attempt could never have been undertaken.

December 1953–September 1956

IN SEARCH OF REALITY

CHAPTER I

INTRODUCTORY

I

THE history of mankind is to be studied epoch by epoch, nation by nation, but philosophy, science and religion must survey it as a whole. From as far back as we can reach to the present day, and all over the globe as it rolls round the sun, it is one story. Now and then a new discovery will bring home to us suddenly the unity of human history: perhaps manuscripts of the Bible that were themselves written in Biblical times; perhaps an early Egyptian tomb with all its royal furniture; or, far more remote, some fossil vestiges of ape-like man. As a searchlight turned first on to one point then on to another, they pierce into the darkness and bring the past vividly to our eyes.

A personal experience of such links is unforgettable. I had the opportunity about thirty years ago of visiting in Galilee a cave newly discovered, which, far back in the Stone Age, had been sealed by a fall of earth blocking the entrance. When the explorers had dug their way through they found that the cave had been a home of Neanderthal man. Probing about with a stick in the floor of fine soft sand I found here and there flint arrow-heads and knife-blades typical of the epoch, undisturbed. I have held in my hand a large fragment of a human skull found in another cave near by with a similar history. The authorities say that it is probably about fifty thousand years old, but perhaps a hundred thousand.

A few miles from there, on the northern shore of the Sea of Galilee, is the site of the town of Capernaum, which figures so largely in the Gospel story. The ruins of a Jewish synagogue of the second or early third century had long been lying there, half-sunk in the ground: much of the structure has been re-erected by French archaeologists. It is possible that some of the stones had been used before in an earlier building on the same site, and even that this had been the very synagogue at Capernaum, 'built by a friendly centurion', where Jesus so often preached.

That Stone-Age man whose cranium I held in my hand – he was himself the product of an evolution of millions of years. During those aeons of time his ancestors had shed their simian characters; they had become erect and large-brained, craftsmen and herdsmen. What thoughts had been active in that brain of his; what were his surroundings, ways of life – fifty, or maybe a hundred thousand years ago? Those crowds of Galileans, who, ages after, had thronged the synagogue by the lake not far away, who had stood near where I had stood and perhaps on those very pavements – what were their emotions as they listened, enthralled by the personality and exalted by the teachings of the great Preacher?

2

Now turn the searchlight on to our contemporary scene – New York, London, Paris. Look with a fresh eye at the aspect of our cities – their buildings, factories, railways underground, airplanes passing overhead. Consider the people as they hurry along the crowded streets – their purposes and habits, their institutions also. Great have been the changes during those long stretches of human history since the Stone Age, even during the two thousand years since the Greeks and Romans – changes that are greater and quicker now than ever before.

Generation after generation the fruits of experience and study have been garnered. Leaders of thought in the past have created and bequeathed to the peoples of today a noble heritage of knowledge; and the peoples, no longer illiterate and ignorant, profit by it. In the art of living together in communities much has been learnt. Over a large part of the globe many evils that had afflicted mankind through all the former ages have disappeared. Tribal warfare, slavery and serfdom have gone long ago and are forgotten as though they had never been. Famine and plague have been eliminated; ways have been found to prevent or to cure many diseases; pain is assuaged, life prolonged. The general standard of living has risen beyond all precedent, and comforts and amenities are within the reach of the ordinary man that in former times would have been beyond the dreams of princes.

Nevertheless, grave defects remain. Even in countries that are in the forefront, the faults of the present civilization are flagrant.

No one denies them: everyone deplores them. Although destitution and starvation have been ended, poverty persists. The community has accepted the duty of ensuring to all its members at least a minimum subsistence, but a large part of the populations remain at that minimum, or little above. Although the squalor that, in the nineteenth century, degraded the lives of millions has mostly been swept away by the sustained efforts of the twentieth, multitudes of homes remain — cramped, ill-kept and overcrowded, destructive of family life, breeding disease and premature death. Law and order are well established and people normally carry on their normal avocations in security; nevertheless most of the nations are still disgraced, in spite of all measures of prevention or cure, by the persistence of crime — ruthless murders, violent assaults, robbery and fraud.

And while all this is still prevailing among the more advanced countries, at least half of the world remains below, and often far below, their standards, faulty as they are. Over large parts of Asia and Africa, undernourishment is chronic, famine often not far away, preventable disease is rife, illiteracy widespread. In some regions, where population is now increasing more rapidly than ever before, the whole future is clouded by anxiety: to some it seems doubtful whether the production of food and materials can keep pace.

Even more formidable and more pressing are the international problems. Peace or war between states, partnership or conflict between races — these are the greatest issues of our time. The future histories of the first half of this century must be dominated by the two world wars. The militarist philosophies of Germany, Italy and Japan, and the upheavals that they caused; the first war; the failure of the League of Nations; the economic collapse of the 1930s; the new force of Communism, dynamic and explosive; the second war, and the dangerous strain between the Communist and the non-Communist countries that has followed it — all this has darkened our times with gloom.

It has been a great age of scientific discovery: but when an ancient dream came true and man achieved the conquest of the air, the first use he made of it was in war — destroying his own cities and slaughtering their inhabitants. And when the skill and persistence of the scientists had made the most wonderful discovery of all time, and the underlying structure of matter itself was revealed, the first use made of that too was the same. So we have, staring us in the face, this strange contrast between some of the noblest triumphs of the human spirit and some of the most sinister and terrible events that the annals of mankind have ever recorded—side by side, within the experience of a single generation.

3

Men's actions are governed by their ideas, but the ideas of our times are confused. The leaders of thought give us no clear guidance. Theology says one thing; science another; philosophy may accept neither; the ordinary man does not know what to believe. After our experiences, honest-minded men and women cannot help asking themselves — If God is Love, and God is omnipotent, why are there wars? If there is a providential order in the world, why do good and innocent men suffer evil?

4

A hundred years ago, after the establishment by Charles Darwin of the principle of Evolution, many thought, in the first flush of enthusiasm, that the answer to all such riddles lay there. In the end it is nature herself who distinguishes between true and false, good and evil, right and wrong. The survival of the fittest is the end and the struggle for existence is the means: these will guarantee the continuous ascent of man, the perfecting both of the individual and his societies. Before long, however, this was seen to be a delusion. The survival of the fittest does not mean the survival of the best, but merely of those individuals that are best fitted to survive in the environment that there is. The struggle for existence is far from ensuring automatic progress. On the contrary, evolution has extinguished as many species as it has developed. It is the same with human societies: empires decline and fall; civilizations dissolve and disappear.

Others have tried to find an explanation and a way of escape in what they term 'the historical process', or in the 'economic forces' that are the basis of Marxism. These, they say, determine 'inevitably' what is to happen. To ask for any reason or purpose is futile and childish. To discover these natural laws, these processes and forces, and then to conform to them, is the only intelligent course; and to persuade, or if need be to compel, all the peoples to pursue this aim is the only way to promote the welfare and the ultimate liberty of mankind, and is therefore the only true philanthropy.

But these laws, processes, forces are themselves no more than figments of the human imagination. They are myths. In the objective universe they do not exist. We cannot find there the guidance that we seek.

So in our age of doubt and bewilderment, 'like gnats above a stagnant pool on a summer evening, man dances up and down without the faintest notion why'.

CHAPTER II

REALITY

I

WE are accustomed to say, with Pope, that 'the proper study of mankind is man', but since his day science has taught us that we shall not get far unless we study also man's environment. Physically, we are what environment has made us. We should not have lungs if there were no atmosphere; we should not have eyes if there were no light, ears if no sound-waves in the air; we could not tread the earth if it were not for gravity holding us to the ground. So it was soon found that our proper study must include the globe that we inhabit and all it contains, together with the universe in which it is one among millions of millions of stars and planets.

Science became so varied and voluminous that it was bound to specialize. It is the principle of division of labour that has made possible the vast expansion of knowledge of the last two hundred years. This specialization is so necessary and has proved so fruitful, we have become so accustomed to it, that we are sometimes liable to forget that it is quite artificial and arbitrary. It is brought in for our own convenience: the universe knows nothing of these man-made compartments. We are turning now more and more to philosophy to help us find a way of escape from the confusions and doubts, the dangers and disasters of our times; and philosophy must stipulate from the outset that the cosmos has to be considered as a unity. Not only must the whole history of man, from the earliest Stone Age up to the present century, be regarded as the single process that it is, but also the entire universe — from the particle within the atom to the star, and from the house where you live to the farthest galaxy visible to the astronomer — all must be considered together, in their totality.

Let us set out then by taking as our proper study nothing less than the whole real universe, with man and his civilizations integrated within it.

2

But before we start we are obliged to consider a preliminary objection that will certainly be raised, and from more than one quarter. Unless we are able to meet it at the beginning, it will be brought up again and again and hinder us all the way.

The very terms in which our purpose has just been stated are themselves challenged. It will be said — 'You speak in an easy way of "the real universe" as the object of your inquiry, as though it could be taken for granted that there is any such thing. Will you please first describe what you mean by "reality"? And if you say that it consists of a given, objective universe, perceived by our senses and understood by our minds, will you explain what ground you have for supposing that this concept of our human intelligence — limited as that is and often wrong — can be accepted as a firm basis for a sound philosophy?'

Already at the dawn of history speculative thinkers in India had tried to peer beyond the veils of sense. They developed a mystic creed which treats the world, not indeed as non-existent, wholly illusory, but as *maya* — mere appearance. The doctrine has persisted all through the centuries with little fundamental change; it is still alive in India today. A recent exposition — in a publication of the Ramakrishna Institute of Culture of Calcutta — ends with this summary: 'So we are forced to the conclusion that the world as we see it has no absolute existence. It exists only in relation to the mind. We see it with our five senses, and if we had more senses it would be an entirely different world. It is, as Professor Frisch said, "a construction of our mind, designed to fit the network of actions and observations which constitute our life". But at the same time the world does exist, and we have to work in and through it. It is a mixture of existence and non-existence. It is *maya*.' Confused as much of this statement may seem, this at least is quite clear, that it is not compatible with the conception of reality held by western empirical thinkers.

Next in the philosophic succession came the Greek schools, and among them the Platonic. Reinvigorated by Bishop Berkeley in the eighteenth century and by the neo-Platonists of the nineteenth, it is still a strong influence in the world of today. It offers the alternative to empirical realism.

B

Now, in the twentieth century, the age of science, this Platonic idealism has received a powerful and unforeseen support from the latest developments of science itself. The revolution in physics, brought about by the discovery of the electronic structure of matter, has opened up many new problems. Among them are some, of fundamental importance, to which physics finds itself unable to give any answers; it holds, moreover, that its own methods of observation and experiment, from the very nature of the case, will never enable it to give answers. Physics here has found itself at a dead-end. To get round it, the school, which has for some years been dominant among theoretical physicists, left what had hitherto been recognized as the field of natural science and struck out into open country, into metaphysics. It now seeks to find a basis for our knowledge of the ultimate structure of matter in the pure abstractions of mathematics. For cosmology it has conceived various hypothetical systems of geometry — giving us a choice of the De Sitter universe, the Lemaître universe, the Einsteinian universe; it selects such features of these as seem likely to be useful, attaches algebraical symbols to them, and then, through those symbols, seeks to link up this world of artefacts with the known world of observation.

When dealing with the inaccessible region where science cannot directly explore the causes of phenomena — with the region of the infinitesimal — the new physics abandons altogether the search for causes. It offers, as a substitute, mathematical probabilities, so-called 'statistical laws', and, in the last resort, 'the laws of Chance.' Here we have, supplementing eastern mysticism and Platonic idealism, the third line of criticism of a realist philosophy.

3

To this controversy I ventured to contribute a short book with the title *Essay in Physics* — published in 1951 in England and in the following year in America. I mention it because it evoked from Dr. Einstein a valuable expression of his own views on the main point at issue. A thirty years' friendship had allowed me to send him a copy of the book in proof, in the hope that it might interest him and perhaps lead him to make some comment. He answered that it did interest him; particularly, he said, because it gave him 'a new illustration of the fact that the philosophic outlook has — under present circumstances — a strong influence on views on physics'. He added: 'To show you this I have tried to formulate, in as short as possible a way, an outline of my own opinions concerning reality and truth in comparison with yours.' A long letter followed, dealing entirely with the one issue of the nature of Reality. Since anything on these subjects from Einstein's pen is of universal interest, and since his letter set out very clearly the present point of divergence between mathematical physicists and realist philosophers, I asked permission to publish it as an addition to my little book, and that was readily granted. (It appeared there as an Appendix, in the original German and in a translation that had kindly been made for me by Dr. F. H. Heinemann.)

But this letter left me unconvinced. Any comment at the time could not fail to be lengthy; the book was in the press and waiting for publication; so it came out, with the letter but without any attempt at a reply. In the course of our correspondence, however, Einstein had said that he thought a talk would be much better, if it were possible, than discussion by letters; and as I had occasion to go to America in the spring of 1952 I gladly seized the opportunity to visit him at Princeton. We spent a long morning discussing the same single point, and from many angles. But we ended with the same disagreement.

Now, if this correspondence and conversation signify, as I believe they do, that there is a clear-cut divergence at the very outset between the main body of theoretical physicists on the one hand and a not unimportant school of philosophers on the other, then some effort ought to be made to resolve it. The situation cannot be left as it is. Where there are two contradictory views, both cannot be right: either one is right and the other wrong, or else both are wrong, and the truth lies in something different from either. But physics is fundamental among the sciences, and this issue is fundamental in physics. If it is left unsettled, there is no prospect of science and philosophy coming together in order to give to the intellectual world that single body of belief which our bewildered age must have if it is 'to learn what is true in order to do what is right'.

I therefore come back to the same issue here. I print again Einstein's letter as an Appendix to this book also. And I take what he said in it, and afterwards in our talk, as a starting-point for this discussion.

4

Einstein's position in its essentials is this: Our knowledge of the universe consists only of our own mental concepts. We ourselves are engaged 'in the construction of physical reality'; we choose for the purpose, out of our experience, whatever elements we find convenient and likely to bring success. Mathematics (including geometry) consists also of concepts of the human mind. Both sets of concepts furnish materials for philosophy and science, and they interact with one another. Furthermore, the only way from the one to the other – from mental concepts to reality – is likewise 'a way of conscious or unconscious intellectual construction, which proceeds completely free and arbitrarily'. It is clear that Einstein does not propose to raise mathematics to the same status of reality as the physical universe of our experience; but the effect of what he proposes would be to reduce that universe to a status of unreality like that of mathematics.

In the course of our conversation Einstein said – and with emphasis: 'We may *hope* that an objective universe exists; we may even *believe* that it exists; but we do not *know* it.'

He asked me to give my reasons for thinking otherwise. I gave them then in outline, and will now set them out more fully.

1. For hundreds of millions of years before man existed an objective universe, of some sort, undoubtedly existed. No scientist would seriously deny this. To do so would be to wipe out as worthless all the facts as to the prehistoric universe that have been so laboriously established by successive generations of astronomers, geologists and anthropologists. To deny that all this is *knowledge* – as distinct from hope or belief – would result in an intellectual nihilism: for no line can be drawn between such a denial and a complete logical scepticism. That, in turn, would challenge the possibility of any knowledge at all – any philosophy, any discussion, including this actual discussion in which we are now

engaged. For, as Dr. Inge has said: 'The logical sceptic has no mind left to doubt with.'

Existence is in no way conditional upon its being perceived by human beings. Existence comes first; perception may not come at all, or, if it does, it comes after. And what is prior cannot be a construct of what is subsequent. Further, the fact that many observers are similarly affected by the same object at the same time is proof that the object exists independently of any one of these: and if of each one, then of them all.

2. It is not the case that we have to depend only upon our own sense-data for knowledge that an objective universe exists. Animal experience proves it also; plant experience as well. The birds I see in my garden, busy with their own affairs in their own section of our common world, bring evidence that is just as valid as my own. About a million species of animal organisms have been identified and named, and about half as many of plants: more are constantly being discovered. The existence of any individual in any one of those species is valid confirmation of the real existence of a universe that is objective for all.

3. Lifeless nature confirms this conclusion. We cannot doubt that the firmament of stars, this globe with its land, air and water, the phenomena of light and heat, are all facts in themselves, and in no way constructs of human minds.

If evidence is needed that the sun and its radiations really exist, a group of cattle on a hot summer afternoon, moving across the field to lie in the cool shade under the trees, will give it. That lightning is real any death or fire caused by a violent thunder-storm is sufficient proof. That the sea is real is proved by the fact that fishes live in it and that we can sail over it.

Every scientific observation bears the same witness. An astrono-mer directs his telescope, with its photographic camera, towards a group of stars and exposes a plate; when he develops it he finds that the sensitive film has been chemically affected by the light rays that have come through the telescope, and shows a number of dots; these correspond in their arrangements with the pattern of the stars which, from his own previous observations and those of others, he knows are situated at that point in the sky. It is true that, as Eddington used to stress insistently, the mind of the astronomer is set in motion, not directly by the stars, but by his own interpretation of the marks on the photographic plate. The fact remains, and cannot be disputed, that there would have been no such marks to give rise to sense-data in his brain if the stars and their light had not factually existed. They preceded the sense-data and did not follow them; they could not therefore have been no more than constructs of the astronomer's mind.

Any number of such examples could be given to confirm the proposition that an objective universe exists, independent of man, real in its own right. We were born into that universe; we live in it, die in it, our fathers before us, our children after us. We are not to be persuaded that we do not know whether it exists or not.

5

This is our indispensable starting-point. But it is no more than that. Our argument so far has only sought to establish that there is given to us a real universe 'of some sort'. The question remains — of what sort? We pass from the objective to the subjective. We have to ask what is the relation between our human perceptions and this cosmos as it is in itself. Is it what it seems to be? This is the fundamental question that is offered as a challenge.

Critics of realism point to the long tale of errors in man's interpretation of what he sees or touches. How then, they ask, can we feel any confidence in whatever ideas about reality may happen to be current among conscious beings on this particular planet at this particular time?

Realists do not dispute that the situation is as so described. It is undoubtedly true that all the cosmologies which seemed to successive ages so plausible, and even convincing, are now discredited. The earth was flat, and the sun, moon and stars revolved round it every day. The firmament, although much bigger than the earth, was still comparable to it in scale. The sun was 'the greater light set to rule the day', and the moon 'the lesser light to rule the night'. The occasional eclipses of the one or the other were, as believed by some peoples, the work of a hostile demon or dragon trying to destroy them; or else, as others thought, portents sent by some god as a warning to mankind of disaster impending. Thunder and lightning were manifestations of divine anger;

drought or flood, earthquake or pestilence, the same; sickness and disease part of the hard destiny of man, against which resistance was vain and hope a delusion. The human race, the various kinds of animals and plants, were each the product of a specific act of creation at a definite moment of time. Material objects were what they appeared to be: a stone by its nature was solid, hard, heavy, cold, stone-coloured. When, already in ancient times, it was guessed that possibly all such things were composed of indivisible atoms, too small to be seen or felt, it was assumed that the atoms themselves had in miniature the same qualities as the objects. In general, the world was made visible by light, habitable by heat, beautiful by colour and variety, odorous by smell, audible by sound — and all for the service of man.

Then compare, say the critics, the universe as we see it today and observe how gross our constant errors have been. The earth is round, rotates on its axis and revolves round the sun; the moon is not a luminary at all, but a reflector; eclipses are regular and are caused by the moon passing in front of or behind the earth in line with the sun. The size of the universe is to be measured in light-years — the distance that light travels in a year at its velocity of over ten million miles a minute (the farthest galaxies visible in the great new telescope, at Mount Palomar in California, are calculated to be a thousand million light-years away). Turn from the immense to the infinitesimal: the stone is made of molecules, the molecules of atoms, the atoms of particles: the particle moves, in whatever way it does move, with frequencies of hundreds of millions of millions in a second. As to the creation of species, the world we perceive is Darwin's world, the product of aeons of evolution. As to pestilence and disease, it is mostly Pasteur's world of bacteria, fought by preventive and curative medicine. On our globe there are no colours — only light-waves of various wave-lengths, and eyes and brains able to distinguish between them; no sounds, but vibrations of air molecules, and ears able to detect them; no odours, but minute scent-particles, and organs able to perceive them; no heat, but again vibrations of atoms and molecules. No beauty is there, and no harmony, save what our own minds have been able to put in. The real universe — if there is one — is utterly cold, dark, silent.

This is the case presented by the idealist; and so far, the empirical philosopher, if he is at all acquainted with present-day science, will in substance agree with it. But he need not agree with the deductions that are commonly drawn. Because our senses are fallible and our minds limited, and the mistakes made in the prolonged effort to understand the cosmos have been many and gross, he will not accept that nothing is known, or even knowable, by us. He will not admit that it follows that the word 'real' has no meaning. He will not concur that all we can do is to compare one set of ideas that have sprung up in our minds with another set; and then, whenever we find them contradictory, change and adapt one or the other, or both, until they become consistent — and that anything beyond that is merely illusory.

Here, then, the realist parts company. He does not agree that, because many beliefs have been found to be false, no belief has been established as true. The world, as studied philosophically and scientifically in a modern university or described in a current encyclopaedia, is indeed very different from the world accepted by the cave-men, or even by the Greeks. But we need not be discouraged by that, or own ourselves defeated.

Everything being governed by the cosmic process of evolution, how was it possible for the acquisition of knowledge to be other than gradual? In the slow ascent from the jellyfish to the marmoset, from that to ape-like man, and from him to the man of today, at what point could all this panorama of knowledge have come suddenly into view? It had to begin in curiosity, followed by speculation: and the first speculations were as likely to be wrong as right. Viewed in the long perspective, we can see that the important thing has been, not that mistakes were made, but that so many were corrected. The speculations were put to the test of experience, of comparison with nature. When they proved to be wrong they were abandoned, and better ones sought for. But how could they have been tested and corrected, proved or disproved, kept or discarded, unless some standards had existed, extraneous and permanent, by which they could be judged? And where could those standards have been found except in a given universe — there all the time?

Because it was folly to think that each eclipse of the sun was fortuitous — a warning from a friendly god or an attack by a hostile demon — it does not follow that we need doubt that all solar eclipses are regular events, caused by the interception of sun-light by the moon in its normal courses, and lunar eclipses by interception by the earth. That this is knowledge – and not merely hope or belief – is made clear by the fact that every eclipse can be, and is being, foretold by mathematical calculation; and that when the day and hour arrive predicted by the calendar, infallibly the moon's shadow begins to sweep over the earth and we see the darkness creep across the sun; and similarly with eclipses of the moon.

To take another example. The belief was held universally for centuries that a disease, which afflicted millions of people and desolated whole provinces in tropical or sub-tropical countries, was due to the unhealthy air at night in swampy districts – to *mal' aria*. This was false, and in spite of remedies and palliatives the disease persisted. Then it was discovered that a brilliant guess was true: the disease was not caused by infected air but by a particular kind of mosquito, which carried in its blood a species of bacteria noxious to man, and could transmit the poison by its bite. Mosquitoes breed in water and fly by night, hence it was natural to attribute the disease to night air in marshy places. The new theory was proved true by the fact that wherever the marshes were drained, or pools sprayed with insecticide, the mosquitoes disappeared, and with them the malaria: where that was not done, it continued.

Every one of the sciences can give similar examples. Indeed they rank as sciences precisely because, by their methods of speculation, observation, experiment, inference and verification, aided by mathematics, they have succeeded in revealing facts of nature, such as the causes of eclipses or of insect-borne diseases. You ask – what is the meaning of truth, the meaning of reality? Here it is. The whole body of scientific achievement – massive, world-wide – brings confirmation. The mistakes of the past may indeed make us diffident about the present: we know that some theories of today may be disproved tomorrow. But if, as constantly happens, the disproof is the first step to the discovery of something better, then the fact of correction is by no means a reason for discouragement, still less for despair. Rather it is in itself a ground for reassurance, for a still firmer hope of fresh successes yet to be won. 'For Nature is the Truth', as Meredith says.

Bearing all this in mind, let us come back now to Dr. Einstein's contention. He says that: 'The most elementary concept in everyday thought, belonging to the sphere of the "real", is the concept of continually existing objects, like the table in my room. The table as such, however, is not given to me, but merely a complex of sensations is given to which I attribute the name and concept "table".' Many theoretical physicists would add, in support of that view, that we now know that our sense-data have completely misled us with regard to the reality of the table 'as such'. All that is really existing in that place at that time is a structure consisting of billions of atoms, each atom made up of its specific particles, the whole held together by binding forces.

But we are not obliged to choose which is real – the table as a piece of furniture made of wood, or the table as a structure of atoms, arranged and combined together in that shape. These two aspects are not mutually exclusive; they in no way contradict one another. On the contrary, they are only different descriptions of the same thing. Both are equally real. The solidity, weight, colour of the table are not figments of our own minds. They are facts, relatively to ourselves, and to the floor on which it stands, to the cups and saucers we place on it, to its environment in general. And why should that be any less significant as an element in the universe than the existence of the table as an atomic structure? A man, at one size-level, consists of many thousands of millions of protoplasmic cells, each with a life of its own. That does not prevent, at another size-level, his being also a unit as a man. The one is as real as the other.

Consider the window of the room. It is solid for the hand that presses against it; if the hand breaks the glass it may cut itself; it is solid for a bee that has blundered into the room and is struggling to get out, or for the rain and the wind beating outside: but it is not solid for the sunlight that passes through it almost as if it were not there. Or consider the walls – solid for anyone who comes against them, or for a nail that is being driven in; but not for broadcasting waves on their way from a distant station to a portable radio-set isolated in the room. The water of the sea is not any less real to the fishes and the ships because every drop of it is made up of molecules consisting of atoms of hydrogen and oxygen.

It is evident that the question is not one of reality and unreality at all. It is a question simply of size-scale. The universe is just as real at the size-level of our familiar experience as it is at the molecular level, or the atomic level, or the sub-atomic. It exists at all of them simultaneously and with equal authenticity. Nor can there be 'degrees of reality', as some writers have suggested. Something may or may not be real: we cannot conceive a state mixing the two. Degrees there may indeed be: but they will be in our own assurance as to the trustworthiness of our interpretations of nature — ranging from doubtful speculation to full conviction. To think otherwise would be to fall back once more into the confusion of subjective and objective, of perception and existence, between our ideas about nature and what nature is itself.

Before passing on, I would refer to one further argument advanced by the critics of realism. That what we take as certain fact may prove to be complete illusion might be illustrated, they say, by the very example that has been given of the astronomer and his photograph. We know that from time to time, though very rarely, stars explode and disappear. Possibly — we cannot tell — one of those stars shown in the photograph may have vanished a million years ago: if we could be now at that place among the stars we should find nothing there. Consequently the actual existence of every distant star is uncertain, photographs or no photographs.

To this it may be answered that all that has been made doubtful is the existence of any particular distant star *at the present time*. That each star shown in the photograph has existed at a previous time, even if not existing now, is definitely proved by the chemical action on the photographic plate of light-waves that had been emitted from that point. The fact that it has taken a long time for the light to arrive here and that the star itself may have vanished meanwhile, does not affect in the least the evidence we derive, from those light-waves among the rest, of the objective existence of a stellar universe. I may read in this morning's newspaper a report, through a reliable source, of an event that had happened in some remote and isolated place a month ago. The date when I get the news does not affect the fact that the event occurred. If, in the other case, the interval between the event happening (the emission of the light-waves), and the news being received (the astronomer's photograph), has been a million years, and if meantime a catastrophe may have wiped out the star — that does not show that the evidence of our senses is worthless and the visible universe unreal.

All these divergences between the realist and idealist schools arise from definite differences of opinion and must be argued out. One more remains — and of great importance. But this one may perhaps be found to be the result of misunderstanding, and that it is clarification that is needed.

The great forward movement in science in the last three centuries began with physics and chemistry — with the study of Things. The successes were so rapid and so striking that many among the scientists, and more among the laymen, jumped to the conclusion that we had only to proceed along the same lines to find the solution of all our problems. By the middle of the nineteenth century the trend in science was strongly materialist. It was in that atmosphere that books such as Haeckel's *The Riddle of the Universe* were written, influencing profoundly the younger generation. When attempts were being made to apply scientific principles to history and politics, Karl Marx based his theories on a dialectical materialism. It was taken almost as a matter of course that any philosophy that sought to be realist must also be materialist.

Then biology, physiology and psychology began to make headway. It soon became doubtful whether, after all, the basic problems of Life and Mind could ever be resolved through physics and chemistry. When before long the insufficiency of materialism was manifest, among the philosophers a sharp reaction set in towards idealism. It became, and has continued almost to the present time, the predominant creed. Meanwhile, realism was discredited. The intellectual world was inclined to say — whoever is a realist will find himself a materialist: materialism is wrong: therefore realism is wrong.

That situation still continues in some degree, and it is here that the misunderstanding arises. For there is a fallacy in that argument. It is not the case that realism necessarily involves materialism. On the contrary, in the countries where there is freedom of thought, few thinkers nowadays, whether philosophers or scientists, still adhere to the materialist theory that was the rising fashion in Marx's time, a century ago.

Materialism has been discarded: realism remains. But it would include within the content of the factual universe, not only things, but ideas also.

That they must be included ought not to be doubted. For ideas are certainly events or processes in human minds, and minds are just as much factual elements in the cosmos as anything else. We see man continually at work moulding in various ways his own material surroundings; those activities are directed by his ideas; thereby their own reality is made manifest. A lightning-conductor deflects flashes of lightning; hot-houses bring on plants before their season; a great hydro-electric dam may change the aspect, and the fortunes, of a whole province. A hundred examples will spring to mind where ideas lead men — who are parts of the real universe — to alter their material environment — which is also part of it. The ideas themselves, therefore, must belong to the real world as much as the men and the environment. And are not all the events of history— political, economic, cultural, religious — the product of ideas? No one can challenge their reality.

Let me offer an illustration — and illustrations as we go along may help to keep us in contact with daily experience and save us from being lost in abstractions.

Consider a fine sunset. The whole sky is a pageant of glorious colour — red and green, blue, purple and gold. People come out of their houses to see the sight; they are deeply moved by its beauty and grandeur. But physical science has told us that in fact there is no colour, and no beauty, out there in the sky. All that is happening over there is that light-radiations from the sun are being refracted by the water vapour and dust particles in the atmosphere, and split up into light-waves of various wave-lengths. And all that is happening here is that human eyes, watching the sky, have the capacity to differentiate between those wave-lengths, and to transmit to the brain impressions which the mind designates as colours. Waves of one set of wave-lengths are seen by us as violet; others, about twice as long, as red; the rest of the spectrum falling, in an invariable order, in between. Further, human minds are so constituted that such combinations of vivid colours on a vast scale, in the fading light of the evening sky, are able to inspire emotions of solemnity and awe.

In that situation — intermingling things and ideas — the materialist and the idealist is each inclined to lay stress on those elements that will support his own preconceived opinions. The materialist will say — nothing is happening that is not purely physical: first the light-waves and their refraction; afterwards the functioning of ocular mechanisms made of organic tissues, with consequent reflex activities in the brain; all else is fantasy. One person may be intensely moved; another will remain indifferent; they have therefore no objective reality; the colours, the beauty, the harmony are no more than auto-suggestions.

On the other hand, the idealist will say that the colour and the beauty are the essence of the situation; they alone give it significance. If they were not there, if they did not exist, no one would have taken the trouble to come out to look. You speak of nature's wave-lengths, but they have been transformed into our colours, and it is just that transformation which matters. You talk of the mechanics of the eye and the brain; but it is not the machinery that concerns us but the product; and the product is, for us, the sense of the sublime and the beautiful, the revelation of the harmony and majesty of the cosmos itself.

Some idealists go further. They declare that, so far from those qualities not really existing, it is they alone that are real. Take them away and the sunset will have lost its meaning. And if, in the case of material objects generally, in obedience to the scientists we deprive them of their qualities of solidity and weight, heat or coldness, roughness or smoothness, and all the rest, nothing would be left. Substance itself would disappear. Then indeed the real world would have been dissolved into illusion.

So we reach the theory of the reality of values, which not long ago commanded much support. One eminent thinker, Dr. Inge, wrote: 'The eternal and ultimate values of Goodness, Truth and Beauty are not inactive thoughts; they necessarily produce an eternal world — a sphere of spaceless and timeless existence — in which they live . . . This is the ultimately real world.' Elsewhere he writes: 'That the attributes of ultimate reality are values . . . seems to be generally accepted by the deepest modern thinkers. For example, Mr. Bradley writes, "Goodness, beauty and truth are all there is which in the end is real. Their reality, appearing amid chance and change, is beyond these, and is eternal". Many others might be quoted to the same effect.

But this view — the Platonic — finds much less acceptance now than it did in Bradley's day. The whole body of empirical thought stands in direct opposition. If it admits the reality of ideas, it is the ideas in human minds, or in other animal minds. The notion that there are some kind of mystical disembodied abstractions floating about the universe, with names attached to them, such as Truth, Beauty and Goodness, is a very different proposition and hard to believe.

Nor is it admitted that, if the various 'qualities', which we ourselves have invented and have chosen to attach to material objects — such as solidity, weight or colour — are taken away again, there will be 'nothing left'. To come back to the sunset, if colours and beauty are denied to the sky and assigned to the observers, there will still be left, extant in the universe, the sun and its radiation, the earth and its atmosphere, the clouds and the dust, the vibrations of various wave-lengths, together with the mechanism of human eyes and brains. These are not illusions.

Nor need realists agree that 'the cosmos in itself is utterly cold, dark and silent'. That would be true of a universe without sentient beings. But the real universe is not without sentient beings. We are here ourselves to prove it. 'Earth was not Earth before her sons appeared.' And since we have left far behind us the primitive notion of a central earth, uniquely created, and are fully aware of the existence of millions of millions of stellar bodies, in all stages, presumably, of evolutionary development, we may well conceive that vast numbers of these may be theatres of organic life, with many grades of mentality. If, in the little sample that we know, we have the habitable earth between an incandescent sun and a frigid moon, and if on that earth we see living organisms, with differing degrees of mental capacity, from an earthworm to Shakespeare, why should it not be the same elsewhere? If one is certain, others are possible. And if others, why not myriads of others?

Here maybe — and not in the physical substratum of particles and atoms, stars and galaxies and electromagnetic radiations — we may touch the inner significance of the whole.

We may now summarize the conclusions reached in this chapter, and can perhaps best do so by condensing them into a few short propositions.

1. We reject, on the one hand, a narrow materialism which does not admit as real anything that is outside the range of the physical sciences; and, on the other hand, we reject also a visionary idealism that would admit *only* abstractions — philosophic constructs of human minds.

2. There exists an objective given universe 'of some sort' — prior to man, independent of man, not a product of human senses or intelligence.

3. We perceive some parts of that universe through our senses, and we interpret it to ourselves by our intelligence. These perceptions and interpretations are such as the character of our bodies and minds makes possible.

4. Our search for knowledge begins in speculation and proceeds to hypothesis and theory. Our attempts are constantly unsuccessful. We know them to be wrong when they are found to be incompatible with features of the given universe already ascertained. As they are discarded and better theories take their place, a vast structure of scientific fact is built up. Even that is open to revision upon further discovery.

5. When we philosophize we are bound to treat ourselves as subject and the universe as object: we fall into constant confusion when we fail to do so. But we know that this is artificial and arbitrary and adopted for our own dialectical convenience. We know that human beings are not external and separate, but are integral elements in the given universe. Consequently human minds also belong to reality; and with them the ideas, which are events or processes in those minds. Mental constructs are likewise real *as such*.

In that sense idealism is to be accepted; not as a substitute for realism, but as part of it. And so we may arrive at a reconciliation of the two.

CHAPTER III

QUESTIONS UNANSWERED

I

WHAT has been said in the previous chapter may lead us now, in our search for the real universe, to make three differentiations: first, between the given cosmos and man's interpretations of it; second, between Things and Ideas — using those terms in their ordinary colloquial senses; and third, within the realm of things, between their different aspects at different size-levels. And let us begin with Things, because that is the easiest; so much more exploration having been done there than elsewhere, and with greater success.

In this book I am limiting myself generally to the matters which are in debate at the present time, and particularly between philosophers and physicists. These disagreements arise mainly in the vast new field opened up by the discovery of the electronic structure of the atom. It will be well, therefore, to start our inquiry into Things at the atomic size-level. Above that we have the level of our own terrestrial experience, long and elaborately investigated by the applied sciences, and raising few new questions from the side of philosophy. Above that again is the level of the stars and the galaxies, which is the sphere of the astronomer and the theoretical physicist — although with regard to certain recent developments, philosophy will have something to say. So we will begin with the atom, and go on from there down to the particle, and even beyond and below that if we can.

2

The conception of atoms as the constituents of matter — exceedingly small, almost infinite in number, invisible and, as was then thought, indivisible also — was familiar to the ancient world: to the Greeks, through Democritus in the great age of Athens, and to the Romans, through Lucretius, four hundred years later.

But it was not possible for it to be anything more than a speculation until the methods of modern chemistry enabled John Dalton
of Manchester, in the early years of the nineteenth century, to
establish its truth. Dalton, by 1835, had identified 12 elements:
fresh discovery gradually increased the number to 92 by about
the end of the century, and since then, by the addition of a series of
radioactive elements, to the present figure of 102.

Some metaphysical physicists, however, raise new doubts as
to the reality of the atom. Heisenberg writes, for instance:
'Modern atomic theory is essentially different from that of antiquity in that it no longer allows any reinterpretation or elaboration to make it fit into a naive materialistic concept of the universe.
For atoms are no longer material bodies in the proper sense of the
word, and we are probably justified in claiming that in this respect
modern theory embodies the principal and basic idea of atomic
theory in a purer form than did ancient theory . . . The experiences of present-day physics show us that atoms do not exist
as simple material objects.'

With this view the empirical philosopher will not concur. If
you ask for proof that the atom is a real entity in the physical
universe, and not merely a useful abstraction created by the
imagination of scientists, you may find it close at hand. For
instance, the rain, the rivers and the sea will provide it. Water
can be disintegrated by an electric current into something entirely
different – into the gases hydrogen and oxygen: and these, if
mixed together in the proportion of two to one and exploded,
can be integrated again to form drops of water. The weight of
the water and the weight of the gases will be found to be the
same. There is no possible explanation of this except to deduce
that there exist units of the two gases, which had first been combined into molecules constituting a liquid – water – then separated
again as gases, and finally recombined. If further proof is needed
you have only to consider the vast industrial enterprises all over
the world, employing hundreds of thousands of workers, which
are entirely engaged in various processes of applied chemistry –
including the production of new substances unknown in nature.
There are also the pharmaceutical laboratories manufacturing the
drugs that relieve or cure our diseases. These products are
realities. So must be the raw materials of those enterprises –

chemical molecules and the atoms of which they consist. If the atoms did not exist, those enterprises could not exist. And if yet another illustration is wanted to clinch the argument, the atom bombs which destroyed Hiroshima and Nagasaki will supply it.

M. Louis de Broglie, for many years one of the leaders in scientific advance, in a book recently published, gives many examples of the verification of the atomic theory by experiments, as well as its value theoretically. Summing up his argument he says: 'Thus the existence of atoms, postulated by the chemists, has been demonstrated by the physicists.'

3

When we come from the atom to the particle we find that doubts have been much more general among physicists. Many, perhaps the majority, hold the view that, in the present state of our knowledge, it is not possible to assert that particles are real entities in the universe, in the same sense that a stone and its molecules are real. This is mainly because, in certain laboratory experiments, streams of what undoubtedly are particles will produce phenomena which, equally without doubt, can only be produced by radiation waves. It is largely this impasse, from which there appears to be no escape, that has given rise to the school of mathematical physicists which, when we reach the sphere of the particle, abandons the mechanistic principles of Newton altogether, and with them the search for causes in nature. In place of physical causes it offers, as already mentioned, arithmetical probabilities, so-called 'statistical laws', and — in the last resort — 'the principle of molecular chaos' and the rule of Chance. We have even been asked to believe that, at bottom, the physical universe consists of 'waves of probability'.

Professor Herbert Dingle,[1] in a lecture not long ago to the Royal Institution, said this: 'The more we have learnt about the relations between our experiences, our observations, the less we have been able to say about the supposedly real entities whose actions we have been said to be observing . . . All we can say

---

[1] He has held, at London University, the first Chair to be established for the History and Philosophy of Science, and has lately been President of the Royal Astronomical Society.

about our foundation stones was summed up in a phrase by Eddington: "Something unknown is doing we don't know what." In another connection, Artemus Ward is reputed to have said: "The researches of many eminent scientific men have thrown so much darkness upon the subject, that if they continue their researches we shall soon know nothing." In the matter of the substance of "the real, material universe", this ultimate accomplishment has now been literally realized: we do, in fact, know precisely nothing at all.' This would be to confess, at least for the time being, to a dead-end in physics.

We would suggest that such surrender is uncalled for. It is legitimate only for those who reject the idea of physical reality altogether. But if we accept the material objects around us as factual entities in a given universe, at what point in our analysis do we pass from the real into the mathematical, theoretical, abstract? If the stone is real, then also the chemical molecules that compose it: if the molecules, then the atoms of which they consist; and if the atoms, then the particles that constitute them. The different characteristics and behaviour of the different chemical elements depend upon nothing else than differences in the number and kind and spatial arrangement of the particles in their various atoms. Or let us reverse our procedure: let us start with the particles. If we deny them reality, where do we suppose it to come in? — with the atom? with the molecule? It is certainly there when we reach the object — the stone, or whatever it may be. At what point in the series does reality enter — at what moment — by what physical process?

There are strong positive reasons also, based upon our direct experience, for holding that the particle is a real entity: and by that I mean a unit, with an internal cohesion that allows it to behave as a unit in relation to other similar units, and to its environment in general.

In the great establishments that the Governments of several countries have set up for research into atomic energy and its practical applications, the most elaborate precautions have to be taken to protect those who work there from bodily injury. The danger comes mainly from flying neutrons and electrons that may have escaped during one or other of the various processes. If there are streams of them and the exposure is prolonged, the effects would be harmful, and might even be fatal. The official publications that have been issued describing these establishments give full particulars of the dangers of radioactivity and of the strict precautions that are taken as a matter of daily routine. We are told that 'the general nature of these effects has been known for fifty years': there may be damage to the skin or to bones: 'more dangerous is irradiation of the lining of the lungs or of bone marrow'; radioactive particles that get established in the system may affect 'the cells that manufacture the red, and most of the white, blood corpuscles, with the result that the blood may be depleted of its corpuscles, resulting in anaemia and leukaemia . . . and in extreme cases a sarcoma or cancer of the bone may be formed'. Safety is only attained by constant vigilance, but (we are assured) when such vigilance is properly exercised the protection is complete. This protection is secured by measures to prevent contamination by the provision of rubber clothing, helmets of transparent plastic, the enforcement of various hygienic rules, and frequent clinical examinations. Further, all the effluents from the buildings, whether liquid from the drains or gaseous from the stacks, are controlled and frequently tested.

Having visited departments of the vast Atomic Research Establishment at Harwell, where one is required to take precautions against possible leakage of neutrons and electrons — protective overalls, caps and overshoes, the hands tested for contamination before leaving; and after seeing the walls screening the apparatus, built of concrete several feet thick faced with blocks of lead, I should need more arguments than have yet been forthcoming to convince me that sub-atomic particles have no real physical existence, but are merely useful mathematical expressions whose habitat is the differential equation. [1]

There is also the evidence of the Wilson cloud chamber, which for forty years has played such a large part in research in electronics. In this apparatus 'when an energetic atomic particle passes through air it leaves behind a trail of ionized molecules.

[1] See *Harwell: The British Atomic Energy Research Establishment, 1946-51*, chap. VII (H.M.S.O., 1952); *Britain's Atomic Factories*, chap. V (H.M.S.O., 1954). Also in American publications: 'Safeguards in Atomic Research: Control and Removal of Radioactive Contamination in Laboratories', *U.S. National Bureau of Standards, Handbook 48*, December 1951; *Assuring Public Safety in Continental Weapons Tests*, U.S. Atomic Energy Commission, January 1953.

If the air is moist, and is suddenly cooled by expanding it, tiny water drops condense on these ions. The row of water drops so formed can be photographed, so revealing the track of a single atomic particle. It can be seen colliding with atoms and thus the dynamics and transformation of single particles can be studied in detail'. Whoever has seen reproductions of these photographs in some textbook of physics will have no doubt as to the reality of the particles. Similar effects are obtained also by other kinds of apparatus.

The study of cosmic radiation brings further proof. The 'hard particles', as they are called, which form part of the streams that come from outer space continuously in countless millions, strike the earth's atmosphere with great velocity and force. They too are very penetrating; they can pass through sheets of iron several inches thick.

Physics tells us also that the electric currents that we are accustomed to use for all sorts of purposes in our homes or in industry consist of streams of particles. If we touch a live wire we feel a shock; a violent shock may kill. One man is electrocuted; another is shot dead by a bullet: the agent in the one case must be physically real as much as in the other.

In presence of these facts it can hardly be necessary to argue further whether a neutron or an electron is a physical fact and not a mathematical or metaphysical assumption. An abstract assumption could not cause anaemia or cancer of the bone. It would not need screens of solid lead, or of concrete several feet thick, to make it harmless. Nor could its track be photographed in a Wilson cloud chamber. Nor could streams of them be used for all the purposes of electrical engineering.

The intensive research of recent years has brought yet another problem. Rutherford established the existence within the atom of particles of two kinds – the proton, with a positive electric charge, and the electron with a negative charge. In more recent investigations at least ten or eleven kinds of particles have been discovered. Most, if not all, of these are unstable. The various types may endure for minutes or for millionths of a second or much less. It is thought that these appearances and disappearances may indicate a fundamental process in nature – the creation and destruction of matter. Physicists have also begun to speak of a Theory of Continuous Creation. It is evident that this opens up new vistas, with great possibilities, for both philosophy and science.

At once the questions arise — where does the new matter come from; where does it go to; of what does it consist? So far the proponents of the new theory have said that they come from nowhere.

Mr. Hoyle writes: 'From time to time people ask where the created material comes from. Well, it does not come from anywhere. Material simply appears — it is created. At one time the various atoms composing the material do not exist and at a later time they do. This may seem a very strange idea and I agree that it is, but in science it does not matter how strange an idea may seem so long as it works — that is to say, so long as the idea can be expressed in a precise form and so long as its consequences are found to be in agreement with observation. In any case, the whole idea of creation is queer.' Professor Bondi says: 'It should be clearly understood that the creation here discussed is the formation of matter not out of radiation but out of nothing.' The Astronomer Royal, while saying that 'The hypothesis of continuous creation is an attractive one and it may in time receive observational support', remarks with regard to it: 'Questions that are often asked are: What is the matter created out of, and what form does it take? It is created out of nothing; it must be supposed that there is literally a true creation going on as a continuous process.' Professor J. R. Oppenheimer, in the course of his Reith Lectures for the B.B.C., says: 'In the last years there have appeared in increasing variety objects heavier than the mesons, other objects heavier than the protons . . . Physicists call them vaguely, and rather helplessly, "the new particles". They are without exception unstable . . . We do not know why they have the mass and charge that they do; why they, and just they, exist; why they disintegrate as they do; why in most cases they last as long as they do, or anything much about them. They are the greatest puzzle in today's physics.'

So far as their origin is concerned, we cannot believe that either science or philosophy is likely to accept 'creation out of nothing' as a final answer. That would be to give up research for magic, science for the Arabian Nights.

The question of the Quantum remains. Is this too a discrete

'thing', having internal cohesion, like the particle, only much smaller? Or is it to be conceived as Planck indicated when he named his discovery 'the elementary quantum of action'? To this we will come back later in a different context.

4

We turn now to waves. The word 'wave' is our name for a form or pattern. It does not denote anything factual. It is no more an entity in the universe in its own right than is 'square' or 'circle'. It differs from these only in denoting a shape that is in motion, that is being transmitted from place to place. It has been well described as 'a moving configuration'.

Whenever there is a pattern there must be something that is being patterned. There could be no waves in the sea if there were no water; no sound-waves in the air if there were no atmosphere. It must be the same with electromagnetic waves – light, heat, radio and the rest. Having found means to measure the velocity of those wave movements, and their frequency (the number that pass a given point in a given time), we are tempted to think that, when velocity and frequency have been stated mathematically, the wave phenomenon itself has been expressed; that this it is which is travelling from one place to another place – say from the sun to the earth. But when we take the other examples of waves – of water or of air, it is clear at once that this is not so.

If we are crossing the Atlantic from east to west and see the great waves apparently rolling past us, we may have only too much reason to know that a very real process of some kind is going on in the sea. But no volume of water is actually leaving the shores of America and travelling towards Ireland. Some ocean current might do that, but not these waves. What the waves are doing may become visible and clear when we arrive off New York, the ship stops, and the pilot's boat comes out. If the rough weather continues, we may watch from the deck of the big ship the tender being lifted up on the crest of each wave and then dropping down into the trough, until the pilot is able to take advantage of a good moment and can swing on to the rope ladder that hangs ready for him. Obviously the motion of each wave is not horizontal, from west to east; it is vertical, up and down: the bulk of water remains there, where it is. The same with sound: a violin played in a concert-hall sets going trains of waves in the air, which travel across and reach the ears of the audience. But the air itself is not like a draught or wind, travelling across. What is happening is that the atoms or molecules of the air at any particular spot swing to and fro, perhaps a thousandth of an inch or less, through alternate compression and rarefaction, the volume of air remaining where it is. And there is no reason to doubt that the process is similar with light-waves, between the sun and the earth, or between a lamp on my table and the book in my hand.

So with all wave radiation. The waves are a pattern: there must be something else that is being patterned; something that conveys a sequence of oscillating movements, that transmits but does not itself travel. What is it that is continuously passing onward those 'moving configurations' — across the room or across the universe?

Physics does not tell us.

5

The question arises whether gravitation also may be part of the general electromagnetic system. Already a hundred years ago Faraday had foreseen that this might be so. In a lecture with the title 'On the Possible Relation of Gravity to Electricity', he described his experiments to find a relation; they had all failed; nevertheless, he said, 'they do not shake my strange feeling of the existence of a relation'. In 1923, Eddington discussed, from the mathematical standpoint, 'electromagnetic gravitational waves' and 'the electromagnetic mode of propagation of gravitational influence'. Since then the study of Relativity Theory has brought fresh support to this view. In particular it indicates that gravitation is a time-process, and not instantaneous as Newton thought. Sir Edmund Whittaker is now able to tell us that 'The problem was finally solved by the discovery of the gravitational waves of the general theory of relativity; the most recent work on the subject makes it clear that the speed of propagation of gravitation is the same as that of light'.

It has long been established that both radiation and gravitation
are subject to the inverse-square-law — the force diminishes in
proportion to the square of the distance of the object at any
moment from the centre of emission or of attraction. To this is
now added that both are wave-processes, and that the velocity in
both cases is the same. All these similarities — the wave pattern, the
time-process, the velocity, the inverse-square-law — might seem
to point to a conclusion that gravitation is of the same order as the
other kinds of cosmic radiation, that are now included in the
Clerk Maxwell wave-band. Physicists, however, give technical
reasons why such a theory should not be accepted, and this is a
matter on which the layman can offer no opinion. But however
that may be, and whatever will be the ultimate verdict on this
particular point, the same problem as before recurs — since every
kind of wave is a pattern in something else, what is that something
in the case of gravity; what is the vehicle that conveys this moving
configuration also? So in the main we are still where we were
with regard to gravity.

With regard also to gravity Newton wrote, 'for the cause of
gravity is what I do not pretend to know'. Whittaker says:
'Although gravity was the first of the forces of nature to be
brought within the domain of exact science and represented by
a mathematical formula, and although a prodigious amount of
highly successful work has been done in the development of the
theory, yet the fundamental physical problems connected with
it are almost as perplexing today as they have ever been.'

6

The last in my list of questions that the empirical philosopher
would wish to put to the theoretical physicist is one which is
seldom raised in this connection. And this not because it is remote,
technical and obscure. On the contrary, nothing is more familiar
or, it would seem, more simple. Indeed it is probably because
the matter appears obvious that few realize that in it lies a mystery.
It is the problem of Impetus.

A boy, walking across the fields, comes to a ditch, say four or
five feet wide and full of water, and has to jump it. He knows
intuitively that if he were to stand at the edge and try to jump

he would tumble into the water. He walks back ten or a dozen paces, turns round, runs as fast as he can, leaps into the air, and the moment after finds himself on the other side. Everyone would say, there is no mystery about that: the boy by running gets an impetus which carries him over the ditch. Quite so: but what was the physical process that was going on between the moment when his body rose into the air and the moment when it landed on the other side? What was actually happening during those instants, at that place, to bring about the result that we see?

Every ball-game is an exercise in impetus. A ball of some kind — soft or hard, large or small — is thrown or kicked or struck, and given an impetus. The player succeeds if the impetus is in the right direction and of the right strength: if not, he fails. In every case the ball is first impelled by some muscular effort; then it is left to itself and goes on 'by its own momentum', as we say. But why does it go on?

If I hold a ball in my outstretched hand and open my fingers and release it, instantly it drops straight to the ground under the influence of the earth's gravity. But if I draw back my arm, make a throwing movement and then release it, the ball does not do that. My hand has ceased to impel it: nevertheless it travels away from me in an almost straight line, until it is either stopped by some obstacle or is brought to the ground by gravity.

A big gun on a battleship may fire a shell weighing perhaps a ton: after it has left behind the expanding gases that had projected it, the shell may continue in its trajectory for several miles over the sea, finally crashing with great violence into its target. It is a legitimate question to ask the physicist — what is the agency that keeps this ton of steel from dropping straight down into the sea a few seconds after it has left the muzzle of the gun? What is it that sustains it, carries it forward all that distance, and finally hurls it against an enemy battleship with force enough to go clean through its heavy armour?

The physicist will reply that all such questions were answered once and for all by Newton in his First Law of Motion. That is: 'Every body continues in a state of rest, or of uniform motion in a straight line, unless it is compelled to change its state by forces impressed upon it.' No one would challenge the truth of that statement. But it does not answer the question. Nor does it purport to do so. Newton offered it as nothing more than an account of what is happening, not as the reason why it happens. The word 'law' does not of course mean in science anything that compels — like a law regulating road traffic or imposing conscription. Laws of Evolution, Gravity, Motion, are no more than our names for natural processes that have been found to produce certain kinds of phenomena. We are now putting the question why an object, once started in motion along a straight line, should continue along it when left to itself. Newton's Law merely repeats our own question back to us. It tells us what the object in fact does — which is precisely what we were inquiring about; but as to an answer, it leaves us where we were.

Let me observe incidentally that this does not justify Newton being cited as though he had thought it useless to inquire into causes. His remark, 'Hypotheses non fingo', is often quoted to that effect. This, however, was clearly an expression of his personal choice; he preferred to devote himself to empirical research and mathematical analysis rather than to the framing of hypotheses. He did not intend this as a limitation upon scientific inquiry where causes could be directly inferred from phenomena and were not proposed as *a priori* general principles. The same paragraph, in the *Opticks*, includes these words: 'To derive two or three general Principles of Motion from Phaenomena, and afterwards to tell us how the Properties and Actions of all corporeal things follow from those manifest Principles, would be a very great step in Philosophy though the Causes of those Principles were not yet discover'd: And therefore I scruple not to propose the Principles of Motion above-mention'd, they being of very general Extent, and leave their Causes to be found out.'

The present-day physicist, however, does not take up the task that Newton left to him. He accepts the principle of Relativity, and he interprets that as exempting him from any such obligation.

When I was writing the previous book in which some of the same points were discussed as in this chapter, I submitted the draft to several scientists who had kindly agreed to go through it and to give me the benefit of their comments. One of the most eminent among them wrote me a letter, a passage from which I afterwards quoted in that book. Others have since endorsed it as expressing the opinion now predominant among physicists; so I reproduce it again here as a statement of the case that I am venturing to question.

He wrote: 'I think my fundamental estrangement from your general approach, which would probably be shared by most physicists, is that I do not feel your need to find a picturable *cause* for phenomena. What I want, and what physics gives, is a *description* which shows them as related but not as effects of hypothetical causes. For one thing, how can you decide what needs a cause and what would happen without one? If a bullet goes on moving, is a cause necessary to keep it going or would a cause be necessary to stop it? I do not see how one can decide except by seeing which assumption is more effective in establishing relations between phenomena. The ancients thought that in the absence of a cause it would be at rest and that a cause was necessary to keep it moving. Newton thought that in the absence of a cause it would go on moving with uniform velocity and that a cause was necessary to change its velocity. Einstein thinks that in the absence of a cause it will move with uniform acceleration and that a cause is necessary to change its acceleration. And so on. We choose the assumption which subsequently provides the best account of the relations between phenomena. Consequently I do not feel the need of an ether to explain things which I am willing to accept as data to be ordered into a rational system.' (The last words relate to the original context of the letter.)

Now I venture to suggest with much respect that there is a fallacy in this argument. It treats 'Motion' as if it were a single and simple process. But it can be caused in four different ways: one makes an object start moving; another keeps it moving; a third makes it go faster; a fourth stops it. We have a choice, it is said, which we regard as *the* cause of the motion; therefore all four can be nothing better than assumptions; and we are free to 'choose the assumption which subsequently provides the best account of the relations between phenomena'. So in the end we cannot establish any 'causes' at all, and all we can do is to accept the data as we find them and leave it at that.

But we are not in fact considering 'Motion' as a single process. In the case proposed we should be considering several events, differing from one another and successive in time: (1) the initiation of the movement of an object, (2) its continuance, (3) its acceleration, and (4) its stopping. It is difficult to find a good illustration, for it is rare to have a case in which a passive object is accelerated while it is in flight. But let us take a football match that is being played on a windy day. At a particular moment the ball is being impelled by the foot of one of the players – that is the first situation; at the next moment it is moving through the air by its own impetus; then, we may suppose, a gust of wind accelerates it; lastly it passes between the goal-posts and is stopped by the net. The situation then, taken as a whole, is not one event, but consists of a series of events. Each of these is the outcome of a combination of prior events, each differing slightly from the others. The first includes the player's kick that starts the ball flying; the second includes the impetus which carries it along through the air; the third adds the gust of wind that accelerates it; and the fourth brings in the net that stops it. Our problem lies in the second of these stages, continuing into the third. We know about the kick, the wind and the net; but we know nothing at all about the physical process in the factual universe that we name the 'impetus'. There lies the mystery. Neither Aristotle, nor Newton, nor Einstein has solved it for us.

The mathematical physicist has one other argument. The whole discussion, he says, is misconceived. Relativity Theory asserts – and no one now disputes it – that there is no such thing as 'absolute motion'. A theoretical observer, with his own frame of reference, isolated in empty space, could never tell whether he was at rest, or was travelling up or down or sideways, in a straight line or in a circle. Therefore it is idle to ask what is the cause of motion as such, for it does not exist. No answer being possible, the question itself is futile and should not be asked.

To this we would offer the following reply. We do not dispute that there is no such thing as absolute motion: Relativity Theory has rendered a great service in establishing this: it has put an end to much empty philosophizing. But we are not concerned now with a non-existent observer in an impossible isolation in a fictional space. He may be a useful, and indeed a necessary personage for the purposes of mathematical calculations. But we are concerned, in the present discussion, not with absolute, but with relative motion – relative to an actual environment, under the conditions of our terrestrial experience. We are concerned with a boy in mid-air over a ditch full of water; with a football that has just been kicked; with a shell in transit over miles of sea. And we ask what is actually happening during the time when the object has ceased to be propelled until the time when it ceases to move. And we persist in asking — what do you mean by the words 'impetus', or 'momentum'? If something — what is it? If nothing, then you are falling back into the sterile scholasticism of the Middle Ages.

In this chapter I have brought together a number of questions to which present-day physics gives no answers.

1. It is found that, in certain laboratory experiments, streams of particles produce effects which can only be due to wave-action, and wave-sequences produce effects which can only be due to particles. How are these contradictions to be resolved?

2. New particles appear and disappear. Where do they come from, and where do they go to?

3. We make constant use of wave-sequences — for light, heat, radio and other purposes. These waves are not entities but patterns. Of what are they patterns? How are they transmitted from one place to another place?

4. What is the nature of gravitation? By what is that too conveyed?

5. We speak of impetus — what actual process in the physical world does that word denote?

In this fundamental department of knowledge here now stands the frontier between the known and the unknown. Along that line the advancing armies of science are halted.

CHAPTER IV

A PROPOSITION

I

IN this chapter I submit a proposition, and in the next chapter a speculation.

The proposition is: That there must exist, as a fundamental element in the real universe — underlying all its phenomena but itself imperceptible and as yet unrecognized — a Continuum, universal and perpetual. This is the medium that conveys all radiations, including gravity. It may also be the seat of all motive force.

The speculation will be as to the nature and the functioning of this prime factor.

2

The proposition is offered as a necessary inference from our own direct experience.

In the discussion on reality I cited the most familiar experience of all — the emission of light and heat from the sun and its effect upon the earth. It cannot be doubted that this involves some continuous physical process between sun and earth. When a cloud comes across the face of the sun the light that we perceive is dimmed and the warmth diminished: if a sunshade is opened, the same happens. We are bound to conclude that a process of transmission had previously been going on which has been interrupted at the level of the cloud, or of the sunshade, and which we shall find going on again the moment the interference is over. What the process actually is may be a matter of doubt, and perhaps of controversy: but that there *is* a process of some kind cannot be denied.

I take a second example from a comparatively new, but now very common, experience, from broadcasting. Looking at the day's programmes I find that an opera is being broadcast at this hour from Milan: I turn on the radio-set in my room, tune in to the Milan wave-length, and at once I hear the music of *La Bohème*. Is it not certain that something is happening between Milan and London that makes that possible? I know also that broadcasting must involve some physical process because programmes may be interrupted during their transmission by 'atmospherics', or by interference from other stations on neighbouring wave-lengths; that reception is often better during the hours of darkness than in daylight; and that beams of radiation directed diagonally towards the ionized strata in the stratosphere may be reflected from there and be received in a distant region. Radio engineers are dealing with these conditions every day. If there were a jump between Milan and London or wherever it may be, across a void in which nothing happened, none of these things would be possible.

I would add another consideration, of a more scientific kind. Radiation is undoubtedly a time-process. If there were a jump across a void in which nothing happened, it would necessarily be instantaneous. But we know that light takes time to travel, and we know what its velocity is. The light of the sun will take about eight minutes to reach the earth; the light from some star may have taken perhaps a hundred years. We are compelled to deduce from this that we are not dealing with a void in which nothing happens, but with a process, a succession of physical events. We believe it to be a sequence of some kind of waves oscillating from crest to trough and back again, each wave an event in time. Its duration is far too small to be perceptible, but it can be measured in the total — as eight minutes, or a hundred years, or maybe a hundred million.

Newton wrote about the conception of 'action at a distance' — 'that one body may act upon another at a distance, through a vacuum, without the mediation of anything else by and through which their action may be conveyed from one to another, is to me so great an absurdity that I believe no man, who has in philosophical matters a competent faculty of thinking, can ever fall into it'. And Einstein says: 'As a result of the more careful study of electromagnetic phenomena, we have come [in modern physics] to regard action at a distance as a process impossible without the intervention of some intermediary medium.' He has written also:

'Physics has to represent a reality in space and time without phantom actions over distances.'

If gravitation is something that is transmitted over cosmic distances, then the same question as to the medium of transmission will apply to gravity also.

The problem of impetus remains. May it be that, if the continuum gives an answer to the other problems, it may furnish the clue to this one as well?

The Greeks recognized the necessity for such a conception, and gave to this invisible element the name of Ether. Newton accepted it; he wrote: 'Is not this medium exceedingly more rare and subtile than the air, and exceedingly more elastick and active? And doth it not readily pervade all bodies? And is it not (by its elastick force) expanded through all the Heavens?' The physicists of the nineteenth century accepted it also; though they were inclined to regard it as 'an elastic solid'. That is to say they supposed every part to be contiguous with the neighbouring parts, but possessing an inner power of expansion and contraction that would permit motion and other phenomena. Science in the twentieth century, however, has discarded the ether altogether.

In my *Essay in Physics* I gave a short summary of the reasons for this, and I need not repeat it here, for the point is not contested. A series of insurmountable difficulties, culminating in the negative result of the critical experiment of Michelson and Morley, led to the conclusion that the existence of any medium such as had hitherto been contemplated, whether quasi-gaseous or an elastic solid, could not be maintained. I do not know that any scientist or any philosopher today would wish to challenge that conclusion.

3

In this situation, the physicists of the twentieth century have sought to replace the ether of the nineteenth by the concepts of Einstein's theory of relativity. The continuum that we seek is to be found in the Space that occupies the whole universe. If we fit to this Space the right geometry; if we assume it to possess characteristics analogous to 'curves and grooves, hills and declensions'; if we use it for purposes of measurement, and thereby confer upon it 'metrical properties' – then we can devise mathematical equations that will symbolize all the phenomena of the factual universe. Equipped with these, we can come back to reality with fresh ideas, leading to fresh discoveries. Certain problems in astrophysics, which the principles of Newton had not been able to solve, were indeed straightway solved by applying the principles of Einstein. The process has been justified by its success. It works: therefore it is sound.

Now it is evident that the whole of this structure depends upon the validity of its conception of Space. Does that word denote any real element in the universe? Can Space play any part at all in physical events? The empirical philosopher is bound to answer those questions in the negative. The real universe knows nothing of Space. And nothing of Time either. The same must follow of their combination as Spacetime.

We are so accustomed to the words 'space' and 'time', they are so essential to ordinary speech, that it comes as a shock to be asked to believe that, as generalizations, they are illusory. We know well what is meant by particular spaces — a room has a cubic space of so many cubic feet; the table and chairs occupy a floor space of so much. And we know what is meant by a particular time — so many hours of time will be needed for a journey; the average length of time in a day differs by so much between summer and winter. We then take it for granted that those spaces are part of a universal abstract Space, those times of a universal abstract Time. We accept as a matter of course that all events take place *in* space and *in* time; we speak now of 'the spacetime system of nature'; and we start our philosophizing from there.

But that little preposition 'in', which looks so commonplace and innocent, when we examine it may be found to be a question-begging little word, deceptive and dangerous. Talking of events happening *in* space and time implies that there must be such things for them to happen *in*. They cannot happen *in* nothing; it follows that Space and Time are something. But that conclusion will not be valid if the original assertion about — 'happening in' — was merely a linguistic phrase and not an established fact.

As Jeans has said: 'Space is a creation of our own minds, and we can make it what we like.' Space and Time are not among the phenomena of nature. No one can observe them; no one can experiment with them; nothing factual can ever emerge from them. They cannot transmit light and heat from a real sun to a real earth; or convey to London a programme broadcast from Milan; or carry a shell, weighing a ton, for miles over the sea.

The system of nature consists of objects or of events that are separated from one another in two ways. They are arranged one here and one there: we say that they are related in extension, or spatially. And they are arranged one then and one now: we say that they are related by succession, or temporally. Afterwards we proceed to measure those relations by means of yardsticks and clocks, and to state the results in mathematical terms. All these are mental devices — of great value, necessary, but of our own making. When, however, we pass from the particular to the general, from the actual to the abstract, we leave reality behind. Reality remains with the objects or the events, and with their physical effects one upon another.

An immense intellectual effort has been proceeding for centuries in order to discover what this Space and Time are and to describe what they do. Poets of genius have drawn inspiration from them. Philosophers have elaborated and magnified them till the discussions fill whole libraries of books. Scientists have tried to track them to the bounds of the universe and to the beginnings of its history. But if you cannot find them in the first inch and the first hour you will not find them anywhere. All these efforts have proved futile. And the reason is simple. The subjects of your whole inquiry — this Space, this Time — do not exist. They are figments.

For our present discussion the conclusion must be that not there can we find the primary continuum that we are seeking.

4

The existing situation in theoretical physics is unstable. For a long time past some of its principal exponents have been uneasy. It is even being said that it may be necessary to reconsider the question of an ether — if only some new conception could be put forward which would be free from the objections that had been fatal to the earlier proposals.

Einstein himself wrote, in a paper entitled *Relativity and the Ether*, published in 1935:

We may sum up as follows: According to the general theory of relativity space is endowed with physical qualities; in this sense, therefore, an ether exists. Space without an ether is inconceivable. For in such a space there would not only be no propagation of light, but no possibility of the existence of scales and clocks, and therefore no spatio-temporal distances in the physical sense. But this ether must not be thought of as endowed with the properties characteristic of ponderable media, as composed of particles the motion of which can be followed; nor may the concept of motion be applied to it.

At about the same time Eddington said, in the course of a series of lectures delivered at Cornell University in 1934: 'As far as and beyond the remotest stars the world is filled with aether. It permeates the interstices of the atoms. Aether is everywhere . . . There is no space without aether, and no aether which does not occupy space. Some distinguished physicists maintain that modern theories no longer require an aether — that the aether has been abolished. I think all they mean is that, since we never have to do with space and aether separately, we can make one word serve for both; and the word they prefer is "space". I suppose they consider that the word aether is still liable to convey the idea of something material. But equally the word space is liable to convey the idea of complete negation.' (Eddington himself preferred to compromise by using the term 'field' — although that does not seem to carry us any farther.) He went on to say: 'The essential truth remains. You cannot have space without things or things without space; and the adoption of thingless space (vacuum) as a standard in most of our current physical thought is a definite hindrance to the progress of physics.'

Recently Professor Dirac of Cambridge, eminent among the mathematical physicists of our time, published a short paper with the title *Is there an Aether?* It opens with this paragraph: 'In the last century, the idea of a universal and all-pervading aether was popular as a foundation on which to build the theory of electromagnetic phenomena. The situation was profoundly influenced in 1905 by Einstein's discovery of the principle of relativity, leading to the requirement of a four-dimensional formulation of all natural laws. It was soon found that the existence of an aether could not be fitted in with relativity, and since relativity was well established, the aether was abandoned. Physical knowledge has advanced very much since 1905, notably by the arrival of quantum mechanics, and the situation has again changed. If one re-examines the question in the light of present-day knowledge, one finds that the aether is no longer ruled out by relativity, and good reasons can now be advanced for postulating an aether.' The paper ends: 'Thus with the new theory of electrodynamics we are rather forced to have an aether.'

Sir Edmund Whittaker, in the Preface to the enlarged edition of his monumental work *A History of the Theories of Aether and Electricity*, writes: 'As everyone knows, the aether played a great part in the physics of the nineteenth century; but in the first decade of the twentieth, chiefly as a result of the failure of attempts to observe the earth's motion relative to the aether, and the acceptance of the principle that such attempts must always fail, the word "aether" fell out of favour, and it became customary to refer to the interplanetary spaces as "vacuous"; the vacuum being conceived as mere emptinesss, having no properties except that of propagating electromagnetic waves. But with the development of quantum electrodynamics, the vacuum has come to be regarded as the seat of the "zero-point" oscillations of the electromagnetic field, of the "zero-point" fluctuations of electric charge and current, and of a "polarization" corresponding to a dielectric constant different from unity. It seems absurd to retain the name "vacuum" for an entity so rich in physical properties, and the historical word "aether" may fitly be retained.' Lord Cherwell in a recent lecture says: 'In the old days one talked of waves in the ether, but it turned out that the ether had to have so many weird and wonderful properties that people no longer talked about it and indeed I am tempted to say seem to want to hush it up.' [1]

5

Some physicists have not only accepted the possibility of an ether but have speculated as to its nature. They have suggested

[1] See note on the spelling of Ether or Aether, p. 213.

that we may not need to look for something novel, strange and complex, but may perhaps find what we are seeking in a factor familiar to mankind for centuries and used daily in the modern world in all kinds of applications. They find it in Energy.

Sir Oliver Lodge published a book in 1925, with the title *Ether and Reality*, in which he advocated that theory. He wrote: 'All pieces of matter and all particles are connected together by the Ether and by nothing else. In it they move freely and of it they may be composed. We must study the kind of connection between matter and Ether. The particles embedded in the Ether are not independent of it, they are closely connected with it, it is probable that they are formed out of it: they are not like grains of sand suspended in water, they seem more like minute crystals formed in a mother liquor. The mode of connection between the particles and the Ether is not known; it is earnestly being sought: but the fact that there is a connection has been known a long time. We know it, because a particle cannot quiver or move without disturbing the medium in which it is. A boat cannot oscillate on the surface of water without sending off waves or ripples; a bell cannot vibrate in air without sending out waves of sound; a particle cannot vibrate in Ether without sending out waves akin to those of light.'

In the same book Lodge quotes J. J. Thomson as saying: 'In fact, all mass is mass of the ether; all momentum, momentum of the ether; and all kinetic energy, kinetic energy of the ether. This view, it should be said, requires the density of the ether to be immensely greater than that of any known substance.' Thomson restated his conviction in a letter, written to a correspondent towards the end of his life, that is quoted by his biographer, Lord Rayleigh. He wrote: 'I differ from you about the value of the conception of an ether, the more I think about it the more I value it. I regard the ether as the working system of the universe. I think all mass, momentum and energy are seated there and that its mass, momentum and energy are constant, so that Newtonian mechanics apply.'

I would also cite Heisenberg, who has written recently in the same sense, although not using the actual word Ether. Referring to the developments of atomic physics in the last few years he says that 'they take us close to the real aim of atomic theory. Just as the Greeks had hoped, so we have now found there is only one fundamental substance of which all reality consists. If we have to give this substance a name, we can only call it "energy". But this fundamental "energy" is capable of existence in different forms. It always appears in definite quanta which we consider the smallest indivisible units of all matter and which, for purely historical reasons, we do not call atoms but elementary particles. Among the basic forms of energy there are three specially stable kinds: electrons, protons and neutrons. Matter, in the real sense, consists of these with the addition of energy of motion. Then there are particles which always travel with the velocity of light and which embody radiation, and finally other forms with a short life of which only a few have been discovered so far. The variety of natural phenomena is thus created by the diversity of the manifestations of energy, just as the Greek natural philosophers had anticipated'.

Whittaker tells us also that 'Faraday himself had enunciated the principle that one and the same aether ought to serve for all purposes: "It is not at all unlikely", he said, "that if there be an aether, it should have other uses than simply the conveyance of radiations." '

The lines of inquiry that we have been pursuing seem all to point in the same direction. Whether you take radiation waves, or gravitation, or particles, or motion — in every case, at the end. you find yourself confronted by manifestations of energy, *and nothing else*. May it not be because, at the end, there *is* nothing else? May it not be that the point where man's analysis stops is the point where nature's synthesis begins? Then the energy, which is our conclusion, would prove to be the stuff which is nature's commencement — making of it radiation-waves, and particles and atoms, with their oscillations and movements; and so fashioning all the material objects and producing all the varied phenomena that had been the starting-point from which we had originally set out.

The idea has much to commend it. But, as stated, it will not suffice. It may indicate where the answer to our questions may lie, but it is not in itself an answer. For the term Energy, in its ordinary usage, implies action, movement, something dynamic. If the universe were that and nothing more, we should have only a raging chaos, like the interior of an incandescent star, and not the ordered cosmos that we know.

None of the scientists whom I have cited offer any answer to that objection. Oliver Lodge in his concluding chapter writes: 'Ether is the seat of prodigious energies – energies beyond anything as yet accessible to man.' (He was writing in 1925.) 'Ether is the universal connecting link; the transmitter of every kind of force. Action at a distance is wholly dependent on the ether, and it is manifestly the vehicle or substratum underlying electricity and magnetism and light and gravitation and cohesion.' A little earlier he had said: 'The ether is a physical thing . . . Its mechanism is unknown to us, its inner nature eludes us; yet mechanism it must have, for it is subject to physical laws.' And he leaves the matter there.

J. J. Thomson, as we have seen, wrote similarly that in the ether all mass, momentum and energy 'are seated'. But what is meant by 'seated'? Heisenberg declared that 'there is only one fundamental substance of which all reality consists . . . which we can only call "energy"', and that this energy is found in various basic forms, among them matter, which itself consists of stable particles, 'with the addition of energy of motion'. But he gives no hint of the kind of process that he conceives to be going on when he speaks of 'the addition of energy of motion'. Einstein, on the other hand, will accept an ether only on condition that 'the notion of movement is not applied to it'.

It is evident that here we have come to another impasse. We cannot accept the hypothesis of a universal ether consisting of energy unless and until we have some conception of its functioning.

We find ourselves now in the field of speculation. But we need not be disconcerted by that. This is usually, indeed, the pioneer stage in any scientific exploration. Professor W. I. B. Beveridge of Cambridge has written a stimulating book, *The Art of Scientific Investigation*, in which he lays stress on the value of speculation. He quotes in his support Newton, who said: 'No great discovery is ever made without a bold guess.' And Karl Gauss: 'I have the result, but I do not yet know how to get it.' And T. H. Huxley: 'It is a popular delusion that the scientific inquirer is under an obligation not to go beyond generalization of observed facts . . .

but anyone who is practically acquainted with scientific work is aware that those who refuse to go beyond the facts, rarely get as far.' And Pasteur: 'If someone tells me that in making these conclusions I have gone beyond the facts, I reply: "It is true that I have freely put myself among ideas which cannot be rigorously proved. That is my way of looking at things." '

Beveridge also, in his opening pages, gives examples of the part that has occasionally been played by 'outsiders' in contributing fresh ideas — sometimes revolutionary — to the advancement of science. The layman, venturing into a field where other people know so much more than he does, is likely at first to be as Shakespeare says, 'made tongue-tied by Authority'. But if he overcomes that diffidence, the layman, bringing to the survey of old problems an innocent mind, not hampered by too much erudition, may sometimes happen upon a clue — perhaps a very simple one — which specialists may find helpful.

CHAPTER V

A SPECULATION

I

THE speculation which I submit for consideration is not merely imaginative: it is not a case of 'intellectual construction, which proceeds completely free and arbitrarily', that Einstein described in his letter. On the contrary, it is based on a combination of some of the most familiar features of the actual universe around us. The first is the existence of the same object at different times in different 'states'. The second is the fact that energy manifests itself in a variety of phenomena, and that it can transform itself, easily and quickly, from one kind into another. The third is the existence of patterns – like the 'moving configuration' of water waves in the sea or sound-waves in the air; or else static, like the lattice structure of crystals.

Let us consider each of these in turn.

2

States. Water, for example, may be, at any particular time, either solid, liquid, or gaseous; almost all substances can be converted from one of those states to another by natural process. Things may be either hot or cold: that is to say, at one time their molecules may be in a state of greater thermal agitation, and at another time of lesser. The surface of the sea may have been rough yesterday and be smooth today. In each case, the things themselves keep their basic identity throughout: the same molecules are there; it is only the state that alters. And these changes come about with great ease and regularity. As soon as the surrounding temperature falls below 32° Fahrenheit – at sea-level atmospheric pressure – we can watch liquid water changing into ice: when it rises above 212°, we can see it in the kettle bubbling away as steam.

3

Transformations of energy. I would ask leave to dwell a little on this, as it is the foundation for the rest of my argument.

Only gradually, and for the most part quite recently, have the distinct forms of energy that we now know so well been revealed by scientific discovery. It is hardly three centuries since the familiar colours of the rainbow were found to correspond with light of different degrees of refraction: the glass prism presented them side by side laid out in a uniform series. This was the beginning of the present electromagnetic wave band. Then the existence of other radiations, with other wave-lengths, beyond each end of the visible light spectrum, was established. The band was extended to include, on one side, the infra-red (which are also the waves of radiant heat), and, on the other, the ultra-violet. Next — suddenly between 1887 and 1893 — Hertz extended the red end much further by the discovery of the radiation now used for broadcasting, and radar; while Röntgen added at the violet end what are termed the X-rays. Soon after, Becquerel and the Curies pushed that side still further with the gamma rays, which are one of the products of radioactivity.

Following quickly upon that era of great discoveries has come the twentieth-century revelation of particles, of many types, existing at a size-level below that of the atoms. And electric currents are found to be nothing else than movements of negatively charged particles. All these have one thing in common — and one only: they are all manifestations of energy.

We are claiming for each of them a place in the real universe. In order to support that claim we may look to see how each takes part in the actual events and experiences of our daily lives.

As I sit at the writing-desk in my library I am surrounded by examples of energy in all sorts of wave-lengths and in many kinds of particles. At the other end of the room is a radio-set: its indicator tells me that it can receive broadcasts on wave-lengths from 2000 metres down to 21 metres. (The entire scale of these Hertzian waves extends, in English measures, from 20 miles to about an inch.) This house has a water-heating system: a small furnace, in a passage outside leading to the garden, burns coke: the combustion of the carbon atoms with oxygen atoms in the air generates waves of radiant heat; these warm the water in the boiler which circulates into the iron radiator near my desk, and so warms the room. These heat-waves merge into those of the infra-red. We happen to have in the house an infra-red lamp bought some time ago for therapeutic purposes; its wave-lengths, including those of radiant heat, may be between a hundredth of an inch and a 30 millionth. In a cupboard upstairs there are some now neglected paint-boxes: if one of them is opened, the paints (which were colourless when the box was closed) will begin to reflect light of wave-lengths from 30 millionths of an inch – red, down to 15 millionths – violet. We have no ultra-violet lamp in the house; but if one were ever required for medical treatment they are easily obtainable: their wave-lengths are from 15 millionths of an inch downwards. I think I still have copies of some X-ray photographs taken after an illness to make sure that no damage had remained: the X-ray camera will have em-ployed wave-lengths of from 1/500 to 1/1000 millionths of an inch. The gamma rays, which are of great penetrating power and of importance in surgery, we have fortunately had no occasion to make use of; but, if needed, the apparatus would be available in some London hospital: their shortest gamma waves go down to 22 million-millionths of an inch. As to magnetism, there may still be in some ancient toy box the little magnet which the children used to have – horse-shoe shaped, painted red, with a steel bar across the open end. You detach the bar and lay it, or a needle, or any small metal object, on a table and hold the magnet close above it, and the object will rise from the table, travel across the intervening space, and cling to the magnet. (Children always ask what makes it do so, and no one is ever able to tell them.) Further, there is gravity, which is in action everywhere and always. It causes this house, and my room as part of it, to adhere to the surface of the earth; and my body itself, when I walk across the room, to remain on the floor, instead of floating up to the ceiling, like the weightless man in H. G. Wells's story.

All these are to be classed as radiations. With regard to particles – there are first the electric currents, transmitted by negatively charged electrons. Near the door is a power connection which works a vacuum cleaner that is busy in the early mornings. Another point brings to the room a weaker current that works the loud speaker in the radio-set; another, the electric heater; others, the table lamps and ceiling light. There is also the telephone by my desk with its connection with the exchange. The electric bell downstairs, which I can ring from the bell-push by the door, has its own battery.

The air in the room, that keeps me alive from one minute to the next, consists mainly of molecules of oxygen and nitrogen, each molecule containing atoms which are complicated systems of various kinds of particles. In the air are also molecules of carbonic-acid gas, each molecule made up of two atoms of oxygen combined with one atom of carbon — these the same as the atoms that cohere together to help to make lumps of coal, or, bound more closely, will make diamonds. If there comes to be in the air more than the right proportion of these molecules of carbonic-acid gas I will say that the room is getting stuffy, and will go and open the window. It is wave oscillations in the air that carry to my ears the sound of the voice of anyone who comes to see me, and of my voice to his. And in the room is also my own body, consisting of some billions of cells, each one a highly complex structure of molecules, each molecule composed again of atoms, and ultimately of particles.

All these things are actual and not abstract. We can speak of them in colloquial language. There is nothing metaphysical about them. They are parts of the real universe.

4

One of the facts of chief importance for our present purpose is that, while from the human standpoint we see going on a number of separate processes that are very different one from another, viewed from nature's standpoint they are not separate and different but are all of a piece. For us, the light of the electric lamp is quite another thing from the current passing along the wire; a broadcast programme is altogether different from an X-ray photograph; heat is different from gravity, the air that I breathe different from the cells of my body. But for nature all these are, at bottom, either waves or particles. An ether theory would go on to say that the waves and the particles are themselves two different manifestations of a single element — of energy.

Another point of great significance is that many of these forms of energy are constantly being converted into other forms. The electric current in the wire becomes heat in the lamp, and the heat, when it reaches a certain intensity, becomes light. The current itself has been produced by an engine and a dynamo where energy has taken the form of mechanical work; and the engine may be worked by steam, produced from water by heat which itself comes from the combustion of coal or oil. Or perhaps the current may come from a hydro-electric power-station, and there it is energy in the form of gravity that brings down the rush of water that turns the turbines that work the dynamo. We can watch the glow in a Crookes vacuum tube when the particles of an electric current, coming in at one end, cause a stream of X-rays to be emitted at the other. Or we may visit a broadcasting station, where the intake is again coal or oil, or electric current, and the output is Hertzian waves emitted from the antenna. We also know that heavy atoms of radium, when they disintegrate, will produce particles combined into lighter atoms of helium gas; together with electrons, and with an emanation of gamma waves as well – three different things produced from the same source at the same time.

Newton, discussing 'the changing of Bodies into Light, and Light into Bodies', says that 'it is very comfortable to the Course of Nature, which seems delighted with Transmutations'.

5

Pattern. I come to the last of the ideas basic to the speculation which follows. In addition to States, and in addition to Transformations, we have to take into account differences of Pattern. (I use these words in their ordinary senses, and make no attempt to give them philosophical or scientific definition.) A piece of cloth may be wet or dry, old or new, clean or dirty – those are its states. It may be thick or thin, large or small, square or oblong – those are its forms. And it may be woven in stripes, or with a geometrical or fanciful design, or perhaps as a tartan – that is its pattern. Throughout it is the same material, it is the same entity. The sea in the tropics may be calm, hot, steamy, flat on the surface, motionless underneath: in the Bay of Biscay, it may be cold and rough, with waves and driving spray on the surface, and currents, tides and eddies underneath. But it remains the sea; it is still a volume of hydrogen and oxygen gases combined as molecules of liquid water, with sodium chloride and other substances mingled in it.

My suggestion is that, if there is a universal continuum — an ether, and if the ether consists of energy, we may conceive that energy may exist, not only in a variety of Forms — as we all know that it does — but also in more than one State and in several Patterns.

6

The energy with which we are familiar is in a state of activity: it is that which produces all the perceptible phenomena of the given universe. We would now postulate that it exists also in another state, hitherto unrecognized — a state of inactivity, of quiescence. This would be the matrix, for which we are in search, of all activity.

Being quiescent, it produces, while in that state, no phenomena that we are able to perceive. It cannot therefore be observed; or described, or defined, for there is nothing beyond itself with which it can be related. Why then should we suppose that quiescent energy exists at all? Because all the phenomena that we do observe lead us to infer that there must be something, outside the range of observation, from which they emanate; and because a mechanism of active and quiescent energy, with easy transformations from one to the other, may be found to be capable of producing all those phenomena.

The Greeks wrestled with the problem whether a thing can at the same time both be and not be: Hinduism is wrestling with it still. Western philosophy of the present day will answer that, simultaneously, both to be and not be is impossible. But there is no reason to question that a thing can, at the same time, both be *and not act*. It may act at one time and not act at another, but exist at both.

This, then, is the suggestion now offered with respect to energy. The word Ether would cover energy in both its states.

On this basis the wave and the particle would be seen as patterns of activity in the ether. The wave is a configuration that advances from one place to another place. The particle is not self-moving. It has an internal coherence which makes it a discrete entity — in some cases stable and enduring, in others unstable and transient. We shall come later to consider Impetus, and will submit reasons for thinking that there is a third normal pattern of ether activation, different from both wave and particle, that would account for it.

From these two states, quiescent and active, and from these patterns, emerge all the various phenomena and processes that we survey as facts in practical experience.

7

A theory such as this would involve important changes in physics — some of them revolutionary.

First, it is evident that energy itself is never in motion. Its structure is continuous; it pervades all matter; it has no interstices; it has no boundaries — other than the boundaries of the universe, if such there be. There is nowhere out of which, or into which, it could move. Einstein's condition for the acceptance of an ether would therefore be fulfilled.

Much of the vocabulary usually employed in connection with energy would not apply. There would no longer be any question of energy itself being emitted or absorbed, transferred or acquired, liberated or spent, conserved or destroyed. While quiescent, it is static and eternal. When active, it is the activation itself that is the cause of the phenomena — the emergence of energy into activity and relapse into quiescence; together with its transmutation from one pattern into another, or from one form into another.

8

The transitions from quiescent to active would appear to be caused by underlying changes in the conditions of the matrix. Although these are not perceptible phenomena and are beyond the range of our knowledge, it does not follow that they do not occur. On the contrary, it is to be inferred that there are

E

variations of conditions, analogous perhaps to the variations of temperature and pressure in our own environment — weather conditions — which, when they reach a certain critical degree, give rise to sudden changes in the state of the ether.

It is evident that activation is also caused by the impact of material bodies already in existence. This will be considered when we come to the question of Impetus.

We must conceive, then, that there is a minimum point at which activation, however caused, becomes effective in stirring quiescent ether into action. Unless there were such a threshold the distinction between the two states of energy could not be maintained, and an ordered universe could not have come into being.

It may well be that this threshold will prove to be identical with Planck's quantum — 'the elementary quantity of action'. Expressed mathematically, in our units of measurement, it gives us the exceedingly small figure of 6.625×10^{-27} erg. sec. This is 'Planck's constant h', which makes so mysterious, and often so unexpected an appearance in many physical observations, experiments and calculations. If that should be so, some of the most difficult of the problems of today in physics might be nearing solution, including that of ultimate indivisibility.

9

We may now be able to form a speculative idea of an ether mechanism.

We may picture a universal ocean of energy, in a state generally of quiescence, and producing no perceptible phenomena. It may, however, be subject to hidden changes in its own condition; and these, or else impacts on one part by material bodies already existing in other parts, may stir it into activity — here and there and from time to time.

This activity may take the form of radiation: that is to say the emission from a given centre of a sequence of spherical waves — or 'pulses', as they are now beginning to be called. [1] The original cause of emission is the oscillation which is now recognized as a

<hr>

[1] This is a better word; but I have not used it in this book because I do not wish to risk confusing the ordinary reader by bringing in terms that are still unfamiliar when familiar ones will serve, even if not quite so well.

given characteristic of the atom. A group of such oscillating points sets going, in the surrounding quiescent ether, a continuous series of expanding spheres. It has long been regarded as established that such spheres, from a great multitude of atoms, aggregate to form trains of larger spheres capable of travelling across the universe. This is somewhat similar in principle to the aggregation of sound-waves. (I remember, in London before the advent of motor cars, how the sound-waves, set up by the beating of the hooves of tens of thousands of horses on the wooden street pavements, were amalgamated into a single continuous noise — the roar of London traffic.)

The process of activation— which is the key to the whole matter — would consist in the spherical layer of ether, immediately surrounding the oscillating atom or atoms, itself becoming active. This activity constitutes a fresh impact, which will similarly activate the next layer. The first simultaneously relapses into quiescence; to be again subject to the same process at the next instant. This sequence will continue indefinitely; until the source of emission ceases to emit, or until the expansion of the spheres, one beyond the other, diffuses the original impulse more and more, until in the end it is spent.

Activation may also be in a pattern different from the radiation waves — a pattern of particles. These are discrete entities. They differ from radiation in that they have internal cohesion, which the waves have not; also they are not auto-mobile. They must need, however, some initial threshold, therein resembling radiation. This would be of the same order as Planck's quantum of action; it might be mathematically the same, or it might prove to be a constant of a different figure.

In the ether-ocean we conceive numberless particles continually forming, and either enduring or immediately or soon dissolving. Some of those that endure may be the free electrons, or other particles, which are now known to exist in vast numbers in what used to be termed 'empty space'. Some of these may afterwards draw together and arrange themselves in various combinations and patterns to form the stable atoms of the chemical elements that we know.

So the material universe will have come into being and may for ever be in fresh creation.

10

I return to the question of Impetus.

It is evident that the continued momentum of massive objects when put into motion and released cannot be explained in terms either of radiation or of particles. The salient point is that which is stated in Newton's First Law, that the object moves in a straight line: the pattern of activation must therefore be rectilinear, and this is not so with either waves or particles.

A second fundamental point is that the movement is always in two successive phases, which are different in their nature – (a) the initial movement out of rest into motion, and (b) the impetus which then takes over and carries the object forward. The ball is first held in the hand while it is being projected, then it travels on 'by itself'; the bullet is first propelled by expanding gases along the barrel of the rifle, then it flies through the air 'independently'. Each of the two phases is a distinct event, each being the result of a different combination of circumstances. Unless we begin by considering them separately we cannot hope to arrive at any sound theory of impetus.

There is another preliminary point which, although obvious, is not always borne in mind. We say, both of a bird and of a ball, 'it flies through the air'; we say, both of a steamship and of a sailing-ship, 'it travels across the sea': but there is all the difference in the world between the motion of a bird, with its muscles and its brain, and the action of an inert collection of molecules such as a ball; between the internal engines of the steamship, and the external winds and currents that carry the sailing-ship along. We are so well accustomed, however, to both kinds of movement that we do not stay to discriminate: almost unconsciously we assume them to be of the same order. An enthralled football or baseball crowd will watch the ball breathlessly to see 'where it will go': the ball becomes an 'it' which is doing something, which has, for the moment, a kind of personality of its own. Whether an object is active or is passive – a bird or a ball – we use the same language about it; we say 'it moves'. To be precise we ought to say 'it moves' only of auto-mobile objects such as the bird or the steamship: of the ball, the bullet or the sailing-ship, we ought to say *'it is being moved'*.

This habit is so ingrained that, when scientists took up the question, it was natural for them to assume that what they were inquiring into was an observed fact — an object doing something, namely, moving from one place to another place. Every possible method has been tried to solve a problem stated in those terms. They have all failed; the reason being that what is assumed to be a fact is not a fact; what is thought to be an observation is an illusion — natural, plausible, like the illusion, accepted for thousands of years, of the sun moving round the earth; but an illusion none the less. If, instead of saying of the inert object that 'it moves', 'it travels on by itself', 'it flies independently', we were to say that 'it is being moved', and that our problem is to find out what it is that is moving it — then we might begin to make progress.

We should be obliged to recognize that the motion is not a function of the object at all. Considering separately the two phases, we see at once that the first, the initiating movement, is caused by some extraneous cause — an arm throwing, a gun firing, or the like: the second, the continuing movement, is a function of the surrounding medium; in the case of the sailing-ship, the air with its winds and the sea with its currents: in the case of the ball or the bullet, the medium is . . . Is what?

That is our problem; there lies 'the mystery of impetus'. Step by step we have argued that there must be a continuum to serve as a medium; that the continuum is an ether, consisting of energy; that energy may exist in two states — quiescent and active, and that all the phenomena that we perceive may come from activations of quiescent ether and relapses; that these activations are in various patterns, of which the expanding spherical waves of radiation are one and electronic particles are another. Now we are reaching the conclusion that motion also must be a function of the ether, but in a pattern — hitherto unrecognized — that is different from radiations and particles. And an essential distinction between this pattern and the others is that it must be linear.

Faraday, who was a pioneer in so many things, may now prove to be a pioneer also in this. Whittaker tells us that Faraday's studies in magnetism 'had suggested to him the idea of lines of magnetic force'. He adds that 'Faraday constantly thought in terms of lines of force. "I cannot refrain", he had written in 1851, "from again expressing my conviction of the truthfulness of the representation which the idea of lines of force affords in regard to magnetic action." '

But if 'lines of force' are one of nature's devices, they need not be limited to magnetism. Again and again we find that a model, discovered in one set of phenomena, is found afterwards in others that had appeared to be quite different. Lines of force may give us the clue to the whole problem of impetus.

We need first to study this new mechanism. What kind of impact is it that will initiate rectilinear sequences of activation? What determines their velocity, acceleration, duration? We shall soon find ourselves immersed in technicalities. These, therefore, are among the matters we have reserved for the Appendices.

CHAPTER VI

LIFE AND MIND

I

LOOKING back over what has been written so far, the first impression is one of incompleteness. We are seeking the real universe: as yet we have been discussing only its material constituents. If an ether were accepted as the matrix or substance of those constituents, that would greatly simplify cosmology: it might also enable physics to give replies to legitimate questions that are now left unanswered. But as a picture of the cosmos as a whole that would still be quite inadequate. It has left out altogether factors that are the most significant of all. It has left out Life and Mind.

For centuries attempts have been made, by some of the ablest thinkers that the human race has produced, to show that living organisms and thinking persons are nothing but the sum of their material components. Again and again we have been told that, wait a little longer, and chemistry and physics will surely produce, from inanimate materials, the rudimentary proto-plasmic cell: once that has been done, evolution would account for the rest. But it has not been done yet: there can be no assurance that it will be done in any foreseeable future. Events may prove this to be wrong: it is possible that, at any moment, some team of biochemists and biophysicists somewhere may make the great discovery. When that happens philosophers will revise their premises and start afresh. But meanwhile they are bound to recognize and accept the tremendous difference that there is, throughout the whole of nature, between the living and the not-living, between the thinking and the not-thinking.

I remember well a personal experience that happened about fifty years ago: unimportant in itself, it was striking enough to leave a lasting impression. In the early days of the motor car, when it was still an unfamiliar, and startling, object in the remoter country districts, I was in the back seat of a car on a road in Yorkshire. We were driving at little more than a walking-pace through a scattered village when there rushed out of the open door of a public house a large rough-haired Irish terrier. It bounded along in front of the car, vigorously barking at this strange object. Suddenly there was silence: we felt a slight jolt; the car stopped; we got out, and there, on the road, lay the dog — quite dead. The owner came out, lifted the body by the feet and dragged it to the side of the road. The contrast between the dog as it had been a moment before — full of life, all its organs and limbs functioning, heart beating, lungs breathing, brain thinking, eyes seeing, throat barking, legs running and leaping; and then as it was now — all those processes stopped on the instant: no longer a dog, with the characteristics of a dog, but the dead body of what had been a dog — this brought home to me, in a startling way, the profound difference there is between life and not-life.

Someone may be walking in a park in the autumn and pick up a chestnut under the trees; he may happen to notice a pebble near by on the path. Picking it up also and laying them side by side on the palm of his hand, he may stay to think about them for a moment. They may be much alike — in size, colour, weight; at first sight the pebble might be mistaken for another chestnut. But the difference between them is fundamental. The pebble is what it is: kept for a hundred years and it will so remain. But the chestnut is not only what it now is, and is seen to be. It has in it also the power to become something else. Let the conditions be favourable, and it will gather materials and activity, from the soil, from the rain and water-vapour in the air, from the light and heat of the sun. In time it will become a great spreading tree; and that tree may produce, year after year, hundreds of other chestnuts, every one of them with the same capacities. This potentiality is as real as the molecules, atoms and particles of which the chestnut is composed. Throughout the vegetable and animal world the case is the same. The difference between the pebble and the chestnut is the difference that there is between the material components of the universe and the universe in its entirety.

Science has done many marvellous things; but so far it has not explained, much less produced, organic growth and reproduction. All the biological sciences together, with all their wonderful processes — chemical, electrical, electronic — cannot do what a single grain of wheat does, germinating in the springtime.

We are therefore left with a deep differentiation between Life and Mind on the one hand and Matter on the other. Whether Life and Mind present a second differentiation, as between themselves, is another moot point. Is there a similar division between the animal and the vegetable as there is between both of them and the mineral? Or are those two of the same order? Is it possible that mind is always present, if only in some embryonic form, wherever there is life — even in the tree, even in the single organic cell? Then, if that should be so, would the converse hold: should we suppose that wherever there is mind there is also life? Are the two in fact inseparable — no life without mind, no mind without life?

These are problems in which many take a keen interest: but whether they will lend themselves to profitable discussion seems doubtful. There is a danger that we should soon find ourselves immersed in arguments about the meaning of words and the classification of species. What do you mean by life? If there were a disembodied soul, presumably it would have mind, but could it be said to have life? Or where should the boundary be drawn — if there is to be a boundary — between living organisms to which mental qualities can be attributed and those to which they cannot?

This is not so with the difference between life and mind taken together, on the one hand, and matter on the other. That difference is not verbal or formal, but factual. It is the difference between the living dog and the dead dog, between the chestnut and the pebble. And this is a problem that cannot be evaded. It forces itself upon us insistently whenever we consider our own experience — the effects which, undoubtedly, our material bodies have upon the working of our minds, and our minds upon the working of our bodies. It is a problem that both philosophers and scientists are studying intensively at the present time — the problem of the mind-body relation.

2

One great step in advance has been achieved in recent years by the workers in this field. They have definitely established that mechanical processes and laws enter into the working of the nervous system. The stimuli that pass along the nerve fibres and provide the sense-data in the brain that enable us to see, hear, smell or feel, are electrical. They can be timed and counted and measured, with great precision. They are as mechanical as an electric current passing along a copper wire, and subject to the same physical laws. And within the brain itself are electrical activities which are closely connected with the processes of thought.

A large part is played in present-day research by an apparatus called the electro-encephalograph — EEG for short. It can record, by oscillating pens on a rapidly moving strip of paper from a reel, the rhythms of electrical processes going on in the living brain. Dr. E. D. Adrian, now Lord Adrian, a leader in this branch of research, was good enough one day to show me, in his laboratory at Cambridge, the working of the instrument, with my own head as the subject of observation. Electrodes, attached to metal head-bands, are applied to various parts of the skull; weak electric currents pass through; in the apparatus near by, the paper strip is run rapidly from one reel to the other; the currents, amplified about a million times, are relayed to an oscillograph which actuates the pens; and the pens trace, along parallel bands, several series of zig-zag lines: each of these records the rhythmical activity of a particular region of the brain. One is asked to shut one's eyes, and after a few seconds to open them; then to do a simple sum in mental arithmetic, followed by relaxation; and other similar tests. When the paper strip is examined afterwards, with the points marked when each of the tests had begun and had ended, there is in every case an unmistakable variation, at that point, in the pattern of the line. The degree of agitation, so to speak, is different when the eyes were closed from when they were open; still more so when one had been doing the arithmetical sum, compared with just before or just after.

Dr. Grey Walter, in his recent book *The Living Brain*, says of this: 'The electrical changes which give rise to the alternating currents of variable frequency and amplitude thus recorded arise in the cells of the brain itself; there is no question of any other power supply. The brain must be pictured as a vast aggregation of electrical cells . . . some ten thousand million of them, through which surge the restless tides of our electrical being . . . It is

when a million or so of these cells repeatedly fire together that
the rhythm of their discharge becomes measurable in frequency
and amplitude.'

3

This helps us to understand how impulses from the outer world
are transmitted to the brain and may constitute its sense-data.
These are the raw material for one part of our thinking — our
perception. And we know that consciousness may be affected by
chemical substances — alcohol, opium, poisons, anaesthetics, also
by concussion. But it gives us no understanding at all of what
happens, in the conscious mind operating normally, as a consequence of perception, or apart from perception altogether. It
does not even begin to explain the processes of reflection, choice,
decision, volition; or the autonomous creation of new ideas,
conspicuous in the arts.

Of the ideas originated by the conscious mind it is evident, then,
that some are based on sense-data and some are not. But in
the later processes the mind seems to treat all alike: manipulating
them, so to speak; arranging corresponding patterns in the brain;
relating these to one another; sometimes also memorizing them.
This handling of different things in the same way proves to be
misleading. We are tempted to say: much of our thinking is
based on the perception of sense-data and is in the nature of
reflex action; sense-data are the outcome of material, mechanical
processes, first outside and then inside the body: we therefore
have a right to infer, in the absence of actual knowledge, that the
rest of our thinking may well be of the same order. More
elaborate, more subtle, perhaps long suspended, it will still belong
to the category of material events.

But the facts preclude that inference. Electrical and chemical
events can evoke related thoughts in the mind: but there are other
thoughts that are not so related, cannot have been so evoked,
and clearly arise independently, from within. We are led to the
conclusion, expressed by Professor Eccles in his recent valuable
work on these subjects, where he says that 'the behaviour of the
individual particles of matter in the active cerebral cortex . . .
may be regarded by us as something "outside physics".' He says

also that we are left 'with an account of the specific events in the brain which are linked with specific states in the mind', but we are told 'nothing concerning the "how" of that linkage'. In other words, in the present state of our knowledge, it is a duality that confronts us.

4

Many of our leading physiologists now recognize this, reluctantly though it may be; and many philosophers accept it from the scientists. In an appendix to this chapter I have brought together a number of quotations from scientific authorities that support this view. I have not attempted to go back to the philosopher-scientists of earlier times — the Greeks, Spinoza, Kant and his successors; for the factual material on which they had to rely has been thrown out of date — largely supplemented, and often entirely superseded, by the new sciences.

The appendix begins with Thomas Huxley, D'Arcy Thompson and Lloyd Morgan, and then comes to writers of the present day — Lord Adrian, Sir Russell Brain, W. E. Le Gros Clark, Wilder Penfield, W. Grey Walter and J. E. Eccles; some brief extracts are added from a recent philosophical lecture by Professor A. S. Ewing.

Sir Charles Sherrington's opinions I would wish to quote here. His lifelong labours in experimental neurology, the brilliance of his discoveries and the clarity of their presentation, won him a world-wide fame. No one will venture to brush aside his considered judgements.

In his *Man on his Nature*, Sherrington wrote: 'The search in that [energy] scheme for a scale of equivalence between energy and mental experience arrives at none . . . The two, for all I can do, remain refractorily apart. They seem to me disparate; not mutually convertible, untranslatable the one into the other.' In his Rede Lecture at Cambridge he said: 'Strictly we have to regard the relation of mind to brain as still not merely unsolved, but still devoid of a basis for its very beginning.' I had the privilege of Sherrington's acquaintance in the later years of his long life, and when I visited him at Eastbourne, where he was then living, we often discussed this question, and others relating to it. (Incidentally,

I made a note of a remark of his that 'the leading physicists in his
day had been materialists, but he thought that was not so now.
They had been so intent on atoms and the like that they were not
interested in the problems of mind'.) I remember very well walking with him one day — in 1946 — along the sea-front: I had been
putting forward the reasons for the dualistic position that I had
expressed in a book a few years before. He agreed in general, and
then, stopping and laying his hand on my arm to emphasize what
he was saying, he added: 'It is perhaps no more improbable that
our being should consist of two fundamental elements than that
it should rest on one only.' He expressed that view, in the same
words, in the concluding sentence of his Introduction, written
in the following year, to a new edition of his principal work, *The
Integrative Action of the Nervous System*. And in his last utterance
of all, when, in his ninety-second year, he recorded the opening
talk in a broadcast symposium on 'The Physical Basis of Mind', his
final words were: 'Aristotle, two thousand years ago, was asking
how is the mind attached to the body. We are asking that question still.'

5

I had intended to insert here some observations on the suggestion that a new line of approach to this stubborn problem of
mind and brain had been opened by the construction of highly
elaborate electrical computing machines. This type of machine
seems to imitate some of the processes of human thought so closely
that it has been popularly called 'the electronic brain'. A lively
discussion has arisen; and the subject has been given the status of a
new department of science under the name of Cybernetics. [1] But
the suggestion has not met with general acceptance; and as the
conclusion reached is negative, I have forgone any discussion
of this subject. And I have not attempted to enter upon
the problems of Extra-Sensory Perception, opened up by the
researches of Dr. J. B. Rhine (of Duke University, U.S.A.), and
his followers, described in his books *The Reach of the Mind* and
New World of the Mind. His results have not so far been accepted

[1] The word was originally coined by André Ampère from the Greek word meaning
'steersman'.

generally by biophysicists and psychologists, and it is not for the layman to venture upon an independent opinion.

Before ending this chapter, however, I would return for a moment to the main point at issue.

A member of a recent parliamentary delegation to Russia, Mr. Christopher Mayhew, was discussing Marxism at an informal gathering with one of the heads of the Russian Government, Mr. Gromyko. 'But what is your own philosophy?' Gromyko asked him. 'Are you a materialist? Is this glass I am holding real or not?'

Here we have a typical example of the persistent confusion between materialism and realism. All material things are real; but much that is not material is also real. Mayhew might well have asked Gromyko in return whether the very conversation that was at that moment going on between them was real or not. If he said it was not real, then he would have to explain what other status it could have in the real universe, in which, un deniably, it was taking place. But if he allowed that the discussion was real — one event in the universal sum of events — then he would have disavowed his own materialist philosophy. For although the wave-vibrations in the air carrying the sound of the voices, and the electric pulses transmitted along nerve-fibres to the brain, belong to the world of matter — as unquestionably as the glass in his hand — it cannot be denied that the conversation, the arguments on each side, their merits and demerits, are not in the sphere of material things. They are events in the sphere of mind. Not material, they are nevertheless real.

We are told that in Russia the ideas of Pavlov are still regarded as authoritative, and accepted as a firm foundation for psychological theory. They are empirical, based on observation and experiment, particularly on certain experiments with dogs. Pavlov's dogs were trained to expect their food when a bell rang. After a time it was found that saliva began to flow in their mouths whenever the bell rang, whether the food was actually forthcoming or not. It was argued that the secretion could only be the consequence of the thought of food in the dogs' minds, and that such thoughts were clearly in the nature of 'compound conditioned reflexes' from an external stimulus. From that and similar examples the conclusion was drawn that thinking in general is a material process; mind is comprised in brain; this is the answer to the mind-body problem.

Lord Adrian in his Presidential Address to the British Association meeting at Oxford in 1954, said of this: 'Pavlov studied learning in animals and explained it in terms of conditioned reflexes, but physiologists ever since Galvani have studied the reactions of nerve fibres and nerve cells, the units of the nervous system, in the hope of explaining what they do in the terms of physics and chemistry. This approach at the lowest level can tell us little about the way in which units are organized, but when we keep to physical and chemical problems we are in the familiar territory of the exact sciences, we know how experiments should be conducted and there are great technical advances at our disposal. It is when we begin to think of organisms rather than molecules that we seem to part company with mechanism.'

Why should we not consider as a test-case, equally relevant, not feeding, but its converse—fasting; and not dogs, but human beings? Every year many millions of orthodox Moslems abstain from food from sunrise to sunset during the whole month of Ramadan; observant Jews do the same for twenty-four hours on the Day of Atonement; Christians in Lent, Hindus and Buddhists according to their customs, are abstinent in various ways. How can any of this be accounted for on the theory of conditioned reflexes? Or think of soldiers deliberately facing death on the battlefield; or martyrs going fearlessly to the stake to testify to their faith; or free men risking years of imprisonment, or even the scaffold, rather than surrender their principles; with tens of thousands of lesser examples — in all these, are not conscious choice and power of will the determining factors? As a foundation for a sound philosophy of life and conduct, such facts as these will carry more conviction than the salivation of Pavlov's dogs.

6

It is true that there is always among philosophers, as T. H. Green said, 'a craving for unity'. They take satisfaction whenever diversity can be resolved by some single principle. In this book we have emphasized the unity of human history, and have been searching for a single substratum beneath the variety of the physical cosmos. To accept a duality, and to take up an agnostic position as to what lies beyond, can never be satisfactory. But sometimes this cannot be avoided. When the existing state of knowledge does not reveal a unity it is better frankly to say so. After all, 'a craving' is irrational, and is itself unphilosophic.

Nevertheless, there are grounds for thinking that there must still be something lying hidden, waiting to be discovered – some 'linkage' between mind and brain. Sherrington spoke of our being consisting perhaps of two fundamental elements and not one, and in this chapter the word 'fundamental' has occasionally made its appearance. But it would be well not to interpret it too strictly. The obvious fact that physical events do affect mental events and vice versa, may lead us to infer that there must be some quality that is common to both; or else that both are products of some underlying element, at present unknown and maybe inconceivable. 'Under every deep a lower deep opens', says Emerson.

Perhaps, however, the endeavour to discover the nature of thought may be doomed to failure from the outset, for the reason that that which is thinking and that which is thought about are one and the same. It may be that no introspection can reveal the process of introspection itself. There is here no subject-object relationship. The mind cannot get a hold on its own thinking.

> The Mind can measure things by scale,
> But what can scale or measure it?

Meanwhile we must struggle to go as far as we can, in this province where physics and psychics meet. Lord Adrian, surveying the scientific progress in this field in recent years, can do no more than say: 'I think we are a little nearer the threshold of mind than we were.' It may prove to be a long and hard task before we reach that threshold, and can cross it, and are able to explore at last the mysteries that lie beyond.

CHAPTER VII

IMAGINATION

I

WE discover that the universe is full of marvels, but is there anything more strange than our own faculty of imagination – the power to create mental figments?

It is innate. It is particularly active in childhood and early youth. In the tombs of children of four and five thousand years ago we find dolls and other toys – images of reality. A child is hardly able to walk when his imagination makes him suppose that there may be something over there – behind the table, round the corner: a first sign of independence is when he insists upon going to see. Later on, every child loves nothing better than to be 'told a story'; fairies and all kinds of magic are the favourites. Those fancies are abandoned reluctantly: it was a typical little girl who said that she knew there was no Father Christmas but she didn't want anyone to say so.

Among primitive peoples the imaginative instinct continues its hold into adult life: spirits of the dead are believed to haunt the woods and the fields; great men become gods or demigods, immortal and invisible, but concerned with the affairs of the living. The earth is full of ghosts; beneath its surface is an inferno of spirits and demons. The great mythologies grow up. For thousands of years their majestic temples, solemn ceremonies and powerful priesthoods determine the beliefs of nations and dominate their history.

The arts arise, creating, within this world of imagination, a realm of their own. The visual arts symbolize the gods and spirits, portray scenes and people, lend beauty and grace to human constructions.

> And, as imagination bodies forth
> The forms of things unknown, the poet's pen
> Turns them to shapes, and gives to airy nothing
> A local habitation and a name.

Out of the cave and the hut evolve the Parthenon and the Taj Mahal. Music, the most imaginative of the arts, opens other vistas. From the chants of the stamping warriors come the *Odyssey* and the *Divine Comedy*, *Hamlet* and *Faust*, the symphonies of Beethoven.

2

Dreams, illusions and myths are fictions: nevertheless, if they are believed to be true, they may affect the events of the real universe. The dream of a somnambulist may lead him to step out of a window and fall to his death. The places and persons and events in a dream are fantasy and may have no relation to reality; nevertheless the dream, as such, is a fact, something that has happened in the mind of the dreamer: a psychologist might find it a useful guide to his mental disposition; a person ignorant of science will study some 'Book of Dreams' to find what he should do or not do. The histories of ancient times are full of dreams of commanders and oracles, of soothsayers deciding whether armies should advance or retreat, accept battle or avoid it.

Wars were waged incessantly for the glory of one god against another: neither existed, but both were believed to exist. A mirage in the desert may lead travellers to disaster. We know the hallucinations that are caused by alcohol and other drugs, and their consequences. To see with the physical eye, or hear with the physical ear, anything that is itself non-material is scientifically impossible: nevertheless many sane and sober people have been convinced that they have seen and heard ghosts (complete with clothes and voices); and such beliefs may affect opinions and actions. In all countries and in all times, including the present, the most absurd superstitions have been rife among the people, making them afraid of empty taboos and mutter idle incantations.

We have recognized that human minds are part of the real universe, as much as things. That being so, the ideas formed in those minds must also be part of it: mental constructs are real *as such*. We now find reason to add that this holds good independently of the truth or falsehood of the particular idea. The consequences of this will be important. As we proceed further and apply these conclusions to philosophy or religion, science or politics, we may discover here a clue to much in human history that is hard to understand. Imagination is a precious faculty and its achievements may be resplendent; but we can see in its errors, when it escapes from the control of reason, one of the main causes of the misfortunes and disasters that beset mankind.

3

But first we must stay for a moment with the arts, for they stand apart. In that realm fancy leads and reason is content to follow. Poetry, drama, the dance, the cinema, the radio and all the prolific literature of fiction, these have their own conventions which are so universally accepted that they have become part of our subconscious minds.

The arts may portray reality if they will, but they are equally free to roam outside it. On the wings of fancy we may soar far beyond the realities of our environment. We take great pleasure in this. Indeed most of the works of literature that have been accepted through the ages as masterpieces have crossed the frontiers of the natural into an imagined supernatural. We think of Homer, the Greek tragedians and Virgil, of Dante, Shakespeare, Milton, Bunyan, Goethe.

We seldom notice how constantly in our daily lives we make this escape from reality. Of the millions of books borrowed from the public libraries every year the large majority are works of fiction. The imaginary characters that populate the volumes on the library shelves, if they were all brought together, would be enough to make a nation: some of these characters are as well known and as widely discussed as the most famous persons in history. We go into a cinema to see some romantic film and find it thronged with people: what they are watching and hearing is three times removed from reality. On the screen are photographic images, ten to fifteen feet high: these portray actors pretending to be other people, who have themselves never existed. Yet the audience follow every word and action of these phantoms with the keenest interest: they rock with laughter at one moment, are moved to tears at the next.

The arts are mostly make-believe; their conventions are no more than pretences; yet we are right to hold them in honour and to praise their achievements. 'Preserve Romance', says Meredith; 'we exchange a sky for a ceiling if we let it go.' Modern civilization recognizes this and is grateful to those among us who, having the ability, dedicate themselves to the arts. It does so the more readily because it is realizing that the age has become too utilitarian and matter of fact: the opposite needs to be emphasized.

But the point I wish specially to make here is that we are so accustomed to this world of make-believe that we are liable to allow ourselves to be conditioned by it. Between factual and fictional the line is blurred. There are philosophies that would give to abstractions the same status as to realities. For centuries philosophers have been ready to pursue the phantoms of Platonic 'Forms'; of the 'Values' of Truth, Beauty, Goodness and the like; or 'The Absolute' of the neo-Hegelians. In political philosophy we are called upon to respect and obey such fictions as 'Destiny', 'The economic forces of History', or 'The State, real in its own right'. And in religion, the same reverence may be demanded for myth as for truth. These matters belong, however, to the subjects to be dealt with in subsequent chapters, and we shall come to them there.

4

But it is not only in philosophy and religion that the imagination is liable to mislead us. It happens also in science: especially now, when physics, although urging the strictest adherence to observation and experiment, has nevertheless been developing a new philosophy of its own that is in essence metaphysical. We have already referred to the theories that would endow with factual reality the fictional abstractions of Space and Time, seeking to impose on the objective universe 'a spacetime framework'. Heisenberg goes so far as to speak of a 'fundamental principle which our science has taken over from antiquity; that is the idea of a purposeful and directive force inherent in mathematical formulations'.

It is well therefore to remind ourselves that the whole of mathematics lies within the world of imagination. It deals, not with things, but with imaginative symbols for things. We become so busy, however, with figures, graphs, diagrams, measurements and calculations, that we sometimes come to confuse the symbols themselves with the objects symbolized. The extreme case is found in Heisenberg's Principle of Uncertainty, which is held to imply that, where the prior events that have given rise to any particular event cannot be identified and expressed mathematically, it must be assumed by science, and accepted by philosophy, that such an event was uncaused.

Whitehead says that: 'The process of thinking ahead of phenomena is essentially a work of the imagination . . . by science the imagination is disciplined and strengthened.' As to the geometrical conception of Space he says: 'Nature is a theatre for the inter-relations of activities. All things change, the activities and their inter-relations. To this new concept, the notion of space, with its passive, systematic, geometric relationship is entirely inappropriate. The fashionable notion that the new physics has reduced all physical laws to the statement of geometrical relations is quite ridiculous.'

'Finally,' says Whitehead, 'we are left with a fundamental question . . . What are those primary types of things in terms of which the process of the Universe is to be understood? Suppose we agree that Nature discloses to the scientific scrutiny merely activities and process. What does this mean? These activities fade into each other. They arise and then pass away. What is being enacted? What is effected? It cannot be that these are merely formulae of the multiplication table — in the words of a great philosopher, merely a bloodless dance of categories. Nature is full-blooded. Real facts are happening. Physical Nature, as studied in Science, is to be looked upon as a complex of the more stable inter-relations between the real facts of the real universe.'

From the symbolism of the mathematical imagination we must come back in the end to these facts of an actual universe, interpreted to us by the help of reason — imperfect no doubt, but it is the best that we have, and always improving. 'We may take Fancy for a companion, but must follow Reason as our guide', says Dr. Johnson, summing it all up in a sentence.

CHAPTER VIII

INSTITUTIONS

I

In our inquiry into the real universe and man's place in it, we have been adding together, one after the other, the elements that we find in it — material things, life and mind, ideas; among those ideas, the figments of the human imagination, and, among those figments, the abstractions of philosophy and science. We must now come to closer quarters with these abstractions. They have a powerful influence, both for good and for evil, on the lives of men and the course of history. Here we link up again with the initial object of our inquiry — to try to detect what are the underlying causes of the misfortunes, disasters and perils of the age in which we live, in the hope of finding better ways.

In his unceasing struggle against the difficulties and perplexities that have beset him, Man acts sometimes alone, sometimes with his fellows in groups or communities. Experience teaches him to form the habits of conduct that are essential to any form of communal life. Personal habits are generalized into social customs. Civilization gradually embodies its customs in Institutions — domestic, economic, political, religious. To these we now turn.

2

The oldest of institutions, and the most fundamental, is the Family. It goes back far beyond the dawn of civilization; it originates in the biological conditions of the race itself. The family arises out of the two-sex mechanism of reproduction, as evolved in the birds and the mammals. A male and a female secrete microscopic germ-cells, which meet by their coition. The two cells amalgamate and develop into a new individual, combining the qualities of the parents. But its survival after birth depends upon the provision, by one or both of those parents, of food and protection during immaturity.

The instincts of self-preservation, sex-attraction and care for offspring, are indispensable to the continuance of the line. Where, in any individual, one or other of these is lacking, the defect will eliminate itself, since no offspring will survive to transmit it to descendants. The same evolutionary causes that had originated the family group will ensure its repetition. A father and mother showing their child the birds in the garden building their nests, feeding their young, teaching the fledglings to fly, are showing the pattern of their own home.

Family groups having come into being, human intelligence puts them to further uses. The children remain with their parents; they all co-operate in mutual defence or attack, in hunting and tilling the soil, in any primary crafts there may be. As population increases, the groups find it to their advantage to come together in clans; the clans grow into a tribe; the tribes into a nation.

The family organization continues throughout, because of its utility. It keeps the child alive and trains him. It helps its members in sickness and old age, in misfortune or disaster. It protects them from violence and prevents attack by being ready to avenge injury. Property accumulates; parents wish to bequeath it to their children; marriage customs arise in order to fix paternity; promiscuous intercourse gives place to a publicly recognized polygamy, and finally, in most countries, to monogamy.

Out of this have developed the principal institutions that we see around us. The elders of the families — 'sitting in the gate', reconciling quarrels, penalizing crimes, deciding the community's attitude to its neighbours — evolve into the jury, the courts of law, the police; delegates are sent to the Council of the Chief, or of the King, finally to Parliaments. Codes of law are enacted: marriage becomes a matter of legal contract, instead only of customary status: the ownership and inheritance of property are legalized and regulated. The State, gathering strength and power, enforces the laws, maintains order, prevents or suppresses crime; if need be, wages war. Then, in the more advanced countries, the State sets up schools, safeguards health, helps the disabled and necessitous. Sometimes anticipating, sometimes supplementing these activities of the State, a vast network of Voluntary Organizations comes into being. They care also for the arts, and all forms of culture and recreation; they uphold religion. The rise of science has been adding in our own day a whole class of new organizations.

These multifarious institutions are bone and sinew of our civilization. When we look around and compare them with the customs and laws of primitive man, or even of the Greeks and Romans, we may stand amazed at the complexity, the vigour, and on the whole the success, of this highly elaborate system. It takes its place as one of the most significant elements in the world of reality.

'Success', but only on the whole. The defects are patent enough. The flow of events carries the institutions along; the older must adapt themselves to the conditions of a changing age; the newer have to consolidate their structure and develop their practice as experience dictates. It is often a painful process. Meanwhile the living generation has to contend with all kinds of difficulties: it is torn by controversies; it may be shattered by wars. In the defects of our institutions we may find a main cause of our distresses.

The family endures at the base of society; but its stability has been shaken, particularly in our own time. This is having important effects on the moral climate.

The family is weakened partly because the new agencies that have come into being have taken over some of its functions. The Welfare State tends for many purposes to supersede the home. (As Lord Beveridge has pointed out, we should rather call it the Welfare *Society*, so as to include the voluntary organizations.) In millions of families, the mother goes out to work; even the rudiments of education are not taught to the child 'at the mother's knee', but at the infant school; later, everything that can be done in the schools is given over to them. Health is the care of the ante-natal clinic, the school doctor and dentist, of the public health service in general. Whoever is in need can look to the community for maintenance. Further, the homes themselves are becoming less and less fitted for family life. Instead of separate houses, often with gardens, more and more of the population are obliged to live in small flats, piled side by side and one on top of another in vast and forbidding buildings, among crowded and noisy streets.

In more placid times most families remained stable, generation after generation, in the same neighbourhood. Circumstances now often lead them to scatter. Local connections have been further loosened by the upheavals of two great wars. And military service, during the most impressionable years of their lives, has taken the young men away from the steadying influences of the home.

In the present century vast changes have come about as the consequence of women's emancipation. That the status of women has been raised and their opportunities enlarged must indeed, in the long run, tend to strengthen the family as an institution. But in these early days it seems to be having an indirect effect that was little foreseen. All through the ages women have regarded marriage as their natural lot, and the bond as unbreakable, except for infidelity. Such difficulties as there might be had to be endured because they could not be escaped. Immemorial custom, the commands of religion, the pressure of public opinion, and, not least, a sense of duty towards children, all combined to make the permanence of the home a matter of course. Now things are different. A higher value is set upon individual liberty. Grievances are not accepted with the old meekness and docility. The same rights are asserted on the husband's side, and not contested. The consequence is that the legislatures of most countries have felt themselves obliged to make the marriage contract less rigid. Although the vast majority of marriages hold fast, the minority that 'come to pieces' has shown a rapid increase.

All this cannot be avoided if gross hardship is not to be inflicted in the exceptional case; but that it is having harmful effects upon the community in general is obvious enough. Easy divorce leads to light-hearted marriage. For an increasing number of the rising generation, the background of a united home, with an atmosphere of lasting affection, will be missing. Children without families lack roots. It is well known that the recent great wave of juvenile delinquency, leading sometimes to violent crimes, has been due more to the absence of parental control, through the break-up of families during the war years, than to any other one cause.

The nineteenth century emphasized social duty and strove to enforce it: the twentieth has laid more stress than before on individual self-expression. In the sphere of morals, laxity is more readily condoned. The tone of novels and plays has been a powerful solvent. A European writer on the contemporary scene has said, of a trend conspicuous in recent fiction: 'Virtue and respectability, so long the objects of praise, become outmoded; they are felt as a source of embarrassed shame . . . Interest is shifted more and more from virtue rewarded to evil-doing unpunished.'

Among the unsettled questions that vex the present age and keep it restless, uneasy, uncertain of itself, are many that relate, in one form or another, to the relations between the sexes and the upbringing of children. And these come from deep down — from the weakening of the family as a fundamental institution of human society.

3

At the base, the family; at the summit, the State. Here the defects are even more obvious, the injuries more grave, the problems more urgent. It is in its politics that our age has suffered its greatest failures. In every country, tension between parties is chronic; in some, revolution is a recent memory and a constant danger. Worst of all, in the international sphere we have the disgrace that, in an age that thinks itself civilized, war has persisted as one of the established institutions of human society.

Two dynamic forces are ever at work — the passion for liberty and the revolt against poverty. These two currents have been sweeping through the modern world; swirling into eddies whereever they are obstructed; clashing in whirlpools wherever they conflict; flowing in an overwhelming flood when they mingle and unite. At one time and place it may be a nation that is struggling to free itself from subjection to an alien Power. At another it may be the uprising of a people against an oligarchy or a King. Or it may be personal liberty that is in question — freedom for the individual from unequal laws and a denial of opportunity. Or lastly — and this is now a dominant issue in most countries of the world in an age of expanding production and abounding wealth — it may be an upheaval of the masses of a people resolved at long last to free themselves from the bonds of poverty and squalor.

> Lazarus, hungry,
> Menaces Dives;
> Labour the giant
> Chafes in his hold.

Constant unrest at home; intermittent, but ruthless wars abroad — that is the overall picture of our times. And these wars have come at a moment when the intelligence of man has surpassed all records in other spheres — in the conquests over nature through the achievements of science. It is the tragic paradox of our generation that, of all the sixty centuries of recorded history, this century has at once the glory of such triumphs and the shame of two wars, the vastest and most destructive ever known.

Men's actions are governed by their ideas. If what they do is bad, it is because what they think is wrong. We have to survey our ideas afresh and try to put our finger on those wrong ideas which have led to the harmful actions. We shall find very soon that, more often than not, the fault lies in what we have just been discussing — mistakes in the form or the working of our social institutions, into which we have been led by strange vagaries of the human imagination, loose from the control of the rational intelligence.

4

I will recall some well-known examples.

The doctrine of the Divine Right of Kings has now been so completely discredited and discarded that the great part it played for many centuries as a frequent cause of revolution and civil war has passed out of memory. The Roman Emperors claimed to be, not only divinely appointed, but divine in their own persons, entitled during their lifetime to worship in the temples of the gods: and this, however questionable the means by which they might have displaced the previous divinity, and however scandalous their own reputations. The myth of divine election was revived in the Middle Ages by the Holy Roman Empire. Asserted again in this country by the Stuarts, it led to the only war in its history between King and Parliament. It was revived once more in the nineteenth century, after the fall of Napoleon, in the self-styled Holy Alliance of the reactionary Emperors and Kings. The tragic deaths of such well-meaning, though misdirected, sovereigns as Charles I, Louis XVI and Nicholas II brought this fiction to an end in the western world. But it was only in 1945 that the present Emperor of Japan formally renounced a divine right to the throne based upon a legend of the physical descent of his family from a Sun Goddess.

Monarchy remains as an institution in our own day, but over a greatly restricted area and with a much more modest title. A hundred years ago all the countries of the eastern hemisphere — except Switzerland (and San Marino) — right across Europe, Africa and Asia from Atlantic to Pacific, were still under Emperors or Kings. Now — apart from territories of the British Commonwealth, Greece, Japan, a few of the lesser States of Asia and Ethiopia — the only ones that remain are the group of monarchies in north-western Europe. These are second to none in the efficiency and stability of their governments. But there is no longer any pretence of 'the Right Divine of Kings to govern wrong'. Their title is not supernatural but purely mundane. The basis is real. It rests, not on imaginations, but on constitutions, written or unwritten, accepted by peoples and administered by Parliaments. Here mankind has rid itself of one cause at least of recurring revolutions and wars.

But hardly had that figment begun to fade away when a new one appeared to take its place. It was the theory of the Original Social Contract. Given prominence at the end of the seventeenth century by Hobbes and Locke, and then powerfully promoted by the eloquence and enthusiasm of Rousseau, it filled the minds of the eighteenth-century intellectuals. It seemed to furnish a philosophic basis for the idea of Natural Rights, which was to inspire both the French and the American Revolutions. The theory was that, since the State exists, it must have had an origin. (This was before the advent of the principle of Evolution.) Its origin could only have been in some agreement between a people and its governors for the promotion of their common interests. Unless this is assumed to have been so, the State could not have come into existence, and there could now be no such thing as Political Philosophy. But the State does in fact exist, in various forms; and Political Philosophy does exist also: therefore we must presume a Social Contract as its basis. From this it follows that, where the governors do not properly care for the welfare of the people, they must be held to have broken the terms of the original agreement, and it is legitimate to overthrow and replace them.[1] Eager reformers seized upon this queer piece of logic. With fervent rhetoric, and contemptuous scorn for any alternative that might be offered, they made it the dynamic idea of their time. But the concept had one considerable disadvantage. It was founded on nothing better than myth. No historian could show that any such contract had ever been made, anywhere. So that when some man of action — a Napoleon, or an Emperor or King of Russia, of Austria, Prussia or France — set out to sweep away democracy and re-establish despotism, he had nothing more facing him in the way of an ideology than a fiction. In the clash with reality the myth went under. It disappeared and has never been heard of since.

Yet such has been the strange attraction of philosophical figments that successors to the Divine Right of Kings and the Social Contract of Peoples soon appeared. In the latter half of the nineteenth century and the first half of the twentieth a profusion of new fictions made their appearance in central and southern Europe. Lacking any other faith, the minds of tens of millions of credulous and uncritical people were captured by these ideas. Where the conditions proved favourable, they succeeded in uniting the two currents seething in our time — the passion of patriotism and the revolt against poverty. They combined them in some form either of National-Socialism or of National-Communism, the first laying chief stress on nationality, the second on social change.

But both were based on myth.

5

Hegel held the doctrine that 'The State' is a living entity, real in its own right, and supreme. 'It is', he said, 'the divine idea as it exists on earth . . . It is the ultimate end which has the highest right against the individual.' Circumstances soon gave to this abstract theory a practical importance. The defeat of Germany

---

[1] In the Revolution of 1688 the House of Commons passed a resolution 'That James, having endeavoured to subvert the Constitution of the Kingdom by breaking the original contract between King and People, and . . . having violated the fundamental laws, and having withdrawn himself out of this Kingdom had deserted the Government and that the throne is thereby vacant'. (January 28th, 1688. House of Lords Records Office, Memo. 9(D), 1955, p. 8).

by Napoleon at the battle of Jena was followed by a recoil; a great patriotic movement among the people not only aimed at redressing the humiliations of the French occupation; its impetus carried it on to asserting the primacy of Germany over Europe. Prussian militarism was revived and exalted: under Bismarck it seized power at home and the initiative abroad.

The Hegelian idea came just at the convenient moment. Its doctrine of an omnipotent state, with a moral law of its own devising, gave an appearance of intellectual justification for Bismarck's three wars of aggression against his neighbours, north, south and west.

The doctrine was incessantly instilled into the German mind by a movement headed by professors at the universities, Berlin in particular. 'Always without exception', said Fichte, 'the most civilized State is the most aggressive.' Treitschke wrote: 'War will endure to the end of history. The laws of human thought and of human history forbid any alternative, neither is one to be wished for.' These ideas, advancing with an ever-increasing momentum, culminated in the National-Socialism of the present century. Hitler wrote in his *Mein Kampf*: 'That this world will in future be subject to the severest struggles for the existence of mankind cannot be doubted. In the end, the urge for self-preservation is eternally victorious. Before it, the so-called humanitarianism, which is merely a compound of stupidity, cowardice and arrogance, melts like snow in the March sunshine. In constant struggle mankind had become great — in eternal peace it must perish.'

All this found an echo in Italian Fascism. The first article in the Fascist declaration of principles entitled, paradoxically, 'The Charter of Liberty', proclaimed that: 'The Italian nation, by its power and duration, is an organism with a being, and ends and means of action, superior to those of the individuals, whether separate or grouped, of which it is composed.' Mussolini said, in one of many such declarations: 'Fascism does not believe in the possibility, or the utility, of perpetual peace . . . War alone brings to their maximum tension all human energies and stamps the seal of nobility on those peoples which have the virtue to face it . . . We are becoming, and shall become so increasingly because this is our desire, a military nation; a militaristic nation, I will add.'

But the concept of a State as a living entity, real in its own right, with an inherent power of action and its own moral code, is also a figment of the imagination — as much as a Divine Right of Kings or an Original Social Contract. For a State is nothing more than a number of men and women, living together in a particular area on this planet, who have organized themselves into an institution for certain purposes of common action. Man is by nature social; but because, after long ages of evolution, human beings have an inborn tendency to co-operate, this does not confer reality on the various forms of co-operation that they find it convenient to adopt. No one would say, if, for example, motor car manufacturers combine in an association to promote their commercial interests, or miners form a trade union, or someone in America gives ten million dollars to establish a university, that a new metaphysical entity in each case has come into being. Similarly when families combine into a tribe, and tribes into a nation, and the members of the nation organize themselves into a State, no 'living entity, real in its own right' has been brought into existence thereby. It is one more fictional abstraction, yet another myth.

Meantime, again in Germany and again under the influence of Hegel, Karl Marx had put forward a social theory of his own. And once more the seed fell on congenial soil. It originated at a time, not of military defeat, but of widespread social misery. The Marxist movement was in essence a vehement protest against the evil conditions of life for the workers that had been among the first results of the Industrial Revolution — low wages for the unskilled grades of labour and for many of the skilled; long hours for all in the factories and the mines; frequent unemployment; squalid housing in the overcrowded working-class quarters of the vast new cities. The remedy proposed was a communist economy based on a materialist philosophy. But here again, in order to give to the whole structure a semblance of scientific authority, Marxism needed a fresh figment. It assumed the existence of 'Historic Economic Forces'. It attributed to them the deplorable state of things that then prevailed. But it also held that the same supposed 'forces' would, by the same inherent necessity, also bring about the cure. The course of past events could be analysed scientifically, and the course of future events predicted with equal certainty. The word 'inevitably' became the key-word in communist propaganda. The faithful were encouraged to believe that they had the universe at their back.

6

This was in essence a reversion to a very ancient idea. The probing mind of the Greeks could not rest satisfied with their old cosmogony of man-like gods. They realized that there must be something beyond, something to which the gods themselves must yield obedience. Thus evolved the super-myth of Anankê — Necessity. Vague, inexplicable, apparently self-created, this was thought of as a Power, ruthless and irresistible, governing in the ultimate resort both the doings of the gods and the fates of men. The belief that has been gaining ground in the modern world is similar. This too follows a decline in the old customary religion — the faith in a personal providence, all-powerful and benevolent, actively controlling at each moment the course of human affairs. For many minds the experience of the two world wars has made it impossible to retain this conviction as a living creed able to control men's conduct. So, under the name of 'Destiny', or sometimes 'History', the ancient Anankê has come back to life. Here, they say, is where final responsibility rests. Here is the explanation for everything that has happened, is happening, or is about to happen.

Writing about the outbreak of the First World War, the former Crown Prince of Germany speaks, in his memoirs, of the year 1914 as a time 'when the enormous pressure of economic and political forces was uncontrollably driving the world towards the catastrophe of war'. Sir Austen Chamberlain, writing of the difficulties of British politics in the same year, says: 'Relentless Fate, as in a Greek tragedy, seemed driving us all to a catastrophe ... The actors were in the grip of forces stronger than themselves, whirled round and downwards like frail craft caught in the maelstrom of inexorable fate.' Lord Grey of Fallodon wrote, in his *Twenty-five Years*, in connection with an earlier crisis: 'There is in great affairs so much more, as a rule, in the minds of the events (if such an expression may be used) than in the minds of the chief actors.'

During the Second World War, Mussolini, orating to a vast throng in Rome in June 1940, proclaims: 'The hour marked out by destiny is sounding in the sky of our country . . . The declaration of war has been handed to the ambassadors of Britain and France.' A month later, the Foreign Office in Berlin issues a statement saying: 'Nobody now contests that Germany and Italy are predestined to reorganize Europe on a new basis.' When things were not going well, Goebbels tells the German people that 'History is quite without grace and mercy, and the nation must make good by a battle full of sacrifices'; but, he adds, the task of this age 'must be viewed by us as a kind gesture by destiny'.

In Dr. Oswald Spengler's monumental work, *The Decline of the West*, which had a vast circulation in Germany in the inter-war period, and considerable influence elsewhere, the key idea, throughout its thousand pages, is again 'Destiny'. He constantly uses phrases such as 'an inherent historic necessity'. He attaches prime importance to 'what is named by us "conjuncture", "accident", "Providence", or "Fate", by Classical man "Nemesis", "Anankê", "Tyche", or "Fatum", by the Arab "Kismet".' He writes, with reference to the territorial expansion of European Powers: 'It is not a matter of choice — it is not the conscious will of individuals, or even that of whole classes or peoples that decides. The expansive tendency is a doom, something daemonic and immense, which grips, forces into service, and uses up the late mankind of the world-city stage,[1] willy-nilly, aware or unaware.'

It must have been somewhat disconcerting, however, for the credulous believers in this Destiny, these Historic Forces, to find that the consequences of their intervention, which were so confidently predicted as inevitable, as often as not did not happen. Germany and Italy, 'predestined to reorganize Europe on a new basis' when 'the hour marked out by destiny is sounding in the sky', failed utterly to do that; the attempt brought them only to utter ruin. The 'Doom, daemonic and immense', which impelled the German people to expand — to annex Alsace-Lorraine, dominate Austria and absorb a large part of Africa — did not save them in the result from the loss of everything they had won.

---

[1] Spengler's term for an industrial civilization.

Most of Karl Marx's predictions of a hundred years ago have proved wrong. He asserted that, in the heavily industrialized countries, the poor would grow poorer and the rich richer. The gulf between the proletariat, on the one hand, and the bourgeois and wealthy classes on the other, would become more clear-cut. The struggle between them would be intensified, until it culminated in each case in a revolution, from which would spring a dictatorship of the proletariat. Such countries as might at first remain capitalist would inevitably soon be driven to plunge into aggressive wars against the communist States; partly for fear of their own peoples being subverted by the success of their rivals, but mainly because they would otherwise be torn to pieces themselves by their own 'inner economic contradictions'. All this was in the living womb of history, and therefore bound to happen.

A century has passed. None of it has happened. In the countries where the Industrial Revolution has gone fastest and farthest — Western Europe and North America — decade by decade most of the poor have grown much less poor; and, owing partly to equalizing taxation, many of the rich much less rich. The line between workers and capitalists has become less and less rigid; the classes more and more overlap. [1]

The only great countries where anything resembling a dictatorship of the proletariat has been established are those that were the least industrialized and least civilized — Russia and China. There is no sign that the others are ready to follow their example. The United States, where the capitalist system is the most highly developed, is not in the least danger of being 'torn to pieces by its own inner contradictions'. No western State has the remotest intention of attacking Russia and China in order to save itself from social revolution: incidentally, it is obvious that that would be the one thing most likely to promote it. The fact is that, since the end of the Second World War, the only victims of aggression have been the unhappy neighbours of the proletarian dictatorships, in the belt of countries from the Baltic to the Black Sea — Estonia,

---

[1] It is not possible to say at what point a working-man passes from the category of the 'have-nots' into that of the 'haves'; but it is known that, in Great Britain for example, working-class investments — in the purchase of their own homes, in co-operative societies, building societies, savings banks, small savings securities and the like — amount to thousands of millions of pounds.

Latvia, Lithuania (Finland only narrowly escaping), Eastern Germany, Poland, Czechoslovakia, Austria, Hungary, Yugoslavia, Bulgaria, Rumania; and again in far-eastern Asia, when the South Koreans were attacked by the North Koreans, supported militarily by China and diplomatically by Russia.

We see, then, how again and again our political institutions have failed to ensure peaceful change, to give us progress with order. We ask why that has been so; we find an answer in this strange readiness of millions of people, now in one country, now in another, to set off, under the leadership of intellectuals with more enthusiasm than common sense, in eager pursuit of some philosophical will-o'-the-wisp. And no sooner is the last one discovered to be the illusion that it is than another is sighted glimmering over the swamps, and a fresh mass movement rushes off to catch it.

Men's actions are governed by their ideas: wrong ideas lead to bad actions: these have been the wrong ideas that have brought us so often to disaster.

7

This is not to suggest that the institutions themselves are fictional. Families, schools, churches, trade unions, voluntary associations in great variety, political parties, Courts of Law, States — certainly they exist, certainly they have their place in the real universe. The mistake is in supposing that they, or any of them, can be regarded as of the same order as living organisms — able to *do* things, able themselves somehow to direct men's actions and decide the course of events.

Then what are they?

Here we may do well to bring in the concept that we have found serviceable before, and say that Institutions are Patterns.

The pattern may sometimes be localized and visible. Schools, universities may repeat the same pattern over and over again in different places: there are teachers and pupils and special buildings. Or you may watch a Parliament at work in its Chamber — the House of Commons, the French Assembly. Indeed it is often easier to visualize and describe an institution by naming its domicile than its composition or functions. In Washington the

Presidency and its activities are spoken of as The White House,[1] Congress as Capitol Hill, the Army Department as The Pentagon. In London we have The Palace, Downing Street, or Whitehall.

In many cases, however, the pattern is not localized, but is diffused and invisible. Trade unions may all be more or less of the same pattern, with the same kind of rules and organization, and given legal existence by registration under a general Act of Parliament. But each union is scattered wherever its members may be – all over the mines, or factories, or workshops of the industry. A great Church – Roman Catholic, Anglican, Methodist – is not only where its headquarters are, or its places of worship. It is universal. Wherever its adherents are to be found, wherever two or three are gathered together, or even where one is, solitary in his own home – the Church is there.

When we were discussing this matter in an earlier chapter, it was clear that, although patterns were realities, they did not exist as entities, self-sufficient in themselves. There must always be something else that carries the pattern. In physics, for example, we found that waves were patterns of – or in – water, or air, or maybe ether – if there is an ether. When we were dealing with the mechanism of mind, we found that it too worked in patterns, this time of electrical activities in the brain and nervous system. In material objects we are accustomed to see the same pattern again and again – printed on wall-paper, woven in cloth, stamped on coins. But there has first to be the paper, the woollen cloth, the metal discs. You cannot have pattern in the abstract – except in the imagination, in the world of thought. So now, if we speak of institutions as patterns, we must at once ask ourselves what it is that is being patterned.

The answer is obvious enough. Human institutions are patterns of individual human beings. These are the stuff, the substance. These constitute the physical reality.

8

The State consists of its citizens. There could be no State if there were no citizens; no House of Commons if there were no

---

[1] The word 'Pharaoh' in the Egyptian language originally meant 'The Great House'. Cf. The Sublime Porte, for the Government of the Sultan of Turkey; The Vatican, The Quirinal, etc.

Members of Parliament; no Law Courts if no judges and lawyers; no army if no soldiers.

Each individual can be — in fact he always is — a unit in more than one pattern at the same time. In any civilized country he will be a citizen of the State. Also, normally, a member of a family. He can be a member of a Church as well, of a political party, of a trade union or professional association, of a club — social, musical, athletic, or the like.

Individuals enter a particular organization; they may go out again and others come in: the pattern persists. As Queen Elizabeth II has said, addressing a parade of the Grenadier Guards: 'The Regiment does not change; it is only the men who stand in its ranks.'

Yet patterns may be modified, perhaps imperceptibly and over long periods. A Church, keeping its name and aspects, may abandon or vary in one century some of the doctrines it had taught earlier. Or an institution may be suspended for a time and then resume; or it may be dissolved or superseded.

We must not picture all this as though it were a rigid system of fixed patterns impressed upon a human society once for all, into which individuals must fit themselves as best they can. It is far more fluid. And it is not imposed by any external agency. Conditioned only by the physical character of the planet we inhabit, the institutions of a nation are the product of the people themselves. No Divine Right, no fictional Destiny or Historic Forces, no evolutionary law of automatic progress, no metaphysical fable of any kind is to be made responsible. It is something much more tangible, more easily understood, closer at hand, that is responsible — the will and actions, or inactions, of the men and women who are the nation.

And it is not enough to say that it is the structure of the institution that matters; that all will be well if we draw up a perfect democratic constitution, or an ideal system of jurisprudence, or even, perhaps, a Charter of World Government logical in every article and unchallengeable. The working is as important as the structure: even more so, for an imperfect constitution, served by men of good sense and good will, will do better than one more perfect in its drafting but less fortunate in its constituents. It has been well said: 'Institutions are like fortresses. They must be well designed *and* manned.'

Lastly, having expelled all the other fictions, let us not allow one of them to slip back surreptitiously, and tempt us to shift our responsibilities on to a figment termed mankind. 'Mankind?' said Goethe. 'It is an abstraction. There are, always have been, and always will be, men and only men.'

And they are not men idealized, as by the French eighteenth-century philosophers, but as they really are; as we see them in the streets or the villages — or, each one of us, in our own looking-glass, every day.

CHAPTER IX

CONDUCT

I

HERE we reach a fresh stage in our search for reality. From now on it is primarily the individual that we have to consider. Postponing, for the time being, theological questions; taking as given our terrestrial habitat in its cosmic setting; shaking ourselves free from the imaginary abstractions that cling to us so persistently; and recognizing that our institutions, the framework of our civilization, are nothing but ourselves, in various patterns, over again — we pause for a moment and look around. What we see is nature, with its varied phenomena, material and mental: among them, human beings thinking and acting. And nothing else.

Each human being is single and autonomous; but he is not solitary. He cannot be thought of — he cannot exist — apart from his environment: or rather we should say environments, for they are many. They are of all dimensions — from the home to the city, the country, ultimately the whole globe. And they extend through all periods of time — from the remotest past to the actual present, and on into an unlimited future. Subject to terrestrial conditions and still leaving in abeyance questions of theology, we reach the conclusion that the individual himself, with others like him — past, present and future — must accept responsibility for everything that has happened, is happening or will happen. For there is nowhere else that responsibility can lie.

The rest of our inquiry will concern itself therefore with individual conduct. It is there, if anywhere, that we must find the causes, and seek the cures, of the evils that afflict us.

2

But here again, as so often before, when we are ready, and eager, to set out into new country, we find ourselves held back by some fundamental problem to which neither philosophy nor science gives any agreed answer. Here it is the question of Freewill.

There are those who say: 'You speak of the human person, his power of choice, freedom of action, moral responsibility: but what do you suppose this personality to be — this Ego, this alleged freedom?' Does it not all begin in a single fertilized germ-cell, with its chromosomes and genes; and do not these embody characteristics, transmitted from prior generations, which have already predetermined its own character? And have not Freud and his successors shown us conclusively that, as part of our heritage, we possess unconscious and subconscious minds, bringing with them primitive racial impulses, accumulated through the centuries, which are constantly breaking through, in instincts and intuitions, to dominate the conscious? Is not the individual born also into contemporary environments which shape and condition his every thought and action? That being so, your supposed freedom of choice, they say, is nothing better than illusion. The will of the individual and its decisions, apparently free and spontaneous, are in fact no more than the necessary consequences of influences, either seated within the mind itself or else external and social, which are altogether beyond his power to control. Here, then, is the message of modern science, and philosophy can do no other than accept it. From this it would follow that the whole structure of our ethics has to be rebuilt now from the very foundation. To talk of personal responsibility is out of date. Praise and blame, reward and punishment are quite outmoded. Our courts of justice are seen to be essentially unjust: it is not the criminal that is to blame but the society that produced him. Every fault, every vice, every crime even, is to be viewed with 'broad-mindedness', toleration and compassion. *Tout comprendre c'est tout pardonner*. The schoolmaster, the preacher, the judge on the Bench or the legislator in Parliament, has no right to censure or penalize; public opinion today, or history tomorrow, must not presume to assess merit and demerit, to approve or condemn.

Are these opinions right or wrong? We shall not get far with our survey of human conduct as a vital factor in the real universe unless we make up our minds about this, one way or the other.

3

Scientists are so busy exploring the obscure and unknown that when, after long effort, they succeed in making some striking and valuable discovery it is not surprising that they should sometimes be tempted to discard the obvious and undervalue the familiar. Freudian psychoanalysis is a case in point. The pioneers, having established the importance of the unconscious and subconscious, may be inclined to present them as all-important. Where, as is often the case, there is a conflict in the mind between present conscious will and inherited subconscious tendency, it would be the tendency that we must expect to dominate. In so far as psychoanalysis is brought into this argument in support of philosophic determinism, it must mean that or nothing. If, however, this is disputed, if it is said that psychoanalysis claims no more than that inherited tendency must be taken into account, and that, though often decisive, it may sometimes be resisted and overcome, then the whole position is surrendered. For that would be to admit that the conscious is still a factor; that the personal will has independence; is real in its own right; can choose whether to surrender to subconscious impulses or to fight against them. It would be an admission that the individual human will is not always the prisoner of a preordained necessity.

No one suggests that this freedom is unconditioned. Of course heredity and environment, 'nature and nurture', always come in. But let us not fall into the mistake of supposing that the autonomous power of the individual person to reflect, to choose and to act, must henceforth be ruled out; that because the unconscious and the subconscious have importance, the conscious now has none.

All these — heredity, the genes, the unconscious and subconscious, the effects of environment — are merged in the personality of the individual. There emerges something new and different. It is his power of choice, what we are accustomed to call his freewill.

All this has led to much learned debate on the nature of Causation. It is asked: 'A cause A is followed by an effect B:

how does that come about: and how, in such a process, can novelty ever appear?' The reply may be simple. This A-B relation never in fact occurs. Never in the history of the universe has any event been the consequence of some single event; always of a combination of a number of events. When something happens and we try to find why, we usually mislead ourselves by looking only for the one abnormal and final event which completes the combination and brings about the result; taking for granted the many normal events that have combined to create the situation itself.

To give an example – let us say a man smells in the night an escape of gas: he takes a box of matches and goes to look for it; there is an explosion and he is killed. The coroner's inquest finds that his own action was *the cause* of the death; and that is sufficient for all practical purposes. But anyone could write down a long list of previous events which are not taken into account because they belong to the usual state of things, although if any one of them had been absent this accident could not have occurred. For instance – the existence of coal and of the mining industry; the use of an explosive gas to light our houses; the fact that this house was lighted by gas and not electricity; the leak itself, due to some defect or negligence; the man having a box of matches at hand and not an electric torch, and his not knowing better than to use them – had any one of these factors been missing the event would not have happened: the moment they all came together, the explosion took place. The causality lay in the combination. And so it is with every event, of every kind.

There is therefore no mysterious 'Law of Causation' that makes things happen and that needs to be described, defined and explained by philosophers. It is a question merely of succession: when the prior events are such that the combination of them will produce a certain result, then, that combination being effected, that result will ensue, and if not, not.

There is, however, one law – or principle, or fact, name it what you will – which is of the essence of the matter; it is usually termed the Law of the Uniformity of Nature. This asserts that if one set of events, when brought into combination, has been followed by a particular event, then any other set of events, if precisely the same, will always be followed, when combined, by another similar event. The prior events are termed causes, the subsequent events, effect. [1]

There is no ground for supposing that causation in this sense applies everywhere else, but not to human decisions and actions.

4

The process of the emergence of novelty is normal in all living organisms. It is usually a gradual process and we can watch it happening any day. Indeed we are so familiar with it that we seldom stop to think how remarkable it is.

Last year I was given, as a present, a hyacinth bulb in an elegant little pot: when spring was at hand we put it on a table in this room and watched it growing day by day. First there appeared at the top of the bulb the two little green specks, which quickly developed into strong shoots, that served as a shield for the sturdy stalk that was pushing its way up between them. Then, at the tip, appeared a compact cluster of embryo buds, which presently unfolded into the column of perfect flowers, with their characteristic colour and scent, each one containing seeds of possible future generation. We called it the daily miracle. In the end was something altogether different from the bulb that we had had at the beginning. There will have been at that time, in other houses or gardens, millions of hyacinth plants doing just the same. But each one was unique, with its own independent life, its own growth and efflorescence and power of reproduction.

Consider now a new-born infant. In nine months it has passed through the successive embryonic states from a single cell to a human personality. The process of development continues uninterruptedly after birth. The infant at first is small, helpless, passive. It is not blind, as most mammals at birth, but it cannot focus its eyes: it accepts and digests food, but only as milk: it cannot masticate: it cries, but cannot talk: moves its limbs, but cannot crawl or walk. In the course of the next few weeks or months it will have doubled its weight, and all those other capabilities will have begun to appear. It develops, as the plant has developed, through its own inherent vitality. With the human organism, mental capacities begin also to show themselves.

[1] 'The philosophy of Hume was nothing more than the analysis of the word "cause" into uniform sequence.' — Benjamin Jowett.

The psychologist tells us that with the child 'there are two critical points in this development which mark the beginnings of new levels; at round about the age of eighteen months representative activity begins: there is evidence then for the existence of ideas or images detached from present reality . . . The second critical point in the development of thinking occurs in general between the ages of seven and eleven, and is marked by the systematization and decentralization of thought . . . Our mature capacity for judgement is a highly evolved instance of the assimilatory activity which is also present at the very beginning of intellectual development'.

The psychologist is describing in technical language what is already common knowledge. Every young father and mother can see this happening in their own children. Month by month, year after year, they watch with pleasure and pride the child developing 'a mind of its own'; later maybe with anxiety also, as the adolescent boys and girls insist more and more upon following their own bent, perhaps at the risk of mistakes and failures. This independent power to choose and will to act does not come at a particular moment as some miraculous gift. It comes gradually and late; but as easily and normally as seeing or hearing, walking or talking. At the end we have the person, the Ego – body and mind interfused. To quote Whitehead again: 'No one ever says, Here am I, and I have brought my body with me.'

Viewing the situation as a whole we conclude that every human action results from a combination of factors. These are – the working of the physical universe; the activities of the surrounding society; the characteristics inherited by the individual; and his own autonomous will. The essential point is that the event that is happening is indeed a combination, not an aggregation; not merely the result of a number of prior causes added together like a sum in arithmetic. Something new and different has appeared. In the vast succession of effect following cause, here at this moment, through the act of volition, a new cause has been born into the universe – real, unique – to give rise in its turn, in conjunction with others, to further events in the future.

Included in our heritage is the capacity to go beyond the heritage. And this is the most important of all, for it is this that keeps the future open. We are not living in a closed system. Within limits that are given, we ourselves are shaping it.

In this controversy, now so ancient, the principle of Freewill, with its consequence of the moral responsibility of the individual, has always been the side taken by common sense. People observe what is happening in their own minds. They know also that, unless such responsibility is accepted, life in communities would be impossible. Philosophers and scientists would be ill-advised to brush this aside as naive and of no account. A practical world, set upon finding solutions for problems that are urgent and vital, will prefer to rely on personal introspection and social experience rather than on logical refinements.

5

Our inquiry has brought us now into the region of ethics. Social institutions are part of the real universe: they cannot work well, or even at all, unless the men and women who compose them act properly towards one another. A study of reality, therefore, must include a study of human conduct.

Ethics seeks to answer two questions. The first is — What is right and wrong? The second is — Why should we do right when to do wrong is more agreeable, or seems more advantageous?

Philosophers have continually been trying to find some formula which will supply a compendious answer to those questions. They speak of the Absolute Good; or the Ultimate Values of Truth, Beauty and Goodness; or the Categorical Imperative. Taking these universals as given, the particulars are to be deduced afterwards. Our intuitions; the dictates of conscience; the innate satisfaction in doing right, or remorse after doing wrong — these are looked upon as a common inheritance, the same for all men. They are to have priority. The applications follow, and give us the code of the Moral Law.

But with this the philosophers of the empirical school are not content. They are sceptical about all *a priori* generalizations. 'Truth, Beauty and Goodness'? — they can find no substance in those terms: not until they have been broken down into particulars will they get any meaning that can be grasped by the mind

'Intuition'? — we may fare badly indeed, as recent world history
has plainly shown, if we are led to put our trust in intuitions
unless they are supported by experience and justified by reason.
'Conscience — the Categorical Imperative'? — but what is to be
done when, as often happens, the conscience of one man, or
creed, or nation commands one thing and other people's con-
sciences command the opposite? In the wars of religion — the
Crusades or the Reformation — have we any right to say that
one side was more sincere, more conscientious, according to its
lights than the other? When, under the Tudors, Protestants sent
Catholics to the scaffold and the stake, next Catholics sent Protestants, and then the opposite again — where shall we find that
'innate sense of right and wrong, common to all men' that is to
be relied upon for guidance? Or to come to an outstanding
instance in our own time, no one was more sincerely guided by
conscience in all his doings than Mahatma Gandhi: but his
murder was not the work of some ordinary criminal, but of a
conscientious devotee of orthodox Hinduism, bitterly opposed to
Gandhi's principles of universal religious toleration. After his
arrest the assassin said: 'Cut me in pieces, and I will still maintain
I did right.' Conscience clashed with conscience.

An eminent writer on these subjects has said: 'Although we
hold it to be wrong of a person to act against his conscience, we
may at the same time blame him for having such a conscience
as he has'; and probably most people would agree with that. But
if so, we shall have abandoned any claim of conscience to be
absolute. If we are justified in blaming someone else for the
kind of conscience that he has, then clearly we are no longer
accepting individual conscience as the touchstone of right and
wrong.

The realist philosopher starts at the other end. He does not
begin by trying to discover The Absolute or to define The Good.
He begins by asking what particular ideas or beliefs, thoughts or
actions, events or objects, are in fact accepted as good. Experience
has taught mankind what they should be, and why they ought
to be accepted.

The primary good for any living organism is to exist. 'No one',
says Spinoza, 'can desire to be happy, to act well and live well,
who does not at the same time desire to be, to act and to live,

that is to say, actually to exist. No virtue can be conceived prior to this, the endeavour, namely after self-preservation.'

Other elementary goods arise from our bodily nature. Health rather than sickness, to be fed rather than starve, a shelter from the weather – that these and the like are 'good' no sane man would deny. Civilization advances, bringing with it new pleasures, intellectual and aesthetic. The arts develop – the arts of language – oratory, drama, poetry, prose; the visual arts; music, dancing. Pleasures like these are among the good that men value. To make life in communities possible, certain qualities in the citizens are also necessary – honesty, truthfulness, orderly behaviour, public spirit. We call good those who possess them, bad those who do not.

Such valuations, however, are themselves not absolute, but must be relative to individuals and circumstances. If mouse meets cat, is that a good thing or a bad thing? Evidently it is good for the cat and bad for the mouse. New knowledge may turn an action that one generation would universally regard as a good deed into one that a later generation would condemn with equal unanimity as anti-social. When Uncle Toby, in Sterne's *Tristram Shandy*, took the fly out of Widow Wadman's eye, and, opening the window, let it escape, saying, 'Go, get thee gone, why should I hurt thee? – this world surely is wide enough to hold both me and thee' – that was praised as a charming piece of sentimentality doing credit to a kind heart. But when Pasteur and the bacteriologists had shown that house-flies may be carriers of diseases, so that Uncle Toby's particular fly, if it had been infected, might have contaminated the food in the larder and per-haps caused the illness or death of a child, then his act was no longer amiable and praiseworthy. To eliminate the house-fly had become a social duty. What had been right in the eighteenth century is morally wrong in the twentieth.

Always and everywhere such discussions about particular cases are going on, and judgements arrived at. Opinion adjusts itself to new discovery. Personal habits and social customs change accordingly. The moral code evolves.

There is indeed a continuous evolution of ideas: it operates – within the minds of men – through much the same process as the natural evolution of organic species – by competition, struggle

for existence, survival of the fittest. Survey the history of the
human intellect from primitive times and we shall see that process in action: we can watch it now. Worship of imaginary gods,
human sacrifice, obedience to omens and portents; attacks of
clan against clan, tribe against tribe, the extermination of enemies;
battle as the arbiter of justice, the duel as the Court of personal
honour; slavery, serfdom, caste untouchability – all these had
been accepted, in one age or another and in one region or another,
as natural and normal. Now they are not. Formerly they were
morally right; now they are morally wrong. At this very hour
we may see among the enlightened peoples a deliberate effort to
eliminate international wars from the recognized institutions of
the civilized world, to put war too under the ban of the
moral law.

We find here the beginnings of an answer to our first question –
What is right and wrong? We have brought together examples
of a variety of ideas, customs and actions that are good. Each one
is recognized as such by a consensus of opinion; and this consensus
has itself been arrived at from long experience. To seek these is
right conduct; the contrary is wrong.

But this is not enough to give us a system of ethics. It only
lays a foundation for a system. It has indeed allowed us to escape
from the futile attempt to find a single formula for the good life.
We see at once that any definition wide enough to be complete
would be too vague to be useful. And we shall no longer be
trying to build first a visionary roof in mid-air, and then to hang
from it a real structure. We have been laying a firm foundation
in the solid earth of fact and experience.

The structure itself, however, has still to be built. For the
ordinary man is not a philosopher, and is too busy with daily
affairs to try to become one. He would be bewildered and helpless if he were given nothing better than a long catalogue of
desirable things, and was left to use his own judgement and
choose his own course in each contingency as it arose.

To begin with some metaphysical abstractions, and to work
downwards by deduction, has not succeeded. But we cannot do
without general principles. Only we may arrive at them best
inductively, from below, from particulars; and these will already
have been found by experience in the world of reality. It is just

this that mankind has been doing ever since civilization began —
and is doing now.

In ordinary daily life everyone can observe among his neighbours examples of truthfulness, let us say, and honesty, of courage
and endurance, of self-control, sympathy and affection; and he
will find them also in himself. Life will have shown him how such
qualities lead to the welfare of the individual and of the community as well, while their contraries prove harmful to both.
Therefore we call such qualities the virtues, their opposites the
vices; the first to be praised and fostered, the second to be blamed
and extirpated so far as may be. That is to say, we go beyond
our list of particular good objects by adding to it the promotion
of right-doing in general.

The overall importance of this is quickly recognized. Right-
doing becomes, not merely one means among others to an end,
but an end in itself. The structure of ethics is completed in the
universal moral law.

6

But before we pass on we must bring into question a view of
the nature of morality which has always been supported by many
ethical teachers and is still widely held, but which may be seen
to be fallacious and a source of confusion.

It is commonly assumed that morality consists in self-sacrifice,
and that self-interest is its opposite; altruism is the only virtue,
egoism always a vice. This, indeed, is held to be the teaching of the
Golden Rule, universally regarded as the essence of the moral
law. And if by egoism is meant mere selfishness — the pursuit of
self-interest regardless of the well-being of others, then that would
no doubt be true. But if we take egoism to include a care for the
interests of the individual which are legitimate in themselves, and
which, by directly promoting his own welfare, will also indirectly
benefit the society in which he is a unit, then the principle is
mistaken and misleading. As Spinoza told us, for the individual
to keep himself alive is a prior condition of the good life; and the
good life itself includes a man's own health, education, efficiency
and happiness. Further, if it is his duty to help make possible a
good life for the members of the society, is he himself not also

H

among the members, and why should he be the only one to whose welfare he should be indifferent?

Nor is this what the Golden Rule requires. The Old Testament says: 'Thou shalt love thy neighbour as thyself', and the New Testament: 'Whatsoever ye would that men should do unto you, even so do ye also unto them.' Confucius says the same: 'Tzu-kung asked: "Can one word cover the whole duty of man?" The Master said: "Fellow-feeling, perhaps. Do not do unto others what thou wouldst not they should do unto thee." ' But none of these says: 'Care for thy neighbour and not for thyself.' On the contrary they take the treatment that one would wish for oneself as the very standard of one's duty to the neighbour: egoism is made the measure for altruism. Both, in proper degree and balance, must be elements in morality.

7

We turn to the second question – Why should we do right when it is more agreeable or seems more advantageous to do wrong?

Here we shall follow the same methods as with the first question, and as indeed we have followed throughout this book. We shall look first to see what is actually happening in the everyday world: we shall examine what are the motives that are in fact leading you and me and our neighbours to act rightly, when we do act rightly, and wrongly, when that is what we do. And we shall not spend our time in trying to discover any single underlying ethical principle when it is clear from the outset that the problem itself is not single but multiple. We shall not look for *the* sanction for ethics, in the singular, but for sanctions, in the plural. And the moment that we begin to look we shall see them in full activity, both within our own minds and everywhere around us.

For there are the two factors engaged – the person and the community. 'All life is a commerce between Self and Not-self', as Dr. Radhakrishnan says. It is so physically, between the body and its environment. It is so in the world of thought. And it is so in morals.

When the individual comes upon the scene the community is already there. The social atmosphere is all about him: he can no more help breathing it in than his lungs can help breathing in air. The moral environment, such as it is at that time in that place, is part of this atmosphere. An infant, he finds it in the family; a child, in the school; all through his life it is in the newspapers, books, broadcasting, in cinemas and theatres, in colleges and universities, in churches, in the Parliament. It is in the talk and behaviour of every person he meets: each one is part of his environment, as he is part of theirs. Whatever ideas — political, religious, scientific, philosophical — are pervading the minds of the people and influencing their behaviour will also affect his own. If the tone and temper of the society is moral, the more likely that he will be moral: if it is immoral, he may soon become the same. The social influence may even transcend, by anticipation, his own life: the statesman will assert his faith in his own action by saying that he is 'ready to abide by the judgement of posterity'.

Perennial and all-pervasive, this social influence is of vast importance. It acts through personal contacts and public opinion, and through the State and other institutions — educational, religious, legal. Its instruments are approval and disapproval, praise and blame, reward and punishment, fame and infamy. These are the social sanctions of ethics.

In return, the individual, consciously or unconsciously exercising his own independent will as one member of the society among the rest, contributes his quota in creating those social sanctions and in applying them.

'One man in his time plays many parts': and not only in the seven ages, but in quite as many distinct capacities.

He (or she) is in the first place a member of a family.

He is a learner: in the early years of life that is his principal concern; but education, in one form or another, is lifelong.

Economically, he is usually a worker, paid or unpaid; a producer of goods or services.

He is always a consumer; and, as such, decides what shall be produced: demand is the arbiter of supply, and the two together determine price.

In a democratic country he is a citizen, shaping the character of the State and its policies; and also a subject, paying obedience to the laws that he has himself helped to make.

He is often the member of a Church, and of other voluntary organizations.

And first and last and all the time, he is his own self: a person, with a freedom of will and choice of action that is independent; emergent from circumstance, conditioned, but real.

The society is concerned with the person in all those aspects; and in all those capacities he has to deal with the society. Hence the enormous complexity of our present civilization. There is an intricate elaboration of rights and duties on both sides. What those rights and duties should be – how to be defined, how safeguarded, how enforced – has become the subject-matter of a whole array of social sciences. So we come into the realm of politics, of economics, of jurisprudence. Within these are a score of auxiliary sciences – education, public health, public administration in general, industrial relations, statistics, social geography, history as science (emerging from history as literature), and many more. All these together form the great department of knowledge to which Herbert Spencer gave the name of Sociology, and which now engages so large a part of the intellectual energies of modern man.

But underlying all this, much older and much simpler, is the primitive practical morality that arose out of the daily needs of life as it is lived. Long before there were religious codes, or statute-books, or ethical treatises, before even writing and reading, there existed, among all peoples at all times, personal habits and social customs setting the standards of good behaviour. They were based on common sense, taught by experience. Homely rules of conduct were passed from mouth to mouth, from generation to generation – as they still are – in maxims and proverbs current in the daily talk of the people.

Then would arise, from time to time, here and there, a sage, a poet, a prophet, able to sum up in a flash the diffused, and perhaps unrecognized, experience of centuries. His teaching is accepted; his authority afterwards points the way. Enthusiasm, passion, the virtue and sacrifice of saints and martyrs and heroes, all go to the making and spreading of the moral law.

Wordsworth says:

Moral truth
Is no mechanic structure, built by rule;
And which, once built, retains a steadfast shape
And undisturbed proportions; but a thing
Subject, you deem to vital accidents:
And, like the water-lily, lives and thrives,
Whose root is fixed in stable earth, whose head
Floats on the tossing waves.

8

What is the upshot of the argument? It is the dominance of the Person.

There are two factors — the individual and the society: but we should never forget that the society, like the State and every other institution, is no more than a pattern, and that the stuff which is being patterned consists of men and women; so that, in the end, we are brought back to the individual again. We are liable to forget it because of our habit of personifying these abstractions. We say of the society, or whatever may be in question, that 'it' does, or should do, this or that; although there exists in fact no 'it' capable of thinking and acting. Each one of the units is part of the pattern, is within it, but is nevertheless distinct, unique.

Physically, he is an individual organism, constituted, at the various size-levels, of particles, atoms, molecules, cells, tissues. He has also life, mind, will, character. He passes, between birth and death, through Shakespeare's seven ages; and he has as well all those various capacities that have been recounted. In each of those aspects he is conditioned and moulded by the society. Yet he may assert his own rights and fulfil his own duties, or may neglect them, according to his own judgement and choice in each case that arises. He can, if he likes, detach himself mentally from his surroundings; look with a critical eye on prevalent ideas and current events, and, if he thinks necessary, join with others to modify the ideas and change the current of events. Public opinion is powerful: but what is 'the public' except himself and his fellows? Each one, therefore, has responsibility for his own actions. And even to remain inactive is itself an action.

This is the beginning of ethics. Politics, economics, jurisprudence, and all the social sciences that derive from them, follow after.

CHAPTER X

MATTERS IN DEBATE

I

RELATING our present age in the western world with those that have preceded it, we see conspicuous in retrospect the special features that have marked the centuries. After the Dark Ages that followed the collapse of the Greco-Roman civilization came the redeeming spirit of the Christian ethic. Then the turbulent feudal period, which ended when the rise of powerful duchies and monarchies inaugurated the modern State, able to maintain order by imposing law. At the same time began the great rebirth of art, science and philosophy. The sixteenth and seventeenth centuries were another period of conflict, dynastic or religious, and on a wider scale. The eighteenth was more tolerant and more placid, but ended with the American and French Revolutions, opening the way to the democracy of the nineteenth. This, with the upsurge of science, began a new economic epoch – the arrival of the machines, the vast expansion of industry, the development of new territories, the accumulation of capital and diffusion of wealth, and the rapid increase in population. Now in the twentieth we are feeling the full force of those mighty changes.

The first half of our century has been convulsed by challenges from an anti-democratic philosophy of power and racial dominance, of repression at home and aggression abroad. The militarism of Germany and her allies having been defeated, twice over, by the rest of the world banded together in defence of freedom, a third threat from a different quarter has been similarly met and may perhaps have been averted. The Marxist creed is strangely self-contradictory. Its end is humanitarian; it strives, with passionate sincerity and often with devoted self-sacrifice, to establish economic justice. But its methods have been the same as those of the Fascists and Nazis – ruthless force, armed expansion, and a cynical disregard for the most elementary human rights. If, however, this peril also is staved off, perhaps the coming decades may prove to be as peaceful for the world at large as, with some minor exceptions, the century from 1815 to 1914 was for this country, and for north-western Europe as a whole.

But democracies are specially exposed to another danger – of an economic kind. It is the inflation of currencies, often gradual but sometimes catastrophic. It is caused in the first instance by a rise in prices. Sometimes this is started by a sudden increase in the demand for essential commodities, as happened at the outbreak of the Korean War. A substantial rise in the cost of living is a necessary consequence, and this is soon followed by a demand for higher wages, which cannot be resisted. An upward movement in salaries and in profits, in costs of production, in the expenses of public administration, in all the operations of the economic system, succeed in due course. Heavier national taxes and local rates form part of the process. Taxation may also be increased unfruitfully by swollen expenditures on war and armaments.

Unless there is an equivalent increase in the efficiency and productivity of industry, all this will give a second impetus to the original rise in prices; and this 'vicious spiral' may be repeated indefinitely. The consumer is the helpless victim. Even when the progress of industry, nourished by science, might help him by the cheapening of goods through a normal healthy competition, the employers and workers, the merchants and retailers, may combine to oust competition, by means of output restrictions, price-rings, and political pressure for protective tariffs. Trade unions hold the employers responsible for putting up the cost of living, and employers accuse the unions; often both are right.

We see clearly enough that in the modern world the influences that tend to make prices rise have been far stronger, almost everywhere, than the influences that would keep prices down. Hence, the depreciation of money, inflation. And inflation is creeping bankruptcy. However, it is possible for such situations to be met.

Skilful financial management by strong Governments, supported by restraint among the people in their demands for goods and services and for cash benefits and allowances, may establish control.

If both war and inflation can be warded off, then the second half of this century may be a time of growing material prosperity, spreading all over the world. It may offer all the conditions needed for a new effulgence of the intellect and the arts, opening an age illustrious in the history of mankind.

2

The present has been termed the century of the common man. You may call it that if you will: or you may speak of the Welfare State, or the Welfare Society. Similar ideas have long been called Liberalism. At one time the word Socialism was widely used, until the Socialist parties in many countries concentrated on a policy of State ownership of industries as a panacea, and the word came to bear that specialized meaning. More recently we often hear the aim expressed as that of upholding the dignity of man.

Whatever the name, the essential creed is the same: that the well-being – physical, mental, moral – of the Person should be the purpose of social action: the welfare both of the self and of the society; and of the self both directly and through the society; and of the society through the self.

But every new situation, or fresh approach to an old situation, brings with it fresh doubts and new problems, and especially this conception of personal and social ethics.

In the first place it is itself open to misunderstanding. It may be said that to lay so much emphasis on the freedom and power of the individual runs the risk of creating, not a world of virtue, but a moral anarchy. What if the individual, emancipated and exalted to that degree, chooses to enjoy all his rights but to repudiate all his duties? To take the extreme case – what if, like Hitler and his accomplices, the 'superman' does things that are sub-human?

The answer would be that every advocate – philosopher or politician – of the right of the individual to personal liberty has also asserted, in the same breath, that it is conditioned by the similar and equal rights of others. Your rights are valid only for the same reasons as make my rights valid. In this scheme of ethics, good behaviour stands, therefore, on the same footing as freedom. There is no room for moral anarchy. Hand in hand with liberty goes discipline.

Discipline may be exercised either from without or from

within — by the society or by the person. Experience shows that
self-discipline is much the more effective. It can be more continuous, and it works intimately at close range. Society uses
every influence therefore to train the individual in self-control
and spontaneous right conduct. The home, the school, the law,
the whole atmosphere, are brought into play.

Habit is the key-word here. The principal means to these ends
is the formation of good habits. We all know that to bring up
children properly they must be trained from their earliest years in
cleanliness, tidiness, truthfulness, honesty, good manners. When,
during the Second World War, in anticipation of the air bom-
bardment of London, some hundreds of thousands of children
were evacuated to small towns and villages all over the country,
many of the people on whom children from some of the worst
slum districts had been billeted were astonished and dismayed at
their evident lack of training in even the most elementary civilized ways. They had been brought suddenly from an atmosphere of bad habits into one with better.

Habit is a product of the mechanism of our bodies and minds.
The nervous system grows into the ways, or 'modes', in which it
has been exercised. Impulses pass along a beaten track with an
ease that increases by repetition. The saying 'Habit is second
nature' is literally true. We learn by use. We see this also
among the animals — the house-training of domestic animals, or
performing animals learning their tricks. A habit becomes
established as the mind gradually relegates it from the conscious
to the subconscious. We say that the action has become 'habitual',
meaning automatic. Compare the laborious efforts of the little
boy or girl learning to read or write with the way an adult does
it, 'without giving it a thought'. And among the habits, usually
formed in childhood, and strengthened or weakened or added to
in later life, is this basic habit of self-discipline, which is the
mainstay of ethical conduct.

Bertrand Russell, however, advances a different doctrine.
He has contributed to a recent symposium on Morals and Religion in a weekly newspaper an article with the title 'Promoting
Virtuous Conduct'. In it he says: 'In spite of all the high-flown
talk, the reason people do not steal is that stealing is illegal and
therefore does not pay in a community where there is adequate

law-enforcement. In fact, of course, in such a community most people do not entertain the merest thought of stealing because it lies outside the pattern of conventional behaviour. But it is the law and the police which produce this pattern.' I would submit, with respect, that this view of ethics ought not to be accepted, for the reason that it is contrary to the facts that are evident all around us.

There is a moral law, which is different from the penal law. It existed long before the penal law, which is one of its many agencies. It is not to be found in any single code; it is far too comprehensive, and too subtle, for that; and it varies in its details from age to age and from country to country, and is always changing and developing. None the less the moral law is fact; as real as the Common Law of England or the unwritten British Constitution. It exists, not as some metaphysical abstraction, but as a set of living ideas, a pattern, in a multitude of human minds. Each of these minds accepts those ideas from others, or itself originates them, of its own will. When fully accepted, the consequent actions become habitual and are carried out by the subconscious mind, without reflection and special effort in each particular case. This is so in regard to not-stealing – the example given – with all normal people in all classes in all countries, except for small minorities, to be found everywhere, of chronic, or casual, or potential thieves.

It is of course true that one of the factors that have produced this state of things is the establishment of 'patterns of conventional behaviour'. But what is a convention? It is not something that appears of itself all of a sudden. Like all else, it is the product of causes: and the causes are the thoughts, the decisions, the actions and examples, of vast numbers of individual people, generation after generation, who have come to the conclusion, as the result of experiences common to them all, that certain kinds of behaviour – stealing being one of them – destroy any possibility of living comfortably together in communities. They have therefore chosen not to steal from one another, and to prevent or punish any among them who would break this general rule. It is not 'the law and police which produce the pattern of conventional behaviour'. It is the other way about – conventional morality produces the penal law.

While these pages were being written, the newspapers were giving prominence to a pronouncement, initiated by Bertrand Russell and signed by several of the world's greatest scientists, who have joined him in appealing to all scientists — since it was science which invented the hydrogen bomb — to take a foremost part in the universal movement for peace and disarmament. Here is a conspicuous example of 'promoting virtuous conduct' — an eminent philosopher acting ethically in a matter of supreme importance. But 'the law and the police' have had nothing to do with it; nor have even 'the patterns of conventional behaviour'. Russell did what he has done by his own volition, according to his own principles, because he thought it the right thing to do. Why should we assume it to be basically different with the innumerable quite moral actions which make up, inconspicuously, the normal life of the ordinary man? Bertrand Russell does less than justice to the human character.

The subconscious is the home of habit. A good habit established there is a mainstay of virtue; a bad habit, once embedded, is hard to get out. We have all had among our friends or acquaintances addicts to habit-forming drugs; especially alcohol, which is a drug disguised as a drink, or sometimes nicotine, a drug concealed in a vapour. [1] But the subconscious mind also can be trained, whether for good or for ill, by the conscious. An adolescent may stray from the right path once, then perhaps repeatedly, and at last become 'demoralized' — an expressive word. On the other hand he may 'pull himself together'; he may practise self-discipline, and be 'reformed' — a revealing word also. The conflict between will and habit is a conflict between the conscious mind and the subconscious. Every man is different today, in greater or lesser degree, from what he had been ten or twenty years before. All through life, but especially in what are properly called the formative years, his own actions have been forming habits, and the habits have been building up his character. It might be said that habit is capitalized action. And since actions

[1] One might mention also the addicts to sleeping-pills and other popular medicines ignorantly thrust into the highly complicated processes of the human body. This is no new thing: Sir Richard Steele wrote: 'But I must confess, for the good of my native country, I could wish there might be a suspension of physic for some years, that our kingdom, which has been so much exhausted by the wars, might have leave to recruit itself.'

are determined by ideas, it is the thoughts behind the deeds that matter most. 'Your thoughts are making you.' Here we have another case of reciprocal action and reaction: conduct makes character, and character determines conduct. And here again we discover that we are not living in a closed system. The individual human will has room for manœuvre. It can bring about change – even in itself.

3

So far with regard to one misunderstanding about an ethic based upon the person. It does not amount to moral anarchy tempered by fear. Discipline is part of it; and the best discipline is self-discipline. This must be an integral element in personal liberty because without it the essential purpose of liberty – the well-being, in the widest sense, of the individual – could not be attained. But there is another misunderstanding, more widespread, and sometimes found among the friends of democracy itself.

A phrase such as 'the century of the common man' is often assumed to imply the dominance of the average. The worst is to be raised to the average, but also the best will be brought down to it. We are to accept average standards everywhere – in education and manners, in books, newspapers, radio, television, in all the arts, in our own homes and cities, in the Parliament and the Government. The man who is uncommon, finding no place, will become extinct. How futile, then, to hold out hopes of an age of greatness, when what you are deliberately doing is to make sure of an age of mediocrity.

This is not admitted. Democracy demands equality of rights before the law and in sharing ultimate authority. But it does not assume an equality of talent, or character, or usefulness to the community, for that plainly does not exist. It demands indeed, so far as it is practicable, equality of opportunity. But it is the equal opportunity to prove unequal merit; and if the value of the service is unequal, reward and status should not be the same. Nor is there any reason why the average demand should be the only one to be catered for. 'Many', said Matthew Arnold, 'are to be made partakers in well-being, true; but the ideal of well-being is not to be, on that account, lowered and coarsened.'

Leaders in every sphere – politics, the professions, industry, culture – are as essential in a democracy as in any other system. And indeed it is there that they are most likely to be forth-coming. For a democracy is able to draw upon whatever apti-tudes there may be, scattered among all sections of the nation, and is not confined to a privileged minority. If the western world has advanced with such astonishing rapidity during the present century in almost every field, it is very largely because the wider opening of the doors of higher education, together with the emancipation of women, has for the first time given access to almost all its resources of character and intelligence, talent and skill.

In the intense competition of these times, no people which allows vast potential resources of leadership to lie idle and unused can hope to keep its place in the scale of civilization. When moving recently in the House of Lords a resolution in favour of a reform in the constitution of that House, which is still based mainly on heredity, I urged that 'a democracy must create from within itself an aristocracy, or it will perish – an aristocracy not of wealth or of lineage, but of talent, wisdom and virtue – manifest in both Houses of the Parliament and diffused among the people'.

There is nothing inconsistent in that with care for the interest of the common man. On the contrary, nothing could be better calculated to promote his interest than to offer him new standards – or preserve for him old standards – that are above the common.

4

The other matters now in general debate to which I would refer do not arise from misunderstandings, but from definite conflicts between one principle and another principle, where both are sound and the need is to find a right balance in apply-ing them.

Political and personal freedom is recognized to be a fundamen-tal element in a civilized society, and the rights of free speech and peaceful combination to be part of it. But if political movements arise which make use of those rights in order to overthrow free-dom itself, what then? Is that also to be permitted? We have seen, in our own lifetime and close at hand, how Fascists, Nazis and Communists have invoked the principles of democracy to cover subversive movements aimed at the destruction of democracy. Many Liberals conscientiously stood by the doctrines they had always professed; until the next thing — and the last thing — they knew was that they themselves were starving to death in concentration camps, or else being tried for their lives before Courts which mocked the very name of justice.

Deception at first, with force following close behind, enabled that simple plan to win easy successes over half of Europe. The question then arose in Britain, the British Commonwealth, France, the United States and elsewhere, whether those who believed in Liberal principles ought to carry their devotion so far as to allow the destruction of the freedon that they 'had loved not wisely but too well'. The answer was an emphatic negative. This was in fact fully justified, not only by practical necessity, but also by political principle. Respect for the freedom of others is always conditioned by their respect for one's own, and the totalitarians had made it abundantly clear that there would be no reciprocity.

War itself raises a similar issue. 'War,' said Gibbon, 'even in its mildest form, is a perpetual violation of every principle of religion and humanity.' This is so obviously true that religious and humane people are bound to ask themselves whether, in any circumstances, they can volunteer for military service; or even submit to conscription by law; or, as citizens and taxpayers, sanction war and sustain it. Some decide that, at whatever cost, to themselves or to their country, they will not do so. But others, not less conscientious, ask first what that cost will be. And this is no remote or hypothetical question. Twice in this century it has confronted us all — stark and inescapable, with no doubt at all as to the cost. It would be a surrender to militarism: it would be the loss of national liberty, and with it political and personal liberties as well. In the long run it would put the control of the world's affairs into the hands of whoever succeeded in establishing dictatorships. It would not get rid of brute force: it would merely ensure its dominance; for the aggressor can have no more effective allies — however unintentionally on their part — than pacifists inside the countries he attacks.

In this dilemma of the human conscience the vast majority of the peoples in the free countries have said: If this is the cost of pacifism we will not pay it: sacrifices — yes, if need be; but sacrifices for resistance, not for submission.

In the next issue that has arisen — the simultaneous renunciation of war and a general disarmament — there is fortunately no such dilemma.

5

There have been, and there still are, other conflicts as to rights. The rights of property have been the subject of long and bitter controversies. Has an owner — of land or houses, a factory or a mine — an indefeasible right 'to do what he will with his own'?

In this country, in the latter part of the eighteenth century and the earlier part of the nineteenth, under the rule of a Parliament in which property was powerful in both Houses, the law ordained that he had. But, as the balance of the constitution shifted, other views gradually gained ground. An unqualified policy of *laissez-faire* had allowed evils so gross and so flagrant to ensue from the Industrial Revolution that such a principle could no longer be maintained. Overcrowded and insanitary tenements; high death-rates, especially among children; child labour in factories and mines and on the farms; widespread illiteracy; unplanned, depressing, air-polluted towns, seeping over the countryside — all classes of the community, including at last many of the property-owners themselves, were forced to realize that such conditions could not indefinitely be allowed to endure.

Again there was a conflict between two freedoms — the right of the owner to use his land, his house, his factory, his machinery as he chose, or to sell them to others for the best price obtainable; and the right of the tenant, the workman, the human being as such, to enjoy decent conditions of life, at home, at work and at leisure. With the advent of democracy it was the right of property that had to give way.

'The Englishman's house is his castle', but the drawbridge had to be let down to admit the sanitary inspector. Then the factory-owner and the mine-owner were subjected to an elaborate legal code for the protection of the health and safety and general well-being of their employees. Very late — not until the present century – laws were passed to ensure that the new quarters of towns should be planned, and the old quarters remodelled, as the public interest required. During the Second World War or since, we have established a special Ministry of Town and Country Planning with wide powers; a number of new towns, airy and seemly, have been built; large areas in the still lovely parts of the island have been preserved for all time as National Parks; green-belts are beginning to encircle the great cities; the streets of London and other towns are becoming lined with trees, with public gardens here and there; the grosser abuses of public advertising are being kept in check; the atmosphere of the industrial cities is being protected from smoke pollution; and new homes are being built at the rate of a million every three years. If it is asked what is meant by social progress, what is meant by moving towards a Welfare Society – here is an example. True that it involves for some the infringing of liberties that had long been established and enjoyed. But it also grants to others new liberties of high value. And the balance is on the right side.

6

I have been discussing some of the issues now actively in debate. These are on the way to settlement. Laws, customs, habits, are adjusting themselves to new conditions and fresh ideas. The broad lines for a consensus of opinion are apparent. But of many others that cannot be said.

One is the question of the relations between the sexes, and in particular whether the monogamous family and home is to endure as one of the basic institutions of human society. On this enough has been written in a previous chapter, and it is unnecessary to add to it here – except to emphasize that, in our time, moral principles, long accepted, have been relaxed, and no new ones established; and that, if present tendencies continue and grow stronger, if they are not checked and reversed, the coming generation may find here one of their most formidable problems.

Another issue with no solution yet in sight is the persistence of crime.

Three thousand years after the Ten Commandments – 'Thou shalt not kill: Thou shalt not steal . . .'; fifteen hundred years since the rise of Christianity; a century, more or less, since the general provision of popular education — we still have the strange survival of a criminal class.

In England and Wales, the number of the more serious offences — indictable offences — 'known to the police', is now annually over 400,000. [1] For years together, great cities of America, leaders in the modern world, had been terrorized and blackmailed by highly organized bands of ruthless gangsters. One feature of present-day civilization has even tended to foster crime. When the small town or village was the social unit, everyone was known to his neighbour; public opinion was alert; any malefactor would soon be discovered and disposed of. But in great cities with hundreds of thousands, or millions of people, it is possible for dark underworlds to come into existence, and to prey parasitically upon the community. They create another social atmosphere of their own, a support and sanction, not for morality, but for vice.

Society protects itself — at great cost in money and manpower — by maintaining an elaborate system of police, magistrates, judges and prisons, of Juvenile Courts, reformatories, probation officers. It develops a new science — Criminology, or Penology — which holds national and international congresses, teaches reclamation rather than vengefulness, encourages voluntary organizations for visiting the prisoners, aiding them on discharge, helping the probation officers. The public conscience turns to this plan and that, does all it can. Nevertheless, crime continues, on a vast scale, generation after generation, perpetrating robberies, frauds, and sometimes acts of brutal savagery.

It would be wrong to conclude that all our measures to stop the sources of crime, to humanize the criminal law and to redeem the criminal, have been so much wasted effort. [2] We may be sure that if they had not been taken the position would be worse than it is. The fact remains that, while the modern world has been able to conquer so many of the old evils that have afflicted mankind, it has failed to conquer crime.

[1] About two-thirds of these have been cases of larceny. In spite of the high standards of efficiency of the Metropolitan Police and the local Police Forces, almost half the total number of offences remain undetected.

[2] 'The statistics of the penal system of this country show that, broadly speaking, some three-quarters of those who go to prison for the first time do not come back.' — Rt. Hon. G. Lloyd George, Home Secretary: Address to the Third International Congress on Criminology, *The Times*, September 13th, 1955.

I

7

The debate goes on, all the time and everywhere, on those questions, and on numberless others which anyone can pick out at his pleasure. Marginal cases and minor points are being argued out continually — in conversation, in the press and on the radio — by students' societies, scientific associations, church assemblies, trade union lodges, party committees, local Councils, Parliament itself. Opinions are formed, conclusions reached, resolutions proposed and carried. New laws may be enacted, new moral conventions established. So one country, and then another, moves into the forefront of advancing civilization, and one century comes to differ from another in character and achievement.

The historian looks at all this in retrospect and from the outside. He sees this vast process as a succession of events that have happened. He disentangles the causes; finding them in political movements, or economic changes, or intellectual trends, influenced perhaps by the emergence of powerful personalities. Summarizing, he speaks of the spirit, or mental climate of the age. But the view of the philosopher is different. While learning much from the past, his concern is with the present; and he sees it, not from the outside as a spectator belonging to another generation, but from the inside as a contemporary. The events that the historian of a hundred years hence will generalize as movements or trends, the philosopher of today finds emerging, one by one, from causes that he can watch all around him in actual operation. And at bottom those causes are nothing else than the choices and actions of the individual men and women who make up the society.

Here is the great process of the evolution of human ideas, their competition for existence, the survival of the fittest. This is how the content of the moral law is built up and the social climate created. And this is the theatre where the individual exercises his will, asserts his rights, fulfils his duties, and takes his share in shaping the public opinion, which in the end is the arbiter.

Let the average man not be dismayed by these responsibilities. All share them, but not equally. We have recognized equal rights of citizenship and of opportunity, but have not been misled by that to assume an equality of knowledge, or talent, or wisdom, which in fact does not exist. The people know this very well. They look about for guidance and choose leaders whom they will be willing to follow. They welcome great men when they appear; are grateful to them and glad to pay them honour. What indeed is the purpose of all social institutions, touching every aspect of life, but to bring out leaders, give them opportunity to formulate their ideas and support in propagating them?

If an institution — especially a State, but also a Church, a Corporation, a learned Society, or the like — has roots that go deep into the past, it will be valued for its traditions and record of service. The ordinary man feels that he is in touch with something greater than himself; and not only in touch with it, but an integral part of it. He is transitory, but the institution has permanence and stability. Through it he links hands with the generations of the past and the generations of the future, and will not feel so lonely as he travels along his own brief stretch on the unending highway of time.

The more novel and strange the modern way of life becomes, the more the people will cherish whatever ancient still remains — so long as it does no harm. And the more, in a democracy, private life becomes modest and simple, the more the State should be stately: it embodies the nation, and the nation is themselves; so that their own status is bound up with the prestige of the State. As Addington Symonds foretold for the peoples of the future —

> They shall be simple in their homes
> And splendid in their public ways.

8

Of the questions that remain in active debate, I will discuss only two others: both relate to the principle of Toleration.

Liberty has always been seen to be essential to the good life, but only in recent times has toleration been recognized as essential to liberty. And we have still not yet worked out its implications. Is the principle so important that we must regard it as an absolute, subject to no limitations or conditions? If so, must we tolerate iniquity? Must we tolerate crime?

Some would say: For the sake of intellectual and moral freedom we must be ready to put up with a great deal. The penal law is a crude weapon: seeking to suppress evil, it may obliterate much that is of value. Lawlessness oppresses, but law can be oppressive also. Democratic majorities have been as tyrannical as any despot, and virtue may be tyrannous as well as vice. The history of Puritanism and of political, religious and literary censorship has proved that abundantly. And after all, how will you define 'iniquity'; what do you mean by 'crime'? One generation will have one view, the next will think quite differently. At what point does a naughty high-spirited boy or girl become a 'Juvenile Delinquent' and a unit for the Criminal Statistics?

All that is very true. Such considerations must always be borne in mind. Nevertheless vice and crime are realities: they do much mischief, both to the vicious and the criminals themselves and to the great body of decent innocent people. Have not these too their rights, with at least as good a claim to be recognized and respected? Have they not the right to lead their lives in freedom and security, without fear of being contaminated or robbed or assaulted? And more than that. The general observance of the moral law is essential for well-being. Sanctions are needed to secure it. They are of the two kinds: internal, through self-discipline, and external, through the action of society; and this effected through its agencies — the penal law and the influence of public opinion.

But what if both of these fail? What if the law is made so mild, so tolerant, that stealing, or other crimes, are no longer found not to pay, in Bertrand Russell's words, but on the contrary to offer, without undue risk, a highly profitable livelihood? And if public opinion, wishing to be — in the present-day vocabulary — 'broadminded, adult, mature, sophisticated', and also being so diffident about its own judgements and so fearful of making mistakes that it condones every fault and tolerates any wickedness — what then?

Force may be used unjustly, but our communities have not become so civilized through and through that Justice can afford to do without it. 'Justice without Force', it has been said, 'and Force without Justice — dreadful disasters.'

Undoubtedly there are fields of misconduct where force is futile and law cannot reach. But society is not therefore obliged to acquiesce and be silent. All around, in the background, is that other agency — public opinion, less rigid, less clumsy, but often more effective; the social atmosphere, with its own influence and its own methods. Here, in our discussion of toleration, we come back to the central point. Public opinion is personal opinion, multiplied and aggregated: in the end it is the individual who is responsible.

9

We have spoken of his many aspects and capacities. He is concerned in this matter in several of them. First as a member of a family, as a parent, he knows his responsibility for the up-bringing of his children: he wishes them to become honourable and worthy people, useful members of society: he has a right to expect that society itself will support his efforts — will at all events not thwart them.

We all know the power of advertisement, with its insistent repetitions: commerce finds it worth while to spend every year vast sums on advertising. But what will happen to the children and the adolescents if, while the family teaches one thing, the environment incessantly familiarizes them with the opposite; if vice is flaunted in public places; and as has happened in various countries at various periods of history, the whole tone of the society is cynical, lax, morally corrupt? If the mental air is polluted how can we expect that minds will grow up clean?

The individual is concerned also as a citizen. There is that grave problem of crime. The penal law is failing. But the serious thing is not so much that our methods for detecting and punishing the criminals have not proved sufficient: it is that such types should be appearing among us at all. To this I shall revert a little later, and inquire whether the present-day approach to this matter is not at fault.

But the individual is concerned also economically — as consumer, setting the demand for goods and services. The news-papers that he reads; the books he buys or gets from the library; the plays or films he goes to see; the broadcast programme he turns on or switches off; the house or flat in town or country that he chooses to live in, and the things he puts into it; the church he attends, or neglects, and the churches he keeps away from; the schools or colleges to which he sends his children – all these help to determine the nature of demand. Demand evokes supply; supply creates the environment, material and mental; the environment moulds people's characters; and character determines action. This is the chain of responsibility between the individual and the course of events. These are the links between what you or I do today or tomorrow and the way the world goes.

Experience shows that the principle of toleration, for all its excellence, may be abused: it may be taken to give a moral justification for indifference when clear-cut opinions and definite action are called for. We often hear someone say in an argument: 'Well, I recognize of course that you are as much entitled to express your opinion as I am mine; and I realize that you are just as likely to be right. Who am I that I should wish to set myself up as a judge? After all there are always two sides to every question.'

That the other person has an equal right to express his opinion is very true. That it follows as a natural consequence that his opinion is as likely to be right as yours is quite false: it may be so, or it may not. And if there are two sides to every question it is not because no question can ever be settled one way or the other, but because, when it has been settled, the argument stops and it ceases to be a question.

It is a mistake, and harmful, to suppose that controversy is objectionable in itself and ought to be avoided. A nation that has no controversies is intellectually moribund and will soon be dead. When you are faced by something that you know to be false and noxious, it having been proved to be so by experience, to subordinate your opinion out of deference to other people should not win praise for broadmindedness and courtesy, but blame for moral weakness – a lie unanswered is a truth betrayed.

10

Throughout this discussion we have laid stress on the social climate of an age and country as an influence of prime importance in forming the habits and customs, the character and conduct, of a people. Many factors contribute to the making of that climate, prominent among them the Arts.

The existence of a social climate depends upon the communication of ideas from one to another; and this is mainly by speech or writing. Civilization develops the arts of language and literature. Oratory and drama, poetry and prose, have grown up through the centuries. The modern world adds the techniques of the newspaper, broadcasting and the cinema. Ideas are communicated also by the visual arts — painting, sculpture, architecture, industrial design, and by music. All these influence the intellect and the emotions.

The social climate is created by the individual members of the community, but contributing not in equal degree. The responsibility is greatest on those who can exercise a wide influence on large numbers. This nowadays is principally through those new techniques, together with popular fiction. The power of the pulpit and of the political platform, which used to be so great, has waned. [1]

How is this responsibility being fulfilled? Those powerful agencies, affecting, here and now, day by day, the opinions and behaviour of tens of millions, how far are they working for good, how far for evil? We seek the causes of the disasters and dangers of our time — is a misuse of the arts among them? While philosophy, religion and science are continually trying to raise the level of our civilization, is it true that journalism, fiction, the theatre, the cinema and the radio, in greater or lesser degree, are constantly tending to lower it?

There are those who say that such questions ought not to be asked. Art, they say, is an end in itself. It will not be subject to the ethical judgement. It is amenable only to its own, the aesthetic, judgement. And this principle of art for art's sake, we are told, is to be accepted *a priori* as an axiom, needing no proof, brooking no argument.

But philosophy has never agreed to this: nor has common

[1] In Great Britain and Northern Ireland, in a population of 50 millions, the circulation of the daily newspapers is about 30 million copies, of the Sunday papers about 34 millions. The admissions to the cinemas number 25 millions a week. Several millions every day listen to sound radio or view television. Only one person in ten goes weekly on the average to some place of worship; and only a small fraction of the voters attend political meetings, even during a General Election; at other times the numbers are quite insignificant.

sense. Both will deny that any particular activity of the human mind can be picked out from the rest and given a position of privilege and self-sufficiency. This is because each activity does in practice influence every other, for good or for ill, and is itself influenced by them. It is with the individual, no doubt, that a work of art originates; it is just that which makes it what it is. But its consequences are social. As Yeats has said, 'a work of art is the social act of a solitary man'. Since the welfare of society depends upon the moral law; since a principal sanction of the moral law is the influence of the environment; and since the arts are part of the environment — we may insist upon the right of the layman, his own welfare being so directly concerned, to evaluate the work of the artist, to praise or to blame, accept or reject.

This is not to say that the artist, whether in literature or in the fine arts, must submit to work in fetters; that whatever originality, talent, or maybe genius, he has shall be continually subject to the ill-informed opinion of a semi-educated public — perhaps to a censorship by local councillors, or even to the judgement of the police and the magistrates, with the penalties of the criminal law in the background. Experience has shown that such controls have often done more harm to the quality of thought and achievement than good to morals.

Nevertheless there are limits. No one suggests that sheer pornography should be allowed a free run in the press, or open indecency on the stage or the screen. Even short of that, there is a province where recourse to official censorship or the penal law may be wrong, but where the alternative — social control through public opinion — would be right. If English people of the twentieth century do not wish their theatres to be degraded to the salacious level of the drama of the Restoration, they have only to use their economic power as 'consumers' and stay away. Similarly with the cinema and the radio, and the newspapers and the novel. We may take warning from the last great period of outstanding brilliance in all the arts — the Italian Renaissance: it was the moral corruption that accompanied it which brought it soon to decadence, and with it the arts.

Bearing these things in mind on the one side and the other, we may come to the actualities of our present situation.

II

The arts reflect the temper of the age: their fashions change with the mood of the nation. We have already recalled the various influences that had given to the two decades between the wars their distinctive character. It was a mood of frustration and scepticism: sometimes merely uneasy, discontented and despondent; sometimes — especially among the younger intellectuals — petulant and embittered. Over it all lay a dark cloud of pessimism.

To the credit of that period, one gain of great value must be recognized. The upheaval of thought was so complete that everywhere the artist felt himself, as never before, liberated from all the old conventions, free to follow, in a buoyant spirit, his own idiosyncrasies wherever they might lead. The consequence was — sometimes — the creation of fine new ideas, of beauty and power, opening fresh vistas of human accomplishment. But the liberation was too sudden and too swift: the release proved too intoxicating; the results, on balance, have often been deplorable.

Originality is a great quality, but not so great as to dispense with all others. Novelty can claim the right to a fair hearing with an open mind, but not an inherent right to be accepted for its own sake. Dean Inge wrote: 'There are two kinds of fools: one says, "This is old, therefore it is good"; the other says, "This is new, therefore it is better".'

Poets began to write in a teasing, puzzling, highly compressed style, of subtle hints, far-fetched images, recondite allusions. With their own minds in a state of confusion, they took refuge in a deliberate obscurity. They belonged to those 'who, because their thought is so muddy that they cannot see its shallow bottom, fancy themselves profound'. Instead of the inspiration of great poetry, they seemed satisfied to imitate the verbal ingenuities of the crossword puzzle. All through this period and since, there have been, indeed, many writers of poetry who disdained the current fashion and pursued their own way. But for a time it prevailed so widely that it seemed as though the noble line of the British poets would peter out, and be lost in arid wastes of laboured verbiage. The wide public of lovers of poetry disapproved profoundly and silently withdrew. By 1950, things

had come to such a pass that a representative literary society, the
PEN Club, declared: 'It is, we suppose, a commonplace that there
is a crisis in poetry, not only in England, but in most parts of
the world.' They appointed a special committee to consider 'the
present deplorable situation in which, owing to lack of demand
for poetry, poets are experiencing great difficulty in finding
publishers for their work'.

Meanwhile, in music, the same revolt from the academic and
classical — wholesome up to a point — was likewise passing to
extremes. We were given much painful music, discordant and
cacophonous. Fritz Kreisler, in a valedictory speech recently on
his retirement, said of modern music that 'it had too much noise,
too much velocity, too much incoherence'.

In the visual arts, the revolt led to an enthusiasm for the non-
representational and the abstract. Nor would anyone wish that
painting and sculpture should limit themselves to copying nature.
New art-forms, transcending the visible material world around us,
with their own patterns, colour arrangements, shapes, conventions, aroused a keen interest among many people in many
countries. If to others these works, or some of them, seemed to
have little or no merit, that is a question of taste: one man is
pleased and edified by works of art of one kind, the next man by
something different and opposite; and there is no reason why
they should quarrel about it.

But there is one exception to this. If you wish not to copy
nature — well and good: you can leave it alone. But you are not
free to falsify and travesty natural forms at your pleasure. Non-
representation if you will: but not misrepresentation. For a
painter to portray a human face with the eyes one above the
other, or the mouth in the forehead; for a sculptor to exhibit
life-size human figures with a cavity through the chest and a
knob where the head should be; or statues 'of caricaturist proportions, gigantic limbs and tiny heads' — this and the like is an
offence. The forms and processes of nature are very wonderful;
millions of years of evolution have made them perfect: they
should be approached with reverence.

The normal man feels instinctively that it is wrong. He finds
such works repellent. Technically they may be excellent; in
craftsmanship admirable. But, spiritually and psychologically

misconceived, there can be no room for admiration of the skill of the work if we resent that it should have been done at all.

No doubt there is a philosophy behind these modernist schools; otherwise they would not have held the attention of so many intelligent people for so long a time. But there are bad philosophies as well as good ones. This is a philosophy which holds that the artist should do no more than accept and reproduce whatever he supposes to be the dominant mood of his own generation. He must be original, but only by catching hold of the current fashions in originality. If his generation, emphasizing the bad and ignoring the good, pronounces this to be an ugly age, then let us write ugly poetry and paint ugly pictures in order to help to show how ugly it is. An age of confusion? — then the arts should be confused; each man, as Sir Desmond MacCarthy said, 'expressing his own private chaos'. An age that has brought misery to millions? — then it is misery, of every kind and degree, that poetry, drama, music, painting should portray. Or, as an alternative, the artist, angry and indignant, may try to detach himself from human affairs altogether. Indifferent to the troubles and struggles of ordinary men, he can rise — or sink — into a private world, of abstractions, of colours, shapes, or sounds of his own creation.

This is a bad philosophy because it ignores social duty. If our age has in it ugly features — and who will deny it? — the duty of the artist should be, not to add to the ugliness, but — for him specially among all men — to strive to redeem it by works of beauty. If the age is confused, it is for the artist — as much as the philosopher, the man of religion, the political thinker, the scientist — to help to give it clarity and cohesion.

And let us not be too humble and diffident, and attribute to our own deficiencies, and not to the incompetence or perversity of the poet, painter or sculptor himself, our failure to be impressed. We may remember the character in Molière who says: 'That must be wonderful; I don't understand it at all.' It need not be in the least wonderful, nor worth the effort to understand.

12

In architecture, the great changes during the present century have not only been influenced by the same vogues of fashion as the other arts: they have been the consequence of a fundamental revolution.

Architecture has had to adapt itself quickly to a complete new range of building materials. At long last, the primitive materials that man had made use of in the Stone Age and ever since — trunks of trees, blocks of stone, lumps of clay shaped by hand and baked by the sun, or later by fire — have given place to things entirely different — to concrete, steel and glass. Machinery has brought in a new technique of construction. Instead of the hodmen climbing long ladders with their little loads of bricks, who were still to be seen in the days of my youth, powerful cranes on lofty scaffoldings swing great girders into the sky. The elevator, with its wire rope, has made buildings possible twenty, thirty, or even a hundred storeys high. The pre-manu-facture of small repetitive units has extended to the building in-dustry the economics of mass-production, countering the heavier costs of labour: the work on the site may be little more than that of the assembly-lines in the factories. This mechanization came just in time to help the nations to cope with the immense task of rebuilding the cities devastated in the Second World War. But the destruction did at least open for the architects of today opportunities of space, light and skyline seldom possible before: and the new codes of Town Planning legislation have often saved those opportunities from being wasted: they have given fresh scope everywhere for bold designing.

Fashions come and go; in painting, sculpture, industrial design we see their quick succession. But the work of the architect may stand for generations, for centuries. Its effect also on the social environment is more direct and more continuous. Consciously or subconsciously the man-in-the-street is being influenced by the street itself all the time. As Mr. Maxwell Fry has said: 'Because of its direct connection with practical living, architecture has be-come the most important of the arts.'

The construction of a building being a public act, vagaries can usually be kept in check. Common sense has a say; local or even national authorities can exercise control. But all these may fail, and then the result may be disastrous. I will give an example.

Many regard the establishment of the United Nations, bearing in mind all its future possibilities, as by far the greatest event in

the history of the modern world. Here is – or should be – the
Parliament of Man. At its headquarters in New York the
Organization has lately had to provide a large new building to
house its multitudinous secretariat. Here was a wonderful
opportunity. Here might be erected a piece of noble architecture; expressing the aspirations of an age which, having been
victorious in war over the enemies of human freedom, was about
to embark, unitedly, in an effort, unprecedented in range and in
scale, not only to preserve world peace, but also to raise the
material and intellectual and spiritual level of all mankind. But
what has in fact been done? On a central site there has been erected an immense slab of steel and glass 505 feet high, 287 feet wide
and 73 feet deep, consisting of small repeating units, absolutely
uniform, featureless, colourless. I saw it not long after its com-
pletion, and was dismayed. I felt in the presence of something
hostile, dominant, completely dehumanized: exactly the kind of
structure that might be built by a race of mechanical robots,
powerful and ruthless, with muscles of steel, minute electronic
brains and no heart. A critic has spoken of 'the starkness of the
new brutalism'. Here it is – plain for all to see.

Size in itself has no merit. It may indeed be made into majesty,
as in the grandeur of a mighty cathedral. But there is nothing
majestic about this building. It is merely an indefinite multiplication of the commonplace. There is a snobbery of size, as there
is of costliness: here may be the classic example.

Is this a portent of the new civilization? Is this the pattern that
is to be stamped on the vast cities of the future, in all the countries
of the world? Already, in Madrid, American architects have constructed, at a cost of £1,000,000, a building to house the staff, 700
in number, of their Embassy; the Spaniards correctly described
the building as 'a pocket edition of the United Nations skyscraper
in New York'. At a meeting of Spanish architects, held in
connection with the inauguration, some protested that 'the
Americans had had little aesthetic appreciation in putting up such
a building overlooking Madrid's beautiful Castellana Avenue'.
A design of the same pattern was proposed by the architectural
advisers of United Nations for a centre that was about to be built
in Paris for one of its agencies; but the Parisians revolted, and the
plan had to be changed.

What has happened in New York and these other cities is of
great significance. We have here a head-on collision between
science and technology on the one hand, and art and the humanities
on the other.

The general situation has been so well described by Mr. Maxwell Fry, architect and critic, in an address from which I have
already quoted, that I venture, with his permission, to reproduce
here some further passages. He speaks of 'the pressures that have
led to the mechanization of building', and says that these 'are
evidence, at the heart of the welfare state, of the dehumanizing,
even devitalizing effect of an over-organized materialist society . . .
In later office designs of Gropius all attempts at differentiation are
abandoned, and the same is true of Corbusier's Ministry of Education building at Rio; while the United Nations Secretariat, on
the biggest scale of all of them, drops all pretence, and the
immense rectangle of glass is identified only by a projecting
entrance at ground-floor level, which, by comparison with the
rest, is barely enough to denote its human occupation: it has
become a vast, impersonal, crystalline monument'. He goes on to
speak of 'the seduction of the machine method and the plausibility
of applied scientific thinking; and how near these are to that same
materialism that turned so much of our early industrial effort
into human desolation. The tendency of reproductive machinery
favours uniformity and rejects variety. Yet art, which is absolutely necessary to life, is various, contrasted, and based on
experiences of feeling'. And he concludes that our policy 'must
knowingly serve two ends: the economic, in exploiting the
machine for what it can bring us; and the aesthetic, setting a limit
to what the machine may do. We must open up a range of experiences through contrast and variety, related forms and textures,
through association with nature, and with works of art – all
considered as components of living as necessary as the components of industry out of which our architecture is to be made'.

13

The mood of the 'fifties of this century has happily changed
from that of its 'twenties and 'thirties. Fashions foisted upon a
reluctant public – too docile and acquiescent – are now spent.

The younger poets of today give us something better than the morose and confused productions of so many of their predecessors. Outrageous pictures and sculptures are losing favour. There are grounds for hoping that the intellectual leaders of the age now opening, while recognizing to the full the need for novel ideas to match changed conditions, will do honour to the arts by seeking to recover, and to express, qualities which do not belong to any place or time, but are universal and eternal – the qualities of sanity, clarity, dignity and grace.

CHAPTER XI

THE RELIGIOUS SITUATION

I

SEEKING reality, we have tried to advance from the known to the unknown. We began with material things, because that was already a well-trodden path. Physical science, by its method of analysis, had penetrated beyond visible objects and had discovered the molecule, the atom, the particle, the quantum. This, however, could not be all. It seemed necessary to infer the existence of a continuum, physically real, underlying these, and we speculated as to its nature. But even some new discovery along that road would still leave behind us a vast field unexplored. Numberless organisms exist, ourselves among them, endowed with the activities that we describe as living and thinking. We generalize and say that Life and Mind, as well as Matter, are parts of reality. But although we see what they do we cannot say what they are.

At that point, pending further discovery, we found ourselves halted. Obliged to pass on, leaving that riddle unanswered, we came — still within the compass of reality — to men's ideas; to institutions; to individual conduct and the social environment; and so to all the varied problems of ethics and politics.

Let us pause again now, and, quitting analysis, try to arrive at a synthesis. Instead of specialization — so useful, but sometimes so dangerous — we shall 'see Nature as not an aggregate but a whole'. We will treat all the size-levels — microcosmic, terrestrial, cosmic — as a unity. We will regard the present time as a momentary cross-section in an unending sequence of innumerable events — 'a whiff of actual being'. And we shall hold the universe to be extant in its own right, and our own perceptions and interpretations to be a part of it — a mirror within, giving a reflection, pale and distorted no doubt, but still a reflection, of a fraction of reality.

Such is our conspectus — so far. Surveying it in a calm hour our first feeling may be one of satisfaction, and at the same time of surprise that the mind of man has been able to accomplish so much. But the next feeling is bound to be a sense of dissatisfaction, of incompleteness. Again we are compelled to say: It is certain that this cannot be all that there is.

2

When in this book we passed on from science to consider the humanities, we postponed for the time being the whole field of religion and the supernatural. Coming now to these matters, we see at once that they are factors, and among the principal factors, in the present world situation — intellectual, moral and political.

Let us begin by offering a broad, but brief, survey of the facts, indicating some of the main ideas on religion that are now current in the modern world, together with the chief criticisms and objections usually raised against them.

But first it may be asked whether it is right to attempt any discussion at all of matters such as these in a book of this kind. Some may object that, having started from an empirical standpoint and kept within the rules of science and philosophy, we seem to be intending now to leave all this behind; to pass beyond the bounds of the reasoning intellect; to try not merely to push into the unknown, but into the unknowable: such an attempt would be out of place, and must in any case be futile.

To this I would answer that whether there is an unknowable, and if so where its frontier lies, is itself among the unknown. The frontier of knowledge moves; it advances century by century. A thousand years ago, or even a hundred, how many of the things that are now familiar were generally regarded as for ever beyond the utmost range of human thought.

The universe, such as we perceive it, does not explain itself, cannot have created itself. It is therefore quite legitimate to infer, from the given fact of its existence, that there must also have existed, and be now existing, something else outside perception. This is a proper field for philosophical inquiry. What would be unphilosophic would rather be a dogmatic negative. It would also be unscientific; for science, which will not accept without proof, will not in such a case reject without disproof, and disproof here is not feasible. There is room then for curiosity, for conjecture, perhaps a chance for discovery. 'Consciousness', says Whitehead, 'does not rest content with a dumb sense of importance behind the veil.'

3

The great religions of today, professed by hundreds of millions of people, are based on beliefs in sacred books, traditions, revelations, that are usually very ancient. The oldest, Hinduism, goes back beyond the dawn of history. Judaism, if we date it from Abraham, is 4000 years old; the universalistic Judaism of the second Isaiah, 2500. At about the same period as Isaiah originated also Buddhism, Taoism and Confucianism, perhaps Parseeism; the pre-Socratic philosophies of Greece were more or less contemporaneous: a great wave of constructive spiritual activity seems to have swept over the then civilized world in the seventh to fifth centuries B.C. Christianity dates back nearly 2000 years, Islam 1400.

But in the present age the universe, and man's place in it, are seen to be very different from what they were thought to be all those hundreds or thousands of years ago. We in our time are beginning to feel the full impact of the discoveries of the sciences during the last three centuries. The books of reference give us impressive totals of the numbers of adherents of the established Faiths in the various countries of the world: they present a tidy statistical façade: but behind that façade the religious state of mankind is by no means so simple and uniform. Among all creeds and in all countries the degree of attachment varies with individuals: it varies through every gradation, from a live, conscious and often passionate conviction, to a merely passive conformity with inherited local tradition. Throughout history, every one of those creeds has been from time to time divided by heresies and torn by theological disputes; they have always competed as rivals, sometimes been enemies fiercely at war with one another. But the present situation is different, unique, and even more grave. It is not a question of some new and more widespread heresy. Now, simultaneously, all the religious faiths are affected by a solvent, intimate and pervasive, which touches directly, one by one, the individual units within each community.

It is the doubt whether, in fact and in substance, the theological doctrines, that former generations had been taught, and had accepted without question, are true.

Each of those creeds has included some kind of theory of the universe. The cosmology has usually asserted a primal act of creation, once for all, by a deity or deities. But we have discovered that the essential cosmic process is a gradual evolution — from what and into what we have no conception. The declaration 'In the beginning God created the heaven and the earth' no longer satisfies the probing mind. For it contradicts itself: that could not have been the beginning since God was already there.

Again, almost all the religions have rested upon supernatural revelations received by their founders, prophets and saints, and these revelations have been held to be confirmed, as authentic messages from beyond the veil, by miracles: that is to say by mundane events which are contrary to the order of nature — their special significance being derived from the fact that they are contrary. But a scientific age is sceptical. It holds that 'Nature never contradicts her own law'. It would rather believe that the witnesses who had recorded such events were more likely to have been mistaken or deceived, or that their records had been tampered with, than that such events had actually occurred. Theologians have tried to allay religious doubts by ways that have created a fresh series of even greater doubts.

Nor is that all. From the first dawning of the religious sense, men's imagination has freely ranged over the possibilities of a continued spiritual life after bodily death. The old mythologies developed eschatologies of the most elaborate kind. The Egyptian Book of the Dead, for example, of which many copies have been found in the tombs and deciphered, is a roll of papyrus, sometimes as much as ninety feet long, filled from beginning to end with magical charms for the use of the dead in the afterworld. The dead man is pictured as being challenged and menaced by terrifying monsters in a series of ordeals, while gods — jackal-headed, ibis-headed and the like — weigh in balances the deeds of his mortal life: if it had been on the whole meritorious, and if he had been provided in the papyrus with the right incantation for each stage, he would be passed on to a new life of eternal bliss. Buddhism, again, supposes for the human soul an unending succession of lives before birth and after death: bad deeds may degrade it, in the next incarnation, into the bodily form of some animal of higher or lower degree; good deeds raise it into an ascending hierarchy of incorporeal spirits. Similarly, 'all systems of Hindu thought accept the idea of the continuous existence of the individual human being as axiomatic'. Islam offers to the faithful and virtuous a sensuous Heaven. The Greco-Roman religion had its Elysian Fields and its Hades. Byzantine theology gave to western Europe the after-life of Paradise, Purgatory and Hell, which Dante, Michelangelo and Milton portrayed so vividly: in all the churches and cathedrals of the Middle Ages, realistic sculptures and pictures instilled terror and awe. But in this century, in the western world – and now in the eastern world as well – how much of this is generally accepted as part of reality?

What is undoubted is that here in this world, in the conditions around us and the lives that we lead, there is much that is evil – much undeserved suffering, cruelty and injustice. If those hopes that all will be recompensed afterwards fade away – or indeed even if they hold good – men ask whether we can still believe in a divine Providence, immanent in this world as well as transcending it, the source of all that has happened and is happening, although all-powerful and all-merciful.

To a generation, already dazed and confused by the impact of the new science on the old theologies, has come the experience of the two world wars. With millions of young men, the bravest and the best, cut off in their prime and promise; with millions more men and women dragged from many countries to mass murder in gas-chambers in Germany, their bodies burnt in refuse incinerators; with tens of thousands blown to pieces in air-raids, or, in the Japanese cities, destroyed in a moment by the first use of the atom-bomb; tortures of physical pain, agonies of anxiety and bereavement; and added to all else, the danger that this, or perhaps still worse, may be repeated, and possibly again and again – where shall we find that living Providence, ever present, ever watchful, caring for mankind as a loving Father cares for his children? Here is a question, stark, insistent, which honesty cannot ignore nor piety evade.

4

In yet another important point the present differs from all former times. Not so long ago questions such as these would not have been permitted. In almost all countries the State upheld the dominant religion, usually in return receiving its support: the doctrines of the established Church were not to be doubted or challenged. Even after the principle of religious toleration had been generally accepted and the penal law had ceased to intervene in matters of faith, public opinion remained active and powerful: custom imposed conformity: parents and teachers were expected to transmit to the next generation the traditions that they had themselves inherited. But now, over most of the world, all this is changing. Individual freedom of thought and expression, beginning with literature, has spread to politics, and from politics to religion. In the communist countries, indeed, this does not apply; but there it is no longer the irreligious who are subjected to disabilities or persecution by the religious: it is the other way about. Generally speaking, almost everywhere sceptics are free to think and act as they like; and the believers, however vehemently they may disagree with their opinions, do not even wish to challenge their right to express them.

The consequence of this, added to the other factors, has been that the ferment of our time in matters of religion has spread with a speed and ubiquity to which no previous age can offer a parallel.

5

Such is the situation; it is complex, confused and changing. Nevertheless we may discern in it three trends of thought, often overlapping no doubt, and with many subsidiary currents, but clearly distinguishable and persistent.

The first is among the faithful. They are content with the ancient ways. Many of them have thought the matter out, have studied, discussed, reflected and have reached the clear conclusion that, in essentials, the religious beliefs they had been taught, or had formed for themselves, were sound and trustworthy. In them they find inspiration, support in temptation, consolation in sorrow. As to science, while not questioning its practical usefulness, they are convinced of its insufficiency and sceptical of its ultimate value. As to philosophy, confused and inconclusive as it is, if it clashes with religion they will prefer to be unphilosophic. Truth itself is seldom certain; the mind of man can never grasp its entirety. And if belief should sometimes stray across the fluctuating line between truth and myth, many will be ready to condone it, if along that way the dimly seeing millions may be led to piety and virtue. In any case, they themselves feel no personal call, and no capacity, to try to revalue religious doctrine. Trusting long-established authority, they feel safe on the trodden paths. In all countries, within all the faiths, these form a solid stable body of sober-minded people, helping to set the standards of the moral law, and to uphold it by their example. Everywhere it is a breeding-ground of disciplined and upright men and women, the soil from which have come saints, heroes and martyrs, the pioneers of the spirit.

The second trend of thought is the opposite of the first. It is modern, critical, adventurous. It is not interested in theological problems. Those who follow it look upon the present theologies as merely belated survivals of the obsolete mythologies: they consist of assertions which are very confident, but are based on nothing better than dreams, visions, trances, or maybe auto-suggestion or self-hypnosis — not messages from without but intimations from within, tricks of the brain. All who try to justify myth as a means of mystifying the people are, they say, accomplices in falsehood. Nor can what is false ever prove, in the long run, to be useful. Sooner or later — and, in an age of freedom of thought and widespread education, sooner rather than later — the delusion, or deception, is revealed for what it is. In any temptation, any dilemma, any crisis, it will fail. In the final choice, men's conduct will not be governed by make-believe. If your system of morals has been built on that foundation, when it crumbles, as it surely will, the structure will fall.

This school of thought, having discarded the current theologies, takes for granted that religion goes with them. The philosophy of materialism remains and holds the field. The only intellectual guide for the modern world will be physical science. Politics becomes a branch of economics. The first aim must be to increase the production of material wealth and to equalize its distribution in order to rescue the masses all over the world from the fetters of landlordism and capitalism, which for centuries have hampered their lives and broken their spirit. In the bitter struggle that this involves, they see the established religions as enemies, fighting on the other side. They say further that, although it is true that religion sometimes tries to bring the faiths together for the preservation of peace and the promotion of welfare, more often it splits them asunder, so that human history has largely been the tale of sectarian conflicts and doctrinal wars. And if it is true that religion has produced the saintly martyrs, is it not equally true that it was the Churches which had produced the persecutors who put them to death? The real saints and martyrs today are, they say, the men and women who have dedicated their lives – and sometimes sacrificed them – in the struggle for political liberty and social justice. But in that battle, almost everywhere the established Churches have ranged themselves, side by side with the monarchies and aristocracies, as allies of the system of class privilege. Clericalism appears on the scene as an active political force; then anti-clericalism (or secularism) arises, claiming to be the necessary reply. The conflict between the two has played, and is now playing, a large part in the politics of many countries; sometimes it dominates them, confusing the issues and hindering progress.

All this has led militant Marxism to declare itself not only socialist, but atheist. There emerges the full communist creed as we see it today. It has seized power right across the Eastern Hemisphere from the middle of Europe to the Pacific Ocean, and seeks to control the opinions and policies of nations comprising a third of the human race.

The third line of thought in religion accepts neither the dogmatic affirmative nor the dogmatic negative. It is not dogmatic at all. It will seek truth freely wherever it may be found.

Since the beginnings of modern rationalism in the time of the Renaissance, its expansion in France and England in the eighteenth century, and everywhere in the nineteenth under the stimulus of the scientific discoveries, this body of opinion has grown steadily and fast. Now in our own century, after the shock of the great wars, it may perhaps – at least among the intellectuals – command a larger volume of support, tacit or expressed, than either of the others.

Fifty years ago, those of this opinion would usually have described themselves as materialists, and often as agnostics: but the development — somewhat tardily — of the biological and social sciences has gradually discredited materialism; and agnosticism has never been a satisfying creed. Francis Bacon reminded us that 'Antisthenes being asked of one, what learning was most necessary for man's life, answered, To unlearn that which is nought!' The saying may be true; but the inquiring mind can never rest there. We may hold with Lowes Dickinson that 'the mistake of agnosticism has been that it has said not merely "I do not know", but "I will not consider!" '

This third school of thought has no name. It has no recognized leader. Its ideas are not formulated in any book. It includes a wide variety of opinions. While many of those who follow it have abandoned all connection with any organized religion, others still conform, though often with mental reservations. A great number, again, belong to unorthodox sects or groups, some old established, some quite new. But on two points all would agree. The first is that no belief may be professed which conscience declares is untrue. There can be no truck with myth or magic. The doctrine that what is known to be false may be pretended to be true, if that is likely to serve a useful purpose, is definitely rejected. The second point is that, on the other hand, they will not be led by their reaction against credulity, barren tradition, make-believe, to blind their eyes to aspects of religious faith which may not be of that order, may not be in contradiction with nature, but compatible with science and based firmly on realities. They hold fast to a conviction that, besides the nature revealed to our perceptions, there must be, in the factual universe, much more that remains concealed. We are asked to believe many incredible things, but that there should be nothing to be believed would be the most incredible of all.

6

We find that the ancient religions, when they try to answer the fundamental questions asked by a mankind bewildered and anxious, are not giving the same answers. To some of them they do; but to others the answers are conflicting. Those differences, strongly, often fanatically, maintained, give rise to estrangement and controversy, to political dispute and international tension, even to war. This has always been so, and — in spite of the acceptance of toleration as a principle and peaceful co-existence as an aim — it remains so today.

Keeping, as we have done throughout, as close to the actual conditions as we can, let us follow a line round the globe and note how frequently and how powerfully religious differences contribute to the present unrest and anxiety.

Starting here with the British Isles, the history of Ireland has been for centuries one of never-ending conflict between the Catholic Irish and the Protestant English and Scots: it is only halted precariously now at the uneasy frontier drawn to separate Ulster from Eire. In western and central Europe, the struggle between clericalism and secularism has been going on for nearly two hundred years. At this moment, in several of those countries, powerful political parties have been established, their names proclaiming their Christianity, and with the defence of religion and all it stands for as their main object. In Spain, it is not long since Catholics and Communists were fighting a civil war — stubborn, fierce and cruel. Down eastern Europe, curving from the Baltic to the Black Sea, runs the embattled frontier between the Soviets — materialist and atheist, authoritarian at home and militant abroad — and the nations of the west, who refuse, at all costs, to subject to that domination their liberties and their faiths.

Cross into western Asia and you see Israel, brought into being and sustained by nothing but its own Judaism, and the support of millions of fellow-Jews all over the world. It is faced and menaced by the Moslem Arab States that surround it: they in their turn supported by an Islamic Front that extends from as far away as Pakistan. For centuries the history of India had been a tale of fluctuating conflict between Moslems and Hindus: when lately the restraining hand of British rule was withdrawn, the two tore themselves apart — the rupture marked by massacres of tens of thousands, and the panic-stricken migrations of millions. Farther east, it has been the ultra-nationalist religion of Japan, Shinto, that made her in our own day the great aggressive Power of the northern Pacific; bringing injury, and sometimes disaster, to China, south-east Asia, Australia, New Zealand and the

United States — finally her own defeat and downfall. (The efforts that have been made in Japan, since the last war, to extirpate Shintoism, seem to have had as yet a very limited success.) Cross the ocean: happily it is true that the whole Western Hemisphere has kept itself free from violent religious strife — an outstanding achievement in human history. But, it may be added incidentally, as an illustration of the continued vitality of religious attachments, that in the present working of United Nations the Latin States of central and southern America form a block, as others do, to promote by peaceful means their own legitimate interests; and are often accustomed, when European affairs are in question, to use their numerous votes to strengthen the position of other Catholic States.

7

To our limited conspectus of the general situation we may now add that bird's-eye view of its religious aspect. It cannot tend to allay the anxiety that pervades our civilization. And if we turn from the Faiths as units to the men and women who compose them and consider what is becoming a normal state of mind in matters of religion, that anxiety is deepened.

The late Archbishop of York, Dr. Cyril Garbett, had written in recent years several short incisive books, in which he considered, with courage and frankness, the present position of the Church of England. He told us that: 'Christianity is now a minority religion; it no longer dominates the Western world. In England today the dominating fact of the religious position is that the majority of our fellow-countrymen have little contact either with the Church of England or any other Church. There has been a great decline in church attendance: churches once crowded are now attended by a mere handful of worshippers. The evidence is overwhelming that the ordinary Englishman, drawn from any class of society, is ignorant of the nature of Christianity and, except for rare occasions of ceremony, regards the Church with indifference or even with dislike as something which is irrelevant to his life.' 'Preaching one day in a town parish church', he wrote, 'rather unexpectedly, I found there a large body of soldiers; after the service, I asked the Chaplain, who evidently knew his men well, what he thought the service meant to them. "Nothing, absolutely nothing", was the immediate reply, with which I entirely agreed.'

'In England', the Archbishop said again, 'there has been a general retreat from Christianity. There has been no open denial on the part of the State. Christianity is still the accepted religion of the nation. The Monarch is anointed and crowned with Christian prayer, exhortation and blessing. Both Houses of Parliament still open with prayer. The judges and the armed forces have their chaplains. On national days of prayer the churches are crowded, and on civic occasions there is usually prayer and dedication. But the great mass of the people are ignorant of the elementary truths of the Christian faith and treat religion as something irrelevant to their lives . . . Within a short period there has been a retreat on an unprecedented scale from Christianity, not only in Russia and countries under Communist domination, but in nations which for over a thousand years have been nurtured in the Christian faith.' [1]

8

We have stressed the importance of the social atmosphere as a sanction for the moral law. Hitherto religion has been one of the principal factors in determining what kind of atmosphere we shall have. Now, with ever-increasing doubts about theological dogmas, and the weakening of the Churches that the Archbishop so forcibly described, we look around and examine what is happening to the social climate, to moral standards today. And if present tendencies persist and perhaps grow stronger, we ask what is likely to happen tomorrow.

Newspapers that circulate in millions pander to vulgarity and sensationalism; daily and weekly they give free advertisement to violence and salacity. Sexual laxity is more readily condoned; marriage is less stable; the family suffers. Among the most successful novels and plays, adultery is a usual theme, and murder a light-hearted topic for a leisure hour. Violent crime persists: organized vice is publicly on sale. Out of this environment can we expect a healthy society, a fine civilization? And is this, then,

[1] See note, p. 213.

a time when we can afford to do without religion, which has ever been the matrix of morality and its safeguard?

Yet the doubts persist. To quote Dr. Garbett once more: 'There are few thoughtful men and women nowadays who are not conscious of the intellectual difficulties in the way of a supernatural faith.' The Professor of Theology at Manchester University says: 'We no longer ask: "Can we make sense of the universe without bringing in the idea of God?" but: "Can we make sense of the idea of God in the light of our experience of the universe?" Does the world we have to live in look as if it were created and controlled by an Almighty God of perfect wisdom and infinite love? This is not just a philosophical question to be debated by experts at a high intellectual level; it is concerned with the total personal relation of each one of us to the total environment of our human existence.'

This brings us directly to the last feature in the present religious situation that we would wish to discuss: it arises from the fact that theology has not been able to find any solution, which the modern world would be ready to accept, to what we have been accustomed to call the Problem of Evil. Can empirical philosophy give any help?

9

Again we are bound at the outset to look closely at the way the problem is posed. The term 'Evil' is an abstract generalization, and the realist is suspicious of abstractions. When we were discussing ethics we refused to join in the pursuit of an intellectual figment called 'The Good' — an absolute, given *a priori*, of which particular goods were supposed to be products and instances. We insisted on looking directly for the particular goods themselves. So now with this other conception termed 'Evil', equally fictitious. *Evils* — in the plural and with no capital *E* — there certainly are: all our lives we have to face them, and strive against them as best we may. But that there should be extant in the universe some vague maleficent Force, formidable but formless; or perhaps symbolized and personified, in a goddess Kali of the Hindus, a deity Ahriman of the Zoroastrians, the Adversary of the Book of Job, the Devil of medieval Christianity, the Satan of Milton, or the Mephistopheles of Goethe — all this is emptiness.

There is no need, therefore, for the theologian to spend agonizing days and nights in trying to reconcile two ideas which are by their nature incompatible — first, the conception of an All-Creator, who is held to be just, loving and merciful; and, second, the existence, as part of his own creation — for, if not, how did it come to be? — of a spirit of injustice, hatred and cruelty, accountable for the calamities that afflict us and the temptations that lead us astray. It might have been obvious from the outset that such an attempt must be futile. It could reach no better conclusion than that 'the ways of Providence are inscrutable', which leaves us at the end where we were at the beginning.

Discussions such as these fascinated the scholastics of the Middle Ages. Modern man is likely to leave them behind and pass on.

Coming to close quarters, then, with the evils, all too real, of actual life, we shall do well in the first place to distinguish between two broad categories which bring in different considerations. One consists of the evils that come upon us from natural causes; the other those that we bring upon ourselves.

All we are and do, all we enjoy or suffer, depends at bottom on astronomical and geological conditions. The earth is a planet as well as a home. The stage of evolution it has reached as a planet makes it sometimes unsafe as a home. The cooling surface of the globe has not quite settled down. Now and then, here and there, an underlying rock-stratum slips a little: up above we have a disastrous earthquake. A volcano erupts: Pompeii is destroyed. The atmosphere also is in a constant state of flux: climate and weather cause all kinds of misfortunes — hurricanes and cyclones, raging floods, droughts bringing famine, fatal strokes of lightning. The lowest forms of life, often our servants, are sometimes our enemies. Microscopic bacteria and viruses, causing diseases and pests, are more formidable than the earthquake and the volcano.

But even against some of these natural evils (as was referred to earlier) man is able to make head. Gigantic engineering works, harnessing the flood and fructifying the desert, save vast populations from misery. Against the storms at sea we build ships large enough and powerful enough to outride them. We can even grasp the lightning and make it harmless. Greatest of all man's triumphs are those won in the constant battle against the micro-organisms. Plague and pestilence, and many diseases that had always been the scourge of mankind, have been almost eliminated. There are high hopes that many among the rest may be conquered soon.

Other calamities arising from the character of the planet will still remain, beyond possibility of control. As to these we can only say — in the concluding words of one of the great Greek tragedies: 'Lament no more: these things are so.'

But by far the larger part of the ills that beset us belong to the second category — those we bring upon ourselves; those that result from our own ignorance or misbehaviour, our own follies and errors, vices and crimes. Here we link up with all that was said before on the reality of freewill — power of choice; and on personal responsibility. Where there is choice there is the risk of wrong decision; when we choose wrongly we suffer for it; and when we suffer we speak of the existence of evil. Seeking the remedies, we now find ourselves back in the field of practical affairs. So the scene shifts from theology and geology to ethics, to the moral law; and then to politics, economics, technology, to social activity and personal conduct.

It is often not the sufferer who is to blame, either wholly or even partially, for his misfortune. Enjoying the advantages of living in a society, we have to incur also its disadvantages. The fault must lie somewhere, but not necessarily with him. We speak of the evils that *we* bring upon *ourselves*; but that is a form of speech, 'we' meaning the generality of mankind as distinguished from Nature. It does not mean that, if something unpleasant happens to you or me it must be because you or I have done something to deserve it. Another person may be to blame, or it may have been society itself through the faulty working of one or other of its institutions. For instance, if a hundred years ago in England some person had died in an epidemic of cholera or of smallpox, it is not probable that he himself had done anything to cause it: it was because medical science and State action had not at that time found the ways to prevent epidemics. If, in some backward country today, however, such an epidemic were to occur, everyone would know where the fault lay. But if in innumerable cases evil is brought about, not directly by the individual who suffers, but by the default of some social institution, we must again remember that all those institutions are themselves nothing more than organizations of individuals, on whom, and nowhere else, the final responsibility rests.

Let not him who suffers undeserved misfortune cry out, then, against the hard lot of man, a cruel universe, or a callous and indifferent God. More often than not, he can find the causes closer at hand: either in himself, or else in the action — or frequently the inaction — of the society which he and his fellows have created and now maintain, or in both self and society together.

CHAPTER XII

RELIGION AND REALITY

I

In the last chapter we suggested that the present anxious religious situation might be attributed mainly to two causes. The first was the failure of the theologies to carry conviction when they try to reconcile the orthodox belief in an active Providence, omnipotent and benevolent, with the facts of practical life, with the existence of evils, such as the two world wars; and we discussed that issue. The second cause was the so-called conflict between religion and science — actually a conflict between some of the conclusions of science and some of the doctrines of theology; to this we now turn. Is there any possibility of arriving — now or ever — at a reconciliation, as a first step to the synthesis for which we have pleaded, between philosophy, science and religion?

It is often said that no one is so rigid as the theologian, nothing so unchangeable as dogma. If that were true, unless science surrendered her position, this conflict would be inevitable and must continue indefinitely. But if we look back down the vistas of history, or around at the present scene, we can see that it is not true. All religious institutions do in fact amend their creeds and formularies. Sometimes this is brought about by a 're-formation'; maybe after much controversy, and perhaps upheavals and secessions. All the great Founders were themselves rebels against the orthodoxies that had gone before — polytheism, Pharisaism, formalism. More often change has come about gradually, and sometimes almost imperceptibly, generation by generation. What is uncongenial to the spirit of the age is no longer emphasized; it is allowed quietly to fade away; the rest is maintained and cherished, in the end perhaps strengthened rather than weakened. In religion — as in philosophy, science, morals, sociology — there is that constant struggle between ideas, that continuous evolution and survival of the fittest. So we find that the orthodoxy of one century is never quite the same as that of the previous century, and may be in many respects quite different from that of five hundred years before.

We see the process going on now, in varying degree, in almost all the creeds almost everywhere. The changes come from within. The opinion of the laity plays a large part. When the ordinary man is led to believe, by fresh discoveries or by discussion, that some new idea has been established as true and its contrary as false; if, nevertheless, the authorities he has been accustomed to follow insist upon keeping it as an article of faith, then his intellect is alienated, his conscience is disturbed, his confidence shaken. He distinguishes between the preacher or leader he thinks enlightened and the one he thinks obscurantist. Little by little the influence of the churchgoers has its effect – and the silent influence of the empty places of those who stay away.

All social institutions that have lasted a long time are in danger of falling into decrepitude. They tend to value past more than future, history more than purpose. It has been well said: 'The noblest movements are apt to outlive their usefulness when their zeal develops into formalism: an ideal creates an institution and then the institution suffocates the ideal.' And again: 'No one can walk backwards into the future.'

Meanwhile, on the side of science, important changes are proceeding, and with greater rapidity. The movement away from materialism during the present century is marked. Throughout the free world the intelligentsia, including the scientists, has not in the main accepted Marxism; and this is due, not only to its political and economic deficiencies, but also to the failure of its dialectical materialism to carry conviction.

It is significant of the present trend of thought in the world of science in this country that, at the meeting at Oxford in 1954 of the British Association for the Advancement of Science, the speaker chosen to deliver the 'Evening Discourse', Professor C. A. Coulson, should have taken as his subject 'Science and Religion'; and that in his conclusion he should have said this: 'Science plays its part in the fulfilling of human life along with many other influences, and cannot be wholly separated from them. The scientist Max Planck could say: "Religion and Natural Science are fighting a joint battle in an incessant, never-relaxing crusade against scepticism and against dogmatism, against disbelief and against superstition." ' He adds: 'Most of us in the scientific movement are deeply troubled . . . I believe that our trouble is that we have forgotten some of those other elements of truth to which we are joined; we have kept blinkers on our eyes when the circumstances of today require us to see the whole of life. The clue to our hesitation will be found in what is, for many of us, an inadequate concept of what is a human being. Here science can help, and help enormously; but it is not enough by itself. We must be willing to open our hearts and minds to the revelation of truth of whatever school or subject.'

With such a disposition now beginning to appear on the one side and on the other, perhaps philosophy may be able to play a useful part as mediator; for it overlaps them both — science, on its left, in the field of theoretical physics; and religion, on its right, in the field of mind and morals.[1] And philosophy itself is also realizing its own limitations, and changing in some degree its interests.

It used, for instance, to be much concerned with Ontology, the problem of Existence — of matter, life, mind, ideas, the cosmos, God — of each separately or all of them together. But it is recognizing more and more that the outcome from all those laborious discussions has been nil; and now, as Professor Gilbert Ryle has said in a sentence of admirable brevity: 'Ontology is out.' In this matter, as in not a few others, the seeker of reality may say with Cowper:

> Defend me from the toil
> Of dropping buckets into empty wells,
> And growing old in drawing nothing up.

2

I do not know that empirical philosophy, depending as it does upon reason, can expect to be able to lead us much further than

---

[1] Whitehead says, in his *Process and Reality*: 'Philosophy frees itself from the taint of ineffectiveness by its close relations with religion and with science, natural and sociological. It attains its chief importance by fusing the two, namely, religion and science, into one rational scheme of thought . . . Philosophy finds religion, and modifies it; and conversely religion is among the data of experience which philosophy must weave into its own scheme.'

the line we have now reached. It does not follow that this is the end of the road. Reason itself convinces us of the existence of a Something Else beyond the perceived universe. Vaguely we can discern the road, still stretching on into an immense unknown. Coulson quotes Pascal: 'The last step that Reason takes is to recognize that there is an infinity of things beyond it.'

But philosophy — with science its ally — is not man's only recourse, nor reason the only faculty at his service. Instinct, intuition, imagination, emotions — all these are constantly at work. They too are realities, playing a part in the real universe, helping to form men's ideas and to decide their actions. Religion enlists them all.

Here, however, we must be on our guard. We are entering on dangerous ground. Experience has often proved that, if we let go of reason and trust to these other, less reliable, faculties, we may be led into disaster.

Instinct? — it can take us back into the animal propensities of the subconscious, rebellious against intelligence and morality. Intuition? — let us remember, for instance, the intuitional philosophy of Nietzsche, and its application by Hitler, his disciple. Imagination? — consider the mythologies of the ancient world, commanding for thousands of years the pious devotion of the credulous millions. [1] Emotion? — it can give us love and joy; but also anger, hatred, quarrel and war. Above all, there is this great difference between reason and those others. When reason makes mistakes — as of course it does, like every human faculty — it can correct them by its own processes — new discoveries, further facts, better arguments; and then it can start afresh. But instinct, intuition, imagination, emotion, often claim finality: for their mistakes there is then no remedy.

Nevertheless, we are obliged to face those risks, and do our best to avoid those consequences, for we have no other recourse; unless we are to give up altogether, and remain unsatisfied, with nothing better than, as Whitehead said, 'a dumb sense of importance behind the veil'.

---

[1] We may see their vestiges even now in the myths and magic that cling so tenaciously to our own rituals; and in the inane superstitions still rife in all sections of society, pandering to nonsense.

3

It is not, however, the purpose of this book to add yet another volume to the hundreds that come crowding, year after year, from the printing-presses of all countries, in the perennial discussion on the relation of man to the supernatural. The philosopher in search of reality must beware of wandering away into those tempting but boundless fields; he would probably soon be lost and never be heard of again. Nevertheless, the religions are facts; influencing, powerfully and constantly, the course of ethics, of politics, even of economics. We should be false to our aim if we were to end at this point. We are bound to make an attempt at least to apply, in this field also, the principles that have emerged in the course of our search. But this inquiry shall be confined to a few points and be kept as brief as may be.

One preliminary point – whether a supernatural does in fact exist – has already been discussed, and we need only to recall the conclusions that we reached. In an early chapter we offered reasons for believing in the reality of 'a cosmos of some sort', prior to man and independent of his perceptions or his philosophies. We know that a Nature exists around us; but we know also that this Nature, as we perceive it, is not self-sufficient, and is therefore, for us, incomplete. It follows that there must also exist other features or factors that are beyond, or outside, the Nature of matter, life and mind, of which we are cognizant. We know a supernatural exists because we see what it does: that existence is not cancelled because we cannot say what it is.

Our basic principles required also a clear distinction between that objective universe as it is in itself, and our own subjective perceptions and interpretations. Without that differentiation, at the outset and all along, everything would be confused: but when philosophy and science have admitted that distinction – first with matter, then with life, then mind – they were able to win great successes. Coming now to religion, we need to make the same differentiation. We must distinguish between that Something Else – given, real in its own right – and man's effort to interpret and describe it.

This distinction is nothing new: indeed it is commonly made in practice already. The metaphysical philosopher leaves the supernatural as a pure abstraction. The ordinary man, seeking to make it concrete, assigns to it qualities akin to his own — sympathies and antipathies, love and anger, approval or disapproval — 'personal' qualities in short. What is 'Deity' to the philosopher is 'God' to the people. The distinction is evident in the fact that we speak of Deity as 'it', of God as 'He'.

This brings us to a question we have not previously considered — the question of the limitations of language.

4

In recent years a group of English philosophers have been stressing the importance of logical precision in the use of terms. Other philosophers, while recognizing the value of their principle, have thought that they have been inclined to carry it too far. They appear sometimes to regard the etymology of philosophy almost as though it were philosophy itself; as if to compile a careful vocabulary and dictionary of philosophical terms would be the best or even the only way to attack the great unsolved problems. But however that may be, in the discussion in which we are now engaged, on religion and reality, this question of language comes at once into the forefront.

In each of our previous inquiries, we carried analysis as far as we could, but sooner or later we reached what had to be regarded, in the present state of human knowledge, as an ultimate. With material things, we called that ultimate Energy; with vital phenomena, we could only call it, tautologically, Life; with mental phenomena, Mind. These we could not describe or define because both ideas and words had failed us. When we come to the edge of knowledge we reach also the limit of speech. It is the same with this other ultimate that we call Deity. Theologians and philosophers invent or adopt terms in which to discuss the supernatural: they speak of Creation; of Omnipotence, Omnipresence and Omniscience; of Infinity beyond Space and Eternity beyond Time; or perhaps of the Absolute. But none of these words enable the mind to grasp or to portray the events that happen, and the processes that go on, in the cosmos. They bring us nowhere.

From this predicament, however, man found a way out long

ago – imperfect, no doubt, but better than none. He has pursued it, and pursues it still, in his religions.

While language is, of course, the principal art of communication, it is not the only one. There are other conventions by which ideas and emotions can be communicated from one to another. The painter does it through his pictures; the sculptor through his carvings; the architect through his edifices –

> Man builds the soaring spires
> That sing his soul in stone.

Music – 'the inarticulate mystic speech of Music', as Carlyle called it – can evoke every mood, express every emotion.

Religion enlists all the arts in its service. Anyone, for example, who has been privileged to attend in Westminster Abbey the celebration of some great national ceremony, will have experienced it. The venerable building itself, perpetuating the traditions of a thousand years in the life of a great people; the colours of the windows, and the shafts of sunlight against the spacious background of the ancient walls; the solemn grandeur or intimate appeal of the music; and the arts of language as well, in the poetry and oratory of the liturgy: all this takes us away – 'the swing of a door from street to temple' – from the familiar realities of everyday life, and brings us into touch with a living cosmos, equally real.

We ask, would it be gain or would it be loss if the cathedrals, churches and chapels, the synagogues, mosques and temples, all over the world, were gradually to be deserted, and finally closed, the ministries of all the Faiths disbanded? Thousands of millions of human beings – men, women and children, of all races and colours, of every degree of ignorance or knowledge, loving and suffering, enjoying or enduring – they are all companions together on this revolving globe, with mystery all about them. They need something beyond and greater than themselves to comfort and sustain them; to fill the imagination, satisfy the emotions; to combat what is evil, strengthen what is good. They are not philosophers. 'Religion', says Meredith, 'has a nourishing breast: philosophy is breastless.'

The peoples turn to religion; and to the arts as its interpreter. They listen to the prophet and to the poet – and more readily than to the philosopher. And if there appears a great prophet or a poet of genius who also has a philosophy, and who has at the same time a gift for leadership and a willingness to undertake its burdens, then he may found a religion, or set going a current of thought, that may endure for thousands of years. All the Founders were of that order.

But we must stress once more the risks that we run when we rely, not upon the intellect alone, but also on the non-intellectual faculties of the human mind — the dangers we shall encounter, the overwhelming disasters that we may invite. Those faculties are so much less trustworthy than reason that it is never safe to allow them the last word. The subconscious may often be reliable, but it is safer to keep the conscious in ultimate control. To follow the vague inklings of intuition may sometimes be right: but it is unlikely, when rational experience clearly says the opposite. The lively visions of imagination may open vistas of great achievement — provided we still keep the firm ground of reality under our feet. And everyone knows that emotion without reflection is dangerous.

History shows that the prophet and the poet are ever inclined to myths, and that a myth, once planted, grows with the luxuriance of a weed. It chokes religion, when 'anything is credible because nothing is true'. We witness it now; for in so far as obsolete mythological elements are still persistently retained in the current theologies, whether eastern or western, religion is discredited. And when intelligent and honest minds — especially among the young, coming fresh to these issues — discard the myths, they often throw religion out as well. Then they are left with nothing better than the blank negation of atheism, or the nullity of agnosticism, which are as far removed from reality on the one side as mythology is on the other.

Let us be careful at the same time not to fall into the opposite error of supposing that all symbolism is nothing but myth. There is a basic difference between the two. Myths, by definition, are fictional. Apollo, Mithras, Pan, the Fates or the Furies; Moloch, Baal, or Ashtoreth; or, again, Adam, Eve and the Serpent — none of these, or the thousands of others of the same order, are real in their own right, facts in the given universe. On the other hand a supernatural, of some sort, does in fact exist: we know it because we know that a natural exists and that it is incomplete. If we have to devise a language in which to think about it and talk about it, and if this involves a symbolic use of terms colloquially used in everyday life, this language is intended to relate to something real. The worship of mythical gods, their invocation, their very names, attach to nothing. And so with every sort of myth, ancient or modern.

But what if the great prophet or the poet of genius has a philosophy, and the philosophy is a bad one? Then, sooner or later, directly or indirectly, immeasurable harm will be done. We may recall the familiar examples. Plato (whose mind was essentially imaginative and poetic), Dante (in *De Monarchia*), Karl Marx, Nietzsche – all yielded, in their political philosophies, to the temptation of taking absolute power as the short cut to their ideals; all advocated despotism as the agent of progress. Their influences were seen in the authoritarianism of some of the established Churches; of Hegelianism, and of Marxism: they have inspired German Nazism, Italian Fascism, Russian Communism. All these, although not theological, are Faiths, with formulated dogmas and creeds, held with passionate conviction and applied with ruthless fanaticism. All of them are intuitive, largely irrational and emotional. All embody political myths. Their consequences we have seen with our own eyes, in the flames of burning cities, the deaths of millions, and, for a whole generation over half of the globe, in the stifling of freedom.

5

We are hoping that present-day thought may move towards a greater measure of understanding between philosophy and science on the one hand and religion on the other. We ask whether our present discussion points to conclusions that might help to that end.

Two conclusions may be drawn. One is the reality of 'a Supernatural of some sort'. The other is the difficulty of getting into touch with that reality through our reasoning faculty, and by means of the language that the intellect creates and employs. We have been led to ask whether there may not be a different line of approach altogether – through the non-intellectual faculties that are always functioning, and through the means of communication of their own that they employ. These involve using the terms by which we denote our human qualities and characteristics *as if* they applied also to Deity. [1]

Now there may be a wide measure of agreement as to the validity of the first, and at least as to the possibility of this second conclusion. For it seems that few philosophers or scientists nowadays would be prepared to dismiss straightway any Supernatural as being, in the nature of things, impossible. The ocean of nescience all around us is so vast, our own little island of knowledge is so small, that the word 'impossible' is out of place.

But these two conclusions — and the second only tentative — seem to be as far as we can go, at present, towards any basis for agreement. For the rest all is controversial.

The three basic problems of religion remain, as ever, in keen debate.

First: accepting Deity, is it allowable to personify it as God, and then to assimilate God to Man?

Second: if it is — should we believe that God is a Providence, actively at work in the world around us, and in ourselves: determining the course of events in the physical universe and in human history, and therefore responsible, at every moment, for individual conduct?

Third: if so, is there direct communion between God and mankind — from God by revelation to individuals, and from men by prayer and invocation?

Hundreds of millions of people, however, are not troubled by any of these questions. Faithful to the beliefs of one or other of the ancient creeds, or of some modern variant, they regard God as identical with Deity; his qualities as portrayed in the Scriptures; Providence as evident around and within us; revelation and inspiration as facts; constant communion established through mystic experience. For them it is not a question of the limitations of human knowledge, of language, of 'as if.' Providence, Revelation, Communion — these are axioms of belief.

Philosophers or scientists among them, having recognized the reality of life and mind in nature (for if they are not real, how is it possible, for instance, for me to be writing these words, or

[1] Cf. *The Philosophy of 'As if'*, by H. Vaihinger (Kegan Paul, Trench, Trubner & Co., 1924).

for you to be reading them?), may find it is easy to recognize also the actuality, however modified and sublimated, of the supernatural. Made planet-conscious by science, cosmic-consciousness is only one step further, with the sense of Deity beyond. Then the whole panorama of nature stretches before them, from the electron to the galaxy, with all its phenomena of life and mind.

From this there may be derived, as a consequence, a transcendent basis for the Moral Law, a unique, and perhaps indispensable, sanction for ethics.

Yet the doubts remain: they too are facts, as much as the beliefs, in the present world situation. Remember Archbishop Garbett: 'There are few thoughtful men and women nowadays who are not conscious of the intellectual difficulties in the way of a supernatural faith.' No one would deny that that is so.

Other millions would give a negative answer to our first question. They would say that it is not allowable to ascribe quasi-human qualities to Deity: it would be a desertion of truth, a slip-back into mythology. The prophet Jeremiah, they might say, rebuked the idolatrous Jews for worshipping the works of their own hands: this is to worship the work of our own minds, and is no better. Reason would have abdicated, to allow Imagination to usurp the throne.

As to the second question — the reality of a Providence, daily and hourly intervening to execute its plan for the ordering of the world, and directing individual human conduct in order that this purpose may be fulfilled — the sceptics would offer an alternative. That is the possibility that the plan of the universe is one which has produced, by a process of evolution, conscious beings on this planet — and, very likely, innumerable others elsewhere — endowed with an autonomous power to frame their own ideas and to conduct their own lives. If this be so, constant intervention would be a contradiction — the plan itself spoilt and defeated by its own author.

Is it impious to hold such a belief? Would it be a derogation from the greatness of God, the destruction of religion? Or might it not rather be seen as an exaltation of the idea of Deity far above any propounded by the old theologies; and at the same time an uplifting of man himself to a nobler status?

When we were discussing the problem of evil, realizing that

the evils from which we suffer are mostly man-made, we offered the conclusion that their causes and their cure should be considered a matter, not for theologians, but for every man. This view has indeed been gaining ground among theologians, particularly since the world wars. They speak of it symbolically, as faith in the Fatherhood of God. We are children, learning by experience the difference between right and wrong. The wise father lets his children learn by their own mistakes, does not direct them at every turn. Struggle and survival, challenge and response, are the conditions of progress: safety is good, but liberty is better. From this it would follow that the grace of God is not to be found in intervention, but in non-intervention; religion reaching its peak when it comes to understand that the silence of God is his greatest gift to us.

As to the third question – on Inspiration and Communion – we see all around us every degree of belief and unbelief. At one extreme are the fundamentalists, who accept whatever is written in the sacred books of the religion in which they have been bred; any uncertainties of authenticity or interpretation being matters, not of faith, but for scholarship. Or the belief may be in a purely personal communion, open to everyone, achieved by prayer and contemplation. Man invokes; God responds; man hearkens and obeys. The universal mind has been brought in, at that moment, in that place: it is again 'a commerce between Self and Not-self'.

At the other extreme are those who reject all such claims. They think that the experiences are more likely to originate within the mind of the worshipper, with no external attachment. It is a wish or resolve already half formed, which leads him to pray: the answer to his prayer is an echo. Intuition, imagination, emotion, a faith deeply established in the subconscious mind by heredity and training – it is these which have led him to accept, as an expression of the will of God, what is really no more than his own endorsement of his own desire.

The phrase, 'the will of God', comes readily to the lips. But when the different religions confront one another – each of them so deeply convinced that it is obeying the will of God that some-times persecution and martyrdom, massacres and long years of cruel war, must be inflicted or endured for conscience' sake – who shall say on which side the will of God truly stands?

The issue is not merely historical and remote. We have traced its powerful effects at this present time all round the globe. The catastrophe of the Second World War had its initial cause in the intuitions of Hitler, continually proclaiming his own mission to have been destined by Providence. Or again, in the controversy that has been raging in recent years over the policy of the present Government in South Africa towards the natives and coloured people; while the Christian Churches of the world have been almost unanimous in condemning it as contrary to the Christian ethic, the Minister of Justice, speaking in a parliamentary debate from the Government bench, no doubt with complete sincerity, could say: 'We believe that we are sitting here at this moment by the will of God.'[1]

Between those two extremes stand many, often perhaps a large majority, who do not accept as authentic all the claims to revelation of communion, nor yet reject them all, but believe in exceptional interventions – not so many as to destroy man's responsibility, nor so rare as to leave the world adrift. The founders of religions, the prophets and apostles, the great mystics, they accept and revere as truly the inspired spokesmen of God. And there are the multitude who hold, with passionate conviction, that assuredly there has been one divine revelation, unique in its fullness and authenticated by its results.

There remain the beliefs in an easy accessibility for everyone, or at least for those psychically endowed, to the abnormal – perhaps supernatural – that lies all about us. Science is now beginning to explore that field – although reluctantly, and with hesitation. Psychical research, the study of telepathy, and of other forms of 'Extra-sensory perception', employ the methods of observation, experiment and statistical measurement. But they have not yet reached conclusions generally accepted by the world of science.

6

Supplementary to the three main problems of contemporary religion is the question of the Moral Law – its origin and its sanctions. Can this be cited as a further proof of the existence of

[1] See note, p. 214.

God and His benevolence? Whatever differences there may be
in theology, all the religions teach substantially the same things
in ethics. Does this prove that they must all have originated from
a common source, which, if we accept Deity, can only be there?
The existence of God, it is held, accounts for the moral law, and
the moral law, in turn, confirms the existence of God.

Here empirical philosophy comes back into the discussion,
bringing its own contribution. When we were considering ethics
and inquiring into the reality of a moral law as a factor in human
affairs, we concluded that a purely mundane basis might be found
for it *a posteriori*, without need for any *a priori* foundation,
metaphysical or theological. The gradual evolution of moral
principles and practices, in response to the needs of life as it is
lived, offers an alternative. The moral law was not promulgated
for the first time at particular dates and in particular places by the
great prophets and sages. Beginning with primeval man, it has
evolved through long ages, and is still evolving. It is the common
experience of human communities of all times and all races that
has taught them what kind of beliefs, habits and customs will
promote their own welfare, what is good conduct and what is
bad. If the moral law is substantially the same among all peoples
the reason is indeed that it springs from a common origin, but that
origin is to be found in the experience of living in communities
that is common to all alike.

But when that has been said, not all has been said. No one can
deny the immensely important part that the religions have played,
and are now playing, as a factor within the evolutionary process
itself. Past history and present observation establish that beyond
question. The religions have crystallized and formulated the
moral law; have brought it to the peoples, persuading their intel-
lects by argument and touching their emotions by fervour and
eloquence. This is why so many thoughtful people who are not
orthodox feel bound to recognize the high value of religious
incentives and sanctions, and are made anxious by their weakening.

7

So the perennial debate continues. In one century, or in one
country, opinion may sway to one side, in another century, or

another country, to the opposite. In the present age, among the great religions, there are no signs anywhere of even the beginning of a reconciliation of theological differences. Apart from the last remaining vestiges of primitive paganism now yielding place before the advances of Christianity or of Islam, there is no prospect of any one of them being displaced by any other. And rarely, if ever, is there any desire in any quarter for the initiation of a new religion, which should attempt to combine them all in some amalgam of theologies essentially incompatible.

On the other hand, the movement towards a reunion of the various sects of the Protestant Churches of the English-speaking world has, in recent years, been making marked progress. And it has been extended further, through the World Council of Christian Churches, to a growing co-operation between the Anglican, the Orthodox and the Armenian. Everywhere, although theology may often divide, ethics can unite: in the present parlous estate of human affairs, this has created a climate of opinion impatient of ecclesiastical disputes and antagonisms, and favourable, wherever opportunity offers, to co-operation. [1]

The word Co-existence has become a key-word in our political vocabulary. The invention of the nuclear bomb has made it clear to everyone that there is only one alternative – Co-extinction. No one can be indifferent or inactive now. The peoples are bound to realize that each other's existence – together with their several cultures and ideologies – is a fact not to be ignored. If those ideologies are to be changed, it must be from within, and by persuasion; not from without, by force.

This idea, which is bound to dominate increasingly the conduct of affairs, ought surely to apply also – and above all – in the sphere of religion. Indeed, in principle, if not always in practice, Religious Liberty, or Toleration, has long been widely accepted. Fellowship and co-operation is only a short step further. Here reason and sen-

---

[1] In 1936, the late Sir Francis Younghusband founded, in England, the World Congress of Faiths, in order to promote a still wider expansion of inter-religious co-operation, in the fields at least of ethics and international politics: not confined within even the wide bounds of Christendom, but extending to all the Faiths, eastern and western. A parallel movement has been set on foot in the United States. Both have branches in other countries. They have won the support of a number of leading personalities belonging to all the organized religions – Christians, Jews, Moslems, Hindus, Buddhists, Confucians, Taoists – and of some not attached to any. But they have not yet aroused that interest among the general body of religious-minded people which the importance and timeliness of their appeal might have been expected to evoke.

timent agree. Active advocacy by the leaders of all the Faiths throughout the world could not fail to have its effect, generation by generation, among the masses of the peoples. Then would come a relaxation, in one at least of the causes of the strain and stress of these anxious times.

8

The debate continues: and the decision, in these matters, as in all others, will rest in the end with the movement of world opinion. And world opinion is nothing else than the collective opinion of this man, and that man, and the other — wherever they may be, whatever their background or their present environment. So that the conclusion that we reach, when we try to relate religion with reality, is that the unit, the focal point, is once more the individual person, his ideas, his actions. It is the same conclusion as we had reached again and again in the course of our inquiry. After we had left the province of material things and passed into the domains, successively, of life and mind, ideas and institutions, ethics and politics, and the arts — at the end, each time, that was the outcome. So we see that after all 'the proper study of mankind is Man'. For even his physical and social environment — given its terrestrial basis — is man-made. And the supernatural itself he can consider only in terms of his own capacities.

I had not set out with this, or any other, general idea in mind. I started from no assumption into which the facts as I came to them would have to be fitted; but only with the principle of keeping empirically, in each context, as close as possible to realities. If we discover at the end that we have reached a philosophic unity, it is because the argument itself has led us there.

Personal responsibility comes into the centre of the picture. For if every man's fate depends upon individual decisions — his own and other people's — he cannot escape an obligation, both to himself and to them. He must do his best to come to right decisions — that is those that will lead to good results; the definition of 'good' to be found in its particulars.

For better, for worse, the modern western world rests intellectually upon a foundation of liberty of thought and action: not as in earlier ages on custom, taboos, enforced conformity to unchanging principles, obeyed without question by generation after generation. This freedom carries with it a corresponding duty: and in our time this duty applies especially to those qualified to be leaders in the free countries of the west. On all those 'matters in debate' which we have been discussing, and the multitude of others stirring men's minds everywhere, theirs is the task of clarifying their own ideas and of seeking solutions to the current problems, in order to give to the age the guidance it so painfully lacks. Here is the growing-point of our present civilization.

Even in the communist-controlled countries the repressions of liberty and denials of equality — political, social, religious — cannot stand indefinitely. The subject peoples will not submit to them for ever. Already, since the death of Stalin, the tyrannies seem to be relaxing. And now for the first time Asia and Africa are taking a fuller part in the general evolution of ideas, on their own initiative, through the force of their own native energies. Hitherto hardly touched by modern science (except in Japan), their vast populations have tarried three hundred years behind the West — sometimes three thousand years. Now their peoples are looking for fresh illumination to the nations that have been in the forefront. But, apart from physical science, they see only the fog of our intellectual confusion.

9

Let us go back for a moment to a question posed, but not pursued, at the beginning — whether there is any purpose in our lives, or whether 'like gnats above a stagnant pool on a summer evening, man dances up and down without the faintest notion why'. We come at once to the same difference of outlook as we have just been discussing. Some believe that our purpose has been set for us by God, and its nature defined in revealed religion. Others, not sharing that belief, must find that the purposes of our lives are whatever men themselves choose to make them — good or bad, worth while or not. But whichever is our approach, and whether taken casually or after long and careful thought, ultimately we come back, yet once more, to personal responsibility. For the believers must bear the responsibility for having accepted the belief which they hold. Even if they wish to renounce their power of choice, and are willing to accept unquestioningly the guidance of religious authority, that renunciation is also a decision: to decide for inaction is itself an action. While for the sceptic, the personal responsibility is clear and direct.

Abstract generalizations are realities only in the world of ideas. In the actual world of nature it is the unit alone that exists, together with its relations with other units. Remember Goethe again: 'Mankind? It is an abstraction. There are, always have been, and always will be, men and only men.' Through the whole of living nature it is the same.

You may travel, for example, by railway across the broad prairie provinces of Canada when the harvest is ripe; and, for nearly a thousand miles, you may see as splendid a sight as any that earth can show. On either side, as far as the eye can reach, stretch the vast unbounded plains of golden wheat. Here, you can say, is Canada feeding the cities of the world. But if you leave the train for a moment at some watering-station and step to the edge of the cultivation, what will you find? Nothing is there but individual wheat plants — each with root, stalk and ear; each with its own separate life; using its environment for its own sustenance; not the less individual because it is repeated a thousand times over — a million times, or a million million.

That plant is the product of an evolution that has lasted for aeons of time. It is the outcome — apart from human intervention — of chance mutations in the genes of abnormal germ-cells, and of changing conditions of climate and weather.

All vegetable and animal — except human — evolution is unconscious of its own processes. With man, there is the same multiplication of individual units to make the race, the species. But outstanding is that vital difference, that he, and he alone, has become aware of himself, his origins, his environment, and of his own shared ideas and institutions. This has not only vastly enlarged his opportunities, but has entirely changed the time-scale of his achievements. Results that would have taken hundreds of thousands or millions of years can be brought about in a century or even a decade. We cannot, 'by taking thought, add a cubit to our stature'; but we can, by taking thought, add an inch, or even two or three inches, to the bodily stature of the next generation. We cannot — fortunately — extend our lives

M

indefinitely; but in the more advanced societies an infant born now may expect thirty years more life than a child born at the beginning of this century: and twice as long a life on the average as a child, born, for example, in India. Our eyesight is not keen enough to let us see the micro-organisms that prey upon our blood-cells; but we have devised microscopes that have enabled us to attack and defeat them. We cannot grow wings: but in fifty years we have created machines that enable us to fly faster and farther than any bird. We have made ways through the mountain ranges, and under the waters of the sea.

All this is the work of individual persons — one here, one there; then of a few — pioneers; then of everyone, everywhere. Supplementing, and sometimes surpassing nature, this is the outcome of an evolution that has become conscious of itself. Indeed, civilization, searching for reality, is discovering that it is itself a process. And the process is just that. Civilization is Conscious Evolution.

LETTER FROM DR. ALBERT EINSTEIN

Princeton, New Jersey, U.S.A., October 13th, 1950

I have now read your book. What impressed me most favourably was your independence of mind which reveals itself in your criticism as well as in your proposals. You demand that physics should describe what is 'physically real'. If physicists attempt to manage with purely fictitious concepts like number, they cannot, you say, reach their goal. You have got the impression that contemporary physics are based on concepts somewhat analogous to the 'smile of the absent cat'.

In fact, however, the 'real' is in no way immediately given to us. Given to us are merely the data of our consciousness; and among these data only those form the material of science which will allow of univocal linguistic expression. There is only one way from the data of consciousness to 'reality', to wit, the way of conscious or unconscious intellectual construction, which proceeds completely free and arbitrarily. The most elementary concept in every-day thought, belonging to the sphere of the 'real', is the concept of continually existing objects, like the table in my room. The table as such, however, is not given to me, but merely a complex of sensations is given to which I attribute the name and concept 'table'. This is a speculative method, based on intuition. In my opinion, it is of the greatest importance to be conscious of the fact that such a concept, like all other concepts, is of a speculative-constructive kind. Otherwise one cannot do justice to those concepts which in physics claim to describe reality, and one is in danger of being misled by the illusion that the 'real' of our daily experience 'exists really', and that certain concepts of physics are 'mere ideas' separated from the 'real' by an unbridgeable gulf. In fact, however, positing the 'real' which exists independently of my sensations is the result of intellectual construction. We happen to put more trust in these constructions than in the interpretations which we are making with reference to our sensations. Thence arises our confidence in statements like these: 'There were trees long before there was a creature able to perceive them.'

These facts could be expressed in a paradox, namely that reality, as we know it, is exclusively composed of 'fancies'. Our trust or our confidence in our thoughts referring to reality is solely based on the fact, that these concepts and relations stand in a relation of 'correspondence' with our sensations. Therein the 'truth' of our statements is founded. Such it is in daily life and in science. If now in physics this correspondence or correlation between our concepts and our sensations becomes more and more indirect, we are not entitled to accuse this science of replacing reality by fancies. A criticism of this sort would only be justified, if we were able to show that it is impossible to correlate the concepts of a specific theory in a satisfactory manner with our experience.

We are free to choose which elements we wish to apply in the construction of physical reality. The justification of our choice lies exclusively in our success. For example, Euclidean geometry, considered as a mathematical system, is a mere play with empty concepts (straight lines, planes, points, etc., are mere 'fancies'). If, however, one adds that the straight line be replaced by a rigid rod, geometry is transformed into a *physical theory*. A theorem, like that of Pythagoras, then gains a reference to reality. On the other hand, the simple correlation of Euclidean geometry is being lost, if one notices that the rods, which are empirically at our disposal, are not 'rigid'. But does this fact reveal Euclidean geometry to be a mere fancy? *No*, a rather complicated sort of co-ordination exists between geometrical theorems and rods (or, generally speaking, the external world) which takes into account elasticity, thermic expansion, etc. Thereby geometry regains physical significance. Geometry may be true or false, according to its ability to establish correct and verifiable relations between our experiences.

But now I hear you saying: 'All right, but the real world exists, independent of the fact whether we have a theory about it or not.' Such a statement has, in my opinion, no other meaning than the following, i.e. 'I *believe* that there exists a satisfactory theory based on the assumption of fictitious objects extended in space-time and their regular relations'. Such a belief is deeply ingrained in us, because it is practically indispensable as a basis of pre-scientific thought. Science accepts this belief, but transforms it radically, leaving it open in principle of what kind these elements are. Within Newton's system they were space, material points and motion. Newton recognized with complete clarity that in his system space and time were just as real things as material points. For if one does not accept, besides material objects, space and time as real things, the law of inertia and the concept of acceleration lose all meaning. 'Accelerated' means nothing but 'accelerated in relation to space'.

Since the days of Faraday and Maxwell the conviction has established itself that 'mass' has to be replaced by 'field' as a basic element or brick for constructing 'reality'. For how should it be possible to reduce light, which can only be represented as a 'field', to material elements in motion? This has been tried strenuously, but unsuccessfully and, in the end, the attempt had to be given up. The conviction of the non-existence of a 'stationary ether', which followed from the special theory of relativity, was only the last step in this transition from the concept of 'mass' to that of 'field' as an elementary concept in physics, i.e. as an irreducible conceptual element in the logical construction of 'reality'. Therefore, I think, it is not justified to regard mass as something 'real', the field, however, as merely a 'fancy'.

The programme of the field-theory has the great advantage that it makes a separate concept of space (as distinguished from space-content) superfluous. The space is then merely the four-dimensionality of the field, and no longer something existing in isolation. This is an achievement of the General Theory of Relativity which, so far, seems to have escaped the attention of the physicists.

As to those who regard contemporary quantum theory as a piece of knowledge which is final in principle, they waver in fact between two possible interpretations, namely:

(1) There is a physical reality. Its laws, however, do not allow of any other than statistical expression.

(2) There is nothing at all which corresponds to a physical situation. What 'exist' are only probabilities of the case of the observation.[1]

We both agree on this point; we regard these two interpretations with diffidence and we believe in the possibility of a theory which is able to give a complete description of reality, the laws of which establish relations between the things themselves and not merely between their probabilities.

But I do not think that this belief of contemporary physicists is *philosophically* refutable. For in my opinion an intellectual resignation cannot be refuted as being logically impossible. Here I simply put my trust in my intuition.

---

[1] The original German is: 'Was "existiert" sind nur Wahrscheinlichkeiten für den Fall der Beobachtung.' An alternative translation suggested to me would be: 'All that exist are probabilities of observation.' (The whole of the letter is given in German as well as English in the Appendix to my *Essay in Physics*.)

FURTHER POINTS IN PHYSICS

1. *Waves and Particles* — 2. *Impetus* — 3. *Gravitation* — 4. *The Theory of an Expanding Universe* — 5. '*The Dying Sun*' — 6. *The Ether* — 7. *The Michelson-Morley Experiment* — 8. *Unity of the Cosmos.*

1. *Waves and Particles*

i

The problem of the wave-particle relation arises from observed phenomena which, it is held, cannot be explained on earlier principles. Andrade states it in a simple example: 'The behaviour of beams of electrons in vacuum tubes when electric and magnetic fields act on them can be explained by supposing that electrons are electrified particles. But when electrons pass through very thin films of metal — or are reflected from crystals — they produce patterns on a photographic plate which remind one of the coloured rings made by light passing through thin films of air or oil, rings which can only be explained by giving wave properties to the light — or to the electron in this case.' Louis de Broglie speaks of 'this strange duality' of waves and particles. Heisenberg writes: 'After the discovery of the quantum of action by Planck the first and most important step was the recognition (achieved by Lenard's investigations and their interpretation by Einstein) that light, in spite of its wave nature as shown by countless experiments of interference, nevertheless does show corpuscular properties in certain experiments.'

Some physicists would account for this incongruity by 'the new conception that every particle has some wave-like properties and every wave has some particle-like properties'. De Broglie himself, as is well known, has put forward the hypothesis that 'there is a wave motion associated with every moving electron'.

Indeed it is usual for present-day physicists to say that the wave-particle problem arises merely from the fact that the phenomena are presenting to the observer different aspects of the same thing, according to the way in which the experiments are carried out. But it is difficult to see how the introduction of the word 'aspect' carries us any farther.

Newton, when he was making his experiments in optics, might have stopped them at an early stage by saying that he found himself confronted by two 'aspects' of light rays — first an aspect of white light, afterwards, when a prism was interposed, an aspect of coloured light.

Had he been satisfied with that, he and his successors would never have made their great discoveries. Or anyone in a boat on a rough sea might say that the water presented two aspects — one of waves and one of drops: the same molecules, at one time and at one size-level, are seen as part of a wave pattern, and, at another time and another size-level, as part of a spray pattern. But this would be no more than to restate the facts in a different wording. It would not explain anything. It would not tell us why we should be seeing, first only waves, next both waves and spray simultaneously, and then only waves again. To do that would have needed a study — such as scientists have in fact made — of the effects of wind pressure on a liquid surface, and of the atomic and molecular binding forces which cause the inner cohesion or the instability of drops of water.

We are constantly tempted to by-pass an objective problem that proves recalcitrant by transferring it to the subjective, and treating it as though it were, not a question of the character of a process in nature, but a question of human perception and scientific method. We may say, if we will, that we cannot give an answer to the wave-particle riddle; even that we do not expect ever to find an answer. But we must not pretend that, when we have said that, the problem has been disposed of and the mystery is no longer mysterious.

ii

In this situation we may do well to bring into the forefront those transmutations in which, as Newton said, nature seems to delight. Physicists are constantly finding, in laboratory observations, particles changing into waves or waves into particles. De Broglie reminds us that, when an electron striking a solid anticathode undergoes a quick stoppage, X-rays appear. He tells us also how two American scientists originally discovered what are described as the wave properties of the electrons. 'By bombarding a crystal of nickel with a beam of mono-kinetic electrons, they clearly detected that the electrons were diffract-ing as a wave of a given wave-length would do.' He says again that 'the simultaneous annihilation of a positron and an electron of opposite signs is really a "dematerialization of matter". The inverse pheno-menon also exists: in certain circumstances radiation can be "material-ized" into a pair of electrons of opposite signs'. Put shortly, waves may change into particles and particles into waves.

Since science has brought us stage by stage from the solid objects of our experience to molecules, then to atoms, and now to particles, we have naturally assumed that all these different kinds of entities have at least this much in common — that, as units, they persist. If a stone remains a stone and a molecule of water remains a molecule of water, then an electron may be expected to remain an electron. If a stream of electrons is directed towards a narrow slit in a screen, and a photograph taken on the other side of the screen shows a pattern of light-waves, then this is regarded as a great mystery. It must show that the electrons 'possess wave properties'; or that they 'have waves associated with them'; or that we have been dealing with some kind of mixed entity, strange and incomprehensible.

But may there not be a much simpler explanation? If you had particles on one side of the screen and waves on the other, may it not be because you have in fact been dealing with particles first and with waves afterwards? The particles, jostling one another as they crowded in thousands or millions through the narrow slit, would have lost their internal cohesion and emerged on the other side as waves of radiation. Or take another example. As the light of stars emerges from the telescope and is able to affect chemically a photographic film, it may consist of particles (or 'photons'). But it does not follow that it has come across the universe in that form. There is strong reason to believe that it has not done so, but as a train of expanding spherical waves. If it manifests itself finally as a stream of particles, may it not be that, at the very end of its journey, it has been changed — not by nature but by man: that the technique of the observation itself has affected the phenomenon that is being observed: that it is the lenses of the astronomer's telescope that have brought about a transformation from waves into particles, followed by chemical processes in the photographic film?

It is highly significant that in none of these observations are waves and particles *found together at the same time*. Niels Bohr is the authority for this. De Broglie agrees with Bohr, and quotes him as follows: 'When the electron has a wave-length sharply enough defined so that it can interfere with itself, it is not localized and does not respond any longer to the corpuscular picture; on the contrary, when the electron is definitely localized, its interference properties disappear and it does not correspond any longer to the wave picture. The wave and corpuscular properties never enter into conflict because they never exist at the same time. We are continually expecting a battle between the wave and the corpuscle: it never occurs because there is never but one adversary present.' From this Bohr developed his theory of 'complementary aspects', which has been widely accepted. But that complex and difficult doctrine of 'complementarity' becomes unnecessary if we put aside the conception of simultaneity and accept that of succession and transformation. We should then no longer say that 'the electron has a wave-length': we should rather say that the electron had dissolved and been succeeded by radiation of a particular wave-length: or, in the reverse case, we should not speak of waves behaving as particles, but of waves forming particles and projecting them forward.

iii

It is often useful to cite analogies from our familiar macrocosmic world to elucidate events in this distant microcosmic world. Consider, for example, ice-crystals forming in the upper atmosphere and falling as hail: the hailstones have strong internal cohesion; the storm may destroy acres of glasshouses. But if they pass through a layer of warm air they may turn into drops of water, with weaker cohesion; and finally the drops may cease to be separate entities altogether, and turn into a film of water on the panes of glass and flow away through pipes and water-courses. Or at the seaside on a rough day, we may watch the advancing waves; each in turn held back at its base by the shelving shore, and its falling crest thrown forward in drops of spray. These possess, if only for a moment, distinct identities of their own — 'And the spat spray stings my eyes to tears', as a present-day poet writes in an effective line.

The assumption of units always persisting cannot be sustained; a theory of transmutations may take its place.

This would have a bearing on the hypothesis, which is not disputed, 'that there is a wave motion associated with every moving electron'. But here there may be two alternative processes. One is that which has just been discussed: the wave sequence is in some way checked or obstructed, particles are condensed out of it, and thrown forward in the direction of the line of advance of the wave-front. In the other alternative the movement of a particle is an instance of the general laws of motion: an inert object is being moved by an extraneous agency. The particle is passive; it does not 'possess energy', but is carried along by something dynamic, usually by a train of electromagnetic waves. The association between wave movement and moving electron may be seen to be a relation of cause and effect. The electron moves because the waves convey it; if there were no waves it would not be moving.

This is not merely a theoretical assumption; it actually happens. Sir John Cockcroft, the Director of the Atomic Energy Research Establishment at Harwell, said in the course of an address to the Parliamentary and Scientific Committee at the House of Commons: 'We have developed at Harwell a new kind of atomic particle accelerator in which electrons are made to surf-ride in front of an electric wave which travels down a hollow tube. The wave travels faster and faster and so do the electrons.'

The conclusion is indicated that, in the long controversy between the partisans of waves and of corpuscles, both sides have been right in claiming that they have truly observed real phenomena, and both have been wrong in thinking that their own discovery excludes the other. And this is because, here as in other cases — impetus for example — everyone has assumed that we are considering a single event, whereas nature offers us a succession of events, differentiated from one another by the intervention of some fresh factor. We can see this succession very clearly when we are dealing with events on our own size-level — the hailstones in the upper atmosphere; then the intervention of a warmer layer, and a transformation into drops of rain; finally the intervention again of a hard surface, causing the drops to dissipate into fluid. Or sea waves, stopped by the shore, will shoot forward hard discrete drops of spray. In the present case, on the electronic size-level, we may begin with a stream of particles in an electric current; we may lead it into a cathode tube; the apparatus stops the stream of electrons and starts instead a sequence of Röntgen waves which we call X-rays. Or we may begin with light-waves from the stars; let them pass through a telescope and they will become particles and interact with atoms in a photographic film. The conclusion may be that it is a matter of stages — particles at one stage, waves at another, or the reverse.

Postscript (April 1956). This section was written some time ago, but I have now had an opportunity of reading another book by M. Louis de Broglie, *Physics and Microphysics*, published in 1955, which is of great importance in this connection.[1] In it he states, more clearly and definitely, a view as to the wave-particle relation which is in part the same as that put forward here. He says: 'In principle there is nothing against the view that energy, while always conserving itself, can pass from the material to the luminous form and vice versa. We know today that it is actually so . . . This final union of the conceptions of light and of matter in the unity of this protoform entity which is energy, has been completely proved by the progress of contemporary physics on the day it discovered that material particles are capable of disappearing while giving rise to radiation, whilst radiation is capable of condensing into matter and of creating new particles . . . All these facts clearly prove that light and matter are only different aspects of energy which can take in succession one or the other of these two appearances . . . Finally, light has just revealed itself to us as capable of condensing into matter, whilst matter is capable of dissipating into light.'

Nevertheless, de Broglie still clings to the assumption of 'simultaneity' as the essence of the problem. He still thinks it necessary to defend the idea of 'the double nature, corpuscular and undulatory,

[1] Published by Hutchinson. See pp. 67-8, 138-9, 240.

which we have been led to attribute to the elements of matter', of 'duality', 'complementarity', 'two aspects', and the like. And this although he clearly recognizes that 'the wave aspect asserts itself only when the corpuscular aspect vanishes and vice versa ... As though by a curious precaution of nature, the two aspects — the corpuscular and the wave — play a sort of hide-and-seek game, so that they never come to oppose one another'. It is strange that it is not yet recognized that these strained metaphysical paradoxes, this attempt to justify a flat contradiction — that an entity can be, at one and the same time, both a spherical electromagnetic wave, diffused and expanding, and also a discrete localized particle — that all this has become unnecessary. Once it is accepted — as de Broglie accepts — that the phenomenon may be one of succession, disappearance and substitution, then it becomes another case of transformation, added to many others. Abandon the assumption of simultaneity — and it is no more than an assumption; accept the fact of succession — and it now appears to be recognized as a fact, and the whole problem vanishes. An incubus weighing upon physics is lifted, and a long-standing cause of conflict between theoretical physics and empirical philosophy is removed.

2. Impetus

We must consider further what kind of impact it will be that will set going in the ether the process of conveying, in a straight line, a massive object.

It cannot be an impact like that made by an aggregation of oscillating atoms, for that acts in every direction simultaneously and produces a rapid succession of expanding spheres. And it cannot be like the cause or causes, whatever they may be, that produce new particles, for these are concentrated on a point; and the particle, in relation to its environment, need not be set moving at all. In order that the activation may continue and the object be carried along in a straight line, the initiating impulse must itself be rectilinear. We see that that always is so — the ball continues along the line set by the thrower's hand, the bullet along the line of the marksman's rifle.

Here I revert to what was said in chapter v about Faraday's 'lines of force'. The term itself is simple and expressive, but it is imprecise. Also it may suggest an association with the Euclidean line of one dimension—length. We are now dealing, however, not with mathematical expressions, but with factors in the real universe, and these can have no existence unless they are three-dimensional. Faraday himself was led on to the conception of *tubes* of force', with three dimensions, and in magnetism he thought that the pattern returned on itself like a loop. But the word 'tube' may be misleading. It brings up an image of a hollow pipe, a longitudinal casing without a core. Faraday clearly envisaged something more in the nature of a rod, with a cross-section that was not a circle, but a disk — or maybe a flat square, or any other shape. The word 'rod', however, would seem to imply a solidity and rigidity that would not at all correspond to a pattern of action such as we are considering. It may be better, therefore, to keep to a purely abstract term, such as 'line of force', while remembering that it is a pattern shaped more like a rod that we have in mind.

We picture then an object being propelled in a straight line by some initiating force, and then released. The impact of the object while it was still being projected will have begun the activation of the quiescent ether surrounding and within the object. After the object is released, the process continues: just as in radiation we conceive that activation, once begun, continues independently of the source of emission, impact after impact, layer after layer.

The velocity that has been established by the initiating force is passed on, therefore, *not to the object as such*, but to the ether in and around and ahead of it. The part played by the presence of the object is only to ensure that the activation is not dissipated in all directions, but is concentrated on a line forward. This is made possible by its internal cohesion. Being a solid, it puts forward, as it moves, a surface (flat or curved). Behind the surface is a coherent aggregation of molecules, which constitutes it an object and makes it massive. All this is in a region of ether that has been thrown into a state of activity: as the object is moved forward, the region ahead is similarly activated: after it has passed, the region behind relapses into quiescence.

An initiating force may be almost instantaneous, as an explosion; or it may be cumulative, taking time to develop. Consider a team of horses straining to start a heavily loaded waggon standing on a road: at first their effort seems of no avail, but gradually the waggon begins to move, slowly 'gathers impetus', and then — a sequence of ether-activation having been established — will run along easily with little strain on the horses. Or think of a boy who has tied a piece of string to a stone: he whirls it round and round his head and then lets it fly. The velocity at which the stone will travel will depend upon the number of times the boy will have circled it round his head, additional speed being accumulated with each effort of his muscles.

The principle of the cyclotron or cosmotron is no different — those very costly electric and magnetic machines, constructed in the great atomic energy establishments to accelerate particles to a very high velocity before discharging them against some uranium, or other substance, in order to effect the fission, or else the fusion, of the nuclei of its atoms. The principle of these machines is that the particles to be accelerated are constrained to follow a circular course by a powerful magnet, and while following this course are speeded up at every turn by electrical forces. 'In a test at the laboratory of the Atomic Energy Commission of America at Long Island, New York, in a machine with a circular track of 204 ft., the atomic bullets made two million trips in seven-tenths of a second; attaining a speed of 175,000 miles a second, only a little short of the velocity of light.'

It would appear that ether transmission may be established at any velocity, from that of a ball in a game to that of electromagnetic radiation, which is nature's own maximum.

3. Gravitation

i

One kind of motion remains to be considered, that caused by gravity. With it we may take magnetism — akin to it in some respects, differing from it in others.

The most obvious point in which these two forces resemble one another and differ from others is that, while their radiation is outward, any object affected by it is not pushed farther in that direction, as might be expected, but is moved back in the reverse direction. The radiation of light exerts pressure on any object on which it falls — too slight to be perceived by our senses, but known to exist: that it results in a movement outwards can be manifested in a simple apparatus. But the more powerful effects of gravitation and magnetism have this peculiar property of giving an impulse backwards.

Consider, as an example, an electromagnetic crane in a modern iron foundry. A large magnet is suspended by a strong chain from a carriage travelling along a gantry under the roof: it is brought to a spot near the entrance of the foundry where a heap of scrap-iron has been dumped, and is lowered to a point close above the heap. The moment that the current of electricity from the main supply is switched on and the magnet is activated, the nearest pieces of iron rise to the magnet and cling to it, and those below cling to the first, the whole forming a cohesive cluster. The crane then transports the magnet with its adhesions to another part of the foundry, close to the furnaces where the metal is to be melted; then the current is switched off, and instantly the whole cluster ceases to adhere and drops to the ground. Here we have — first, an outward current passing from the magnet in a wave formation; secondly, a quite different process evoked within, and probably around, each individual piece of iron near enough to be affected, which operates in the opposite direction. And this is not merely a reflection of the current, since its effect is different, being a massive movement, lifting up the pieces of iron to touch the magnet, or to touch the overlying pieces of iron that are in immediate contact with it. The whole can then be raised, countering the attraction of the earth's gravity, but yielding to gravity again the moment that the electric current is discontinued. Are we not witnessing before our eyes the exact process which has been suggested as that of gravity — an outward wave radiation eliciting as response an inward molar movement?

It is evident from this that gravital or magnetic phenomena are not the result of a single process, as we are accustomed to assume, but of two processes, one succeeding the other. The first is an outward radiation from an emitting centre: this has an impact upon any material object — or, as we should say here, upon the ether in and around an object. This impact activates the ether in that region and establishes a second movement. The problem is why that movement does not continue forwards along the line of the radiation wave-front, but is opposite. And we have to ask by what mechanism that reversal can be brought about.

In my previous book, *Essay in Physics*, I discussed this and other speculative points relating to gravitation at some length. At that time I was inclined to think that this dual process might be unique, without any analogies among the known mechanisms of nature. I did not then fully realize the importance either of the incessant transformations of energy in many of the normal processes of nature, or of the conception of 'lines of force'. These two, together with the familiar mechanism of reflection — as with light-waves on a mirror or sound-echoes — may perhaps, in combination, open a way of approach to the basic problems of gravitation and magnetism.

ii

Suppose an object dropped from a height — say a stone over the edge of a cliff. We conceive that gravital waves, produced by atomic oscillation, are rushing upwards in the ether from every point on the surface of the earth with the speed of light. When such waves strike the stone, which is free to move in any direction, they do not drive it upward. Our speculation is that the impact may have a reflex effect upon the volume of ether where the stone is. This ether is not quiescent as in 'empty space', but is already in a state of activity. The activity is in the patterns of the particles that constitute the atoms of the stone, and of the electrical forces that make those atoms cohere as molecules, and bind the molecules together as a stone.

Newton's Third Law of Motion asserts that: 'To every action there is always opposed an equal reaction.' If that is so in this case, we may suppose that the object — that is to say the activated ether in and about it — will react, and will thereby give rise to a new activation in the opposite direction. For the reason already given, the presence of a material object will not allow this activation to follow the pattern of expanding spheres, but will make it rectilinear — a line of force.

We may add to this that, as in the case of other initiating movements, the amount of force transmitted may be cumulative. The outward waves of radiation, as they impinge upon the surface of the stone, are relatively weak; but the total reaction that they set up, by the time that they have passed through its bulk, will be many times as great. It may be above the threshold needed to establish the self-repeating sequence of activations that will give rise to a continuous movement. (If the bulk of the object were not sufficient for this, movement would not take place — as, for example, with a feather floating in the air.) As soon as the threshold is passed the stone starts falling, and the quiescent ether that lies between the stone and the earth's surface is put into action in a new line of force.

iii

At first presentation, such a conception will no doubt seem far-fetched and difficult to understand. But all physicists, and a considerable part of the general public, have become quite accustomed to something that would have been considered in past times as far more extraordinary: to the idea that all the material objects around us — human bodies, or rocks in the mountains, or what you will — while solid for us at our own size-level, are also, at the remote size-level of the microcosmos, nothing other than atomic systems of whirling particles, with frequencies of hundreds of millions of millions in a second. And such transmutations of energy as here suggested need not astonish us more than the successive changes that we can observe any day at a hydroelectric power station and in its connections: transformations from gravity, pulling down the water from the reservoir; through mechanical work; to magnetic induction and electric currents; finishing in one's own room, in light, or heat, or work, say in a vacuum cleaner.

Further, we have nowadays in radar a reflex action not very dissimilar from that which we are suggesting as a possible explanation for gravitation; and in magnetism also; although there is the important difference that in radar the returning echo is of the same wave order as the outgoing pulsation, while that is not so in gravitation.

iv

The physicist, however, will naturally ask, before he will give a hearing to such novel propositions, how they will fit in with the principle, long-established and still generally supported, of the conservation of energy.

As has already been said, with quiescent ether no question of conservation can arise. It is universal and eternal, and cannot be either increased or diminished. When it becomes active the position is different. Active energy may pass through the various transformations of pattern that we have been discussing, and the question is whether the amount of force in the originating impact, whatever that may have been, must remain constant.

Observation and experiment, continued over a long period of time, are believed to show that in fact it does. The amount of force that is being exercised throughout the successive manifestations, measured so far as possible by the methods suitable to each, is found to be the same. But that principle of conservation has had to be sustained sometimes by making assumptions that are not supported by observation and experiment. Energy is regarded as though it were a thing which moves from place to place; can be stored for long periods; can be released, acquired, expended and absorbed; it can be dynamic, or become kinetic and cause material objects to move. The same dose of energy, so to speak, is conserved and persists throughout. No doubt the 'dose' will constantly be merging with others; but it is supposed nevertheless to retain its quantitative value — and it is to be traced mathematically through all its vicissitudes.

The test of observation is regarded as all-important: but can it be claimed that all this has actually been observed? The only evidence in support of the theory is the fact that the amount of activity, measured in a manifestation in one pattern, had been the same in the previous manifestation, and will be found to be the same in the one that comes after. For example, in a series — work, heat, electricity, and work again — if the first is increased the others will be greater also, if diminished they will be less. But as to storage between whiles in a state of 'potential energy of position'; as to being acquired by an object, and then expended in moving it along; as to its being successively, for example, in the rays of the sun, in water vapour rising from the sea, in clouds in the sky, in a fall of rain, again in water collected in a reservoir, then in the revolutions of a turbine, then in a dynamo, next in an electric current, and finally in a street lamp or the brushes of a carpet-sweeper — is there any evidence of all this? Is it not more probable that, after Joule, Rumford and others had discovered conservation in some of such transformations, scientists assumed too hastily that it was a universal principle? When it could not be traced, it became necessary to assume that the principle applied nevertheless. Finally, with a strange relapse into medieval scholasticism, terms had to be devised — energy of position, dynamic, kinetic, acquired, possessed, and the like — to cover the gaps and conceal their emptiness. The latest example is the postulate that the system of the atom includes a particle, to which the name 'neutrino' has been given, which is without mass or charge, but is assumed to exist and to carry energy and momentum in order that the principle of conservation may hold.

An ether theory would by-pass the whole of this argument. It regards the mechanism of nature as a system of processes; each of which begins, and continues, either indefinitely or else coming to an end.

A candle is lighted, thereby starting a chemical process of combustion. This process will continue, self-renewing, as long as the wax will last. But if someone blows out the candle, the chain is broken and the process ends. There is no reason to ask what has become of the activity, where has the energy gone? The energy has not gone anywhere: the activity has simply stopped; the process has ended; and that is all that need be said about it. Whether at the end there is the same amount of energy functioning in the universe — or less — or more, becomes a matter of no importance.

When modern science took its rise, it began mainly with chemistry, with the study of things. It was natural for the chemists to wish to trace the materials that they were investigating through their various states and combinations: many valuable discoveries were made in doing so. And now that science is dealing fundamentally with action, physicists, as naturally perhaps, have taken over from the chemists the idea that nothing is ever destroyed, if something disappears from view it has only to be carefully tracked down in order to be found again, perhaps in some form very different from the first. But that need not be so with action. A process may end as well as begin; and physicists may come to see that the persistent effort to jusify the assumption of universal conservation and continuity has become out of date, and should now be abandoned.

In any event, in a system such as we are conceiving here, it would be impossible to ascertain, as it would be unnecessary, whether the amount of energy active in the universe is, or is not, constant. For at every moment new radiations are being emitted, new particles are being formed, and, if there are lines of force, new ones are being established; while others, of all of these, are ceasing and disappearing. Whether there is equality between beginnings and endings, and, if not, which are gaining, is a question that cannot be answered; and even if it could, it is difficult to see what advantage would be gained.

N

As to the corpus of quiescent energy itself – the total physical universe – scientific curiosity would no doubt wish to know whether it has boundaries; and, if so, whether they are constant, or expanding, or shrinking. But that is part of the ultimate problem of the existence of anything at all, which is now – and may well remain – outside the range of the human mind. So that our curiosity, in this also, is not likely to be satisfied.

v

One can imagine a critic at this point raising an objection to the whole of our argument. He might say: 'You reject the present belief in "potential energy", but you put forward yourself a notion of "quiescent energy", and indeed make it the basis of your scheme. Where is the differer.ce? If the one is a mere assumption, unsupported by evidence, so is the other.'

But there is a great difference. An ether theory does not require a belief in doses of energy; which may be acquired by a material object, will move with it when it moves, remains localized in it when at rest, and will leave it only when it can transfer itself somewhere else. And if it be aŋswered to this that these 'doses' are only thought of as quantitative and mathematical, we may reply that mathematics must follow reality and can never replace it, that what has no existence in practice cannot be given it by theory.

Further, as has been said throughout, a primal ether of quiescent ether is not put forward as a convenient assumption: it is put forward as a necessary inference from our observation of the whole body of nature's phenomena. And if it is also possible that the ether conception might give us a clue, a single clue, to the several riddles that still remain unanswered – the medium for radiation, the mechanism of gravity, the wave-particle relation, the appearance of new particles, and impetus – it might be found worth pursuing as a working hypothesis. The idea of the passage from one state to another and back again, whether gradual or instantaneous, puts no strain upon the imagination, for we are accustomed to it through the whole range of nature's processes. The alternation of activity and relapse may in the future be seen to be, in physics, as usual and easy as, in biology, is the breathing of a lung or the beating of a heart.

vi

I come from these more general considerations to some specific questions relating to gravitation.

Why is it that it obeys the inverse-square rule – that the effect of the force of gravity on any outlying object should always diminish in ratio to the square of its distance at any moment from the gravitational centre? Why is it never in simple proportion; or as the cube of the distance; or any other multiple or fraction? Some people seem inclined to think that this is a proof that events in nature obey the laws of mathematics; that Jeans may have been right in his suggestion that the universe may perhaps be nothing more than 'a thought in the mind of a Mathematician'.

But there is no need to bring into science any such mysticism. The inverse-square rule applies equally to the diffusion of light. It applies also to the diffusion of sound in the atmosphere. It applies in fact wherever the mechanism is one of expanding spheres; and this is because it follows, simply and necessarily, from the geometrical construction of a sphere. Mathematicians discovered long ago that the area of the surface of a globe was equal to the square of its diameter, multiplied by the factor π (which is the ratio of the diameter of a circle to its circumference). The distance of the surface of a sphere from its centre is the length of its radius; since a diameter is twice a radius the square of a diameter is equal to four times the square of a radius. Hence we get the arithmetical formula for the superficies of an expanding sphere at any moment, namely $4\pi r^2$ where r is the distance of the object from the centre at that moment. All the other factors being constants and r the only variable, we say that the area of the surface of a sphere varies directly as the square of its radius.

Let us translate this arithmetic into terms of an actual process, for example an expanding soap-bubble. I take a saucer of soapy water; dip into it a glass tube; a drop clings to the end of the tube; I blow, and a bubble forms. When the radius of the bubble is, say, one inch, the area of its surface is that determined according to the formula, r being one inch. The film of the bubble would then have a certain thickness, which could if necessary be calculated. I now again blow into the tube until the radius of the bubble becomes two inches. The area of its surface is then not twice what it was before, but the square of it, that is four times. The material that was in the drop of soapy water remains the same in amount, but it is now spread over a much larger area, and the film becomes thinner in proportion. If the bubble were blown out to a radius of four inches, the film would become so thin that it would probably lose its cohesion and burst. Now apply this process to a sequence of expanding spheres of light or of gravity. We shall have a succession of activations of quiescent energy in a pattern of expanding spheres. No question of cohesion arises here: but just as the film of the bubble was spread out over a larger area and grew thinner at every moment in proportion to the square of the distance from the centre, so will the intensity of the light, or the strength of the gravitational force, grow less, and in the same proportion.

The inverse-square law is not something given by nature, discovered empirically by scientists, and to be accepted as fact without inquiry as to the reason for it. What is given by nature is the mechanism of expanding spheres. The inverse-square law is the necessary consequence. It is no more than an arithmetical measurement of what is going on in the real universe from moment to moment.

The important point for our present purpose is that wherever you have radiation — throughout the electromagnetic wave-band or in sound — you also find the inverse-square law. The converse is, if not certain, at least probable, that wherever you find the inverse-square law you will also find radiation. This is a strong support for the theory that gravity is a form of radiation.

vii

Another question that arises is, how can we account for the fact that the velocity of a falling object is continually being accelerated, and again in the proportion of the square of its distance from the centre? If a stone is thrown horizontally, its velocity will be diminished as the strength of the initiating impact is spent, or owing to air resistance; but a velocity can never be increased, unless exceptionally by some fresh force 'impressed upon it'. If, however, the stone is dropped, as over the edge of a cliff, it will increase its speed cumulatively, until it strikes the earth with violence. Why should that be so?

From the standpoint of an ether theory this question presents less difficulty than those that have preceded. It may be seen at once that the difference between the two cases arises from the different kinds of initiating motion. When I throw the stone the movement of my hand that starts it operates once for all: the moment my hand releases the stone its function is over: there is nothing to accelerate the object and it travels on at a uniform speed in a straight line. But when I drop the stone it is otherwise. The mechanism of gravity is continuing to operate all the way: the original first impulse propelling the stone downwards is followed and reinforced by a series of others; and these are stronger and stronger at every point as the stone draws nearer to the gravitational centre.

viii

The last question to which I need refer in connection with gravity asks why it is that a heavy object and a light object will fall from a height with the same velocity and arrive at the same time.

If we have been able to free ourselves from the notion that it is the object that conveys energy, and to realize that, on the contrary, it is the energy that conveys the object, the answer will be plain enough. A line of force, of adequate strength, having once been set up, it will carry along whatever objects, large or small, light or heavy, may lie in its path. It makes no difference to a river whether it is the trunk of a tree or a cork from a bottle that is floating on its surface; it makes no difference to the westerly current in mid-Pacific whether it is a great sailing-ship or the Kon-Tiki raft that happens to come its way. Big or small, heavy or light, are carried along at the same speed and will reach a given point at the same time. It is the active medium, not the static object, that decides. The same applies to gravity.

4. *The Theory of an Expanding Universe*

These notes have related to matters that are either on the microcosmic level — from quantum to molecule, or on the terrestrial level — that of our own experience. Passing on to the astronomical level two questions remain, of great philosophic interest, on which the ideas that have been current among physicists appear to be open to criticism. One is the theory that the galaxies are receding from one another at a high velocity, so that the universe as a whole is rapidly expanding. The other is the conviction, until lately universally held, that the incandescent stars, including the sun, are by their radiation continuously dissipating their energy, so that 'the universe is running down like a clock'. I venture to submit some observations on each of these.

i

The expansion theory rests upon a single fact, discovered about thirty years ago, that the lines in the spectra of distant nebulae, compared with those from the nearby stars, are shifted towards the red, and that the amount of the shift increases with the distance of the nebulae that are being observed.

It was already known that when a star is moving away from an observer directly along his line of sight, there is also a red-shift—named the Doppler effect after the Austrian physicist who had predicted it, in 1842: this is often compared to the change in the pitch of the whistle of a railway-engine when the train is approaching or receding. It was thereupon assumed that this new red-shift must be of the same order. It was to be regarded as a velocity effect, and the cause of it must be a general recession of the sources of the light; that is to say an expansion of the galaxies of the universe.

That this red-shift is a fact is not disputed. To recount the proof here would involve technicalities that would be out of place; and it is unnecessary, for the reality of the phenomenon is not the question in debate. Although no red-shift is detected in the spectra of the nearer galaxies, it is very evident to astrophysical observers when they study those farther away: its increase with the distance rises to about 20 per cent of the original wave-length, at the farthest range of perception. But as to interpretation there is no such unanimity.

Many physicists have long had doubts. Conspicuous among them was the late Dr. Edwin Hubble, of the great American observatories at Mt. Wilson and Mt. Palomar, who was one of the leading researchers in this field. Hubble described the Expansion Theory as leading to conclusions that are 'rather startling', and 'strange and dubious'. Not long before his death he wrote that the results of the exploring work that had been done were 'a definite step in the observational approach to cosmology . . . But the essential clue, the interpretation of red-shifts, must still be unravelled. The former sense of certainty has faded and the clue stands forth as a problem for investigation'. In another paper, presented to the Royal Astronomical Society in 1953, he was careful to make qualifications, such as '. . . if red-shifts are interpreted as Doppler shifts . . .'; or '. . . if red-shifts do measure the expansion of the universe . . .' Another writer on this subject, Dr. G. J. Whitrow, in his book *The Structure of the Universe* (1949) — says that 'The whole problem bristles with complications, although in time new criteria may help to resolve them'; meanwhile 'the ultimate verdict' has not been given. Similarly M. A. Ellison, in a review in the scientific quarterly *Endeavour* of a book by Professor George Gamow of Washington University, *The Creation of the Universe*, makes this observation: 'Here and there the author writes so persuasively that he allows his speculations to derive quite unwarranted support from uncertain observations. Thus, for example, we read: "Hubble found that the galaxies populating the space of the universe are in a state of rapid dispersion ('expanding universe')." Or, again: "The relationship between recession velocity and distance is given by Hubble's law . . ." Now, Hubble has been most careful to point out (*The Realm of the Nebulae*) that all we can observe are red-shifts in the nebular lines and that these appear to increase with distance. The red-shifts may be interpreted as indicating velocities of recession, and they have been seized upon in this sense by many cosmologists in order to save the theory of the expanding universe. Equally well, they may arise from the action of some unrecognized principle leading to loss of photon energy in intergalactic space. Our ignorance in this field is so complete that it is wise to suspend judgement until further observations can decide the issue.'

Recently a new suggestion has been made by Professor E. Finlay-Freundlich, of the University of St. Andrew's Observatory, which has received much attention. He says: 'I propose to introduce as an additional hypothesis that light passing through deep layers of intense radiation fields (in stellar atmospheres) loses energy.'[1] This he says 'may even permit an interpretation of the cosmological red-shift other than that of an expanding universe'. And he concludes: 'One may have, therefore, to envisage that the cosmological red-shift is not due to an expanding universe, but to a loss of energy which light suffers in the immense lengths of space it has to traverse coming from the most distant star systems.'

In this situation it may not be presumptuous to suggest that an ether theory may have a contribution to make to the discussion.

ii

Let us, in the first place, try to understand clearly what the phenomenon is that we are examining; for the term red-shift may easily give a false impression. It might lead us to suppose that the red waves in the spectrum have in some way been moved from their position in relation to the other waves. But that is not what is meant. It is the whole band that is shifted, including not only the coloured light that we see, but also the ultra-violet and the infra-red. The spectrum has moved bodily towards the red side.

What is actually happening, then, is an all-together shift of the whole spectral band from the region of the shorter waves to that of the longer. Where there had been ultra-violet rays there are now violet; where there had been blue there are now green, and so on to red; while the former red rays have become infra-red. Our senses cannot be aware of this because the final result is a removal of the whole series so that there is less of it in the ultra-violet and more of it in the infra-red; and those regions are to us invisible. The process might be properly, and more simply, described as a simultaneous lengthening of all the waves that make up the spectrum.

Whitrow, giving the comparison of the whistle of an engine which is shriller when approaching than when receding, goes on to say: 'This is due to the fact that in the former case the sound-waves are more compressed. Similarly, Doppler argued that the light-waves from an approaching source are also compressed and those from a receding source correspondingly elongated, the degree of compression or elongation depending on the speed. A general shortening of wave-length

[1]The cause, he thinks, may be attributable to 'photon-photon interaction', but this, I am informed, is not accepted by other physicists.

would mean that the spectrum would be shifted bodily towards the violet, while a lengthening would shift it towards the red.'

We have seen in other contexts that changes in wave-lengths are a feature in many of nature's mechanisms. They are the cause of most of the transformations of energy, as we have been accustomed to call them. These are processes that are not only observed and produced in the laboratories, but are continually used in the electrical and chemical industries. Another example is included in one of Einstein's three famous predictions, the verification of which first gave to the theory of Relativity its present status. Professor Philipp Frank in his *Life of Einstein* says: 'The third prediction that Einstein made was on the change in wave-length emitted by a star. His calculation showed that light, in leaving the star where it is emitted, has to pass through its gravitational field, and this passage shifts the wave-length towards the red. Even for the sun the effect turned out to be hardly observable, but in the case of the very dense companion star to Sirius it seemed to be of observable magnitude.'

In recent years the exploration of the upper atmosphere by the help of rockets and by radio methods has resulted in some remarkable discoveries; among them is yet another example of change in wave-length. A paper published in April 1954 recounts that at high altitudes there is a process of transformation of ultra-violet radiation from the sun into heat radiation. 'The thermal effects of the atmosphere depend upon its properties over a wide range of altitude. This is because a number of processes are involved — absorption of the short-wave soler radiation, which takes place at great heights, its degradation to long wave-length heat radiation, and the subsequent effects of these heat-waves.' (The word 'degradation' relates to the lessening of frequencies — short waves having high frequencies and long waves low frequencies.) The term 'red-shift' is itself unscientific: it is a picturesque, shorthand expression for a process which in fact is only one more example of wave-length variation.

Let us recall that our ether speculation conceives that each individual wave of radiation is, first, a separate activation of a layer of quiescent energy; causing, secondly, a fresh impact on the next sphere of quiescent energy, and thereby activating it; with a return, thirdly, to quiescence. The process of radiation continues, self-repeating, over such vast distances in the cosmos, that it would be reasonable to imagine that each wave is the exact equivalent of the one before: that the repetition, from one wave-crest to the next, must be without loss in the strength of the pulses. (This would be apart from the effect of diffusion under the inverse-square law, and unless some kind of interference occurs.) But natural as this would be, it is an assumption and nothing more.

Suppose now that the assumption is wrong. Suppose that the process itself, the effort of transmission, involves an infinitesimal weakening of impact from one wave-crest to the next. (Present physics would term this a 'loss of energy'.) At first far below the range of perception, repeated cumulatively millions of times in a second, and over a period of hundreds of millions of years, it would attain an observable effect. And the greater the distance, the greater would be the effect, in exact proportion.

iii

Hubble allowed an alternative to the Expansion of the Universe theory. In his Oxford lectures published under the title *The Observational Approach to Cosmology* he speaks of 'the phenomena of red-shifts whose significance is still uncertain'. He says that 'alternative interpretations are possible . . . Red-shifts are produced either in the nebulae, where the light originates, or in the intervening space through which the light travels. If the source is in the nebulae, then red-shifts are probably velocity-shifts and the nebulae are receding. If the source lies in the intervening space, the explanation of red-shifts is unknown but the nebulae are sensibly stationary'. In that case, he says, 'they represent some unknown reaction between the light and the medium through which it travels'.

An ether theory might offer a suggestion as to the nature of the reaction, hitherto unknown, between the light and the medium through which it travels — the suggestion of a lengthening of wave-lengths. If this alternative proves acceptable, this 'strange and dubious' hypothesis of an expanding universe — so vast a new cosmogony built on so narrow a foundation — could be discarded, and modern physics would be relieved of a troublesome complication.

5. 'The Dying Sun'

i

Sir James Jeans gave that title to the opening chapter of one of those scientific books of his which commanded the attention of the English-speaking world. It stated the conclusion, universally held among physicists, that the sun, and the hot stars in general, are continuously losing their energy through radiation. The Second Law of Thermodynamics asserts this, and no one doubts that it is true. It follows that — immensely long as the process will be — the sun, together with its planets, must end in death. Upon the earth an age will come of absolute cold; another ice age, but far more intense, and one that will not pass away. Man's life, his achievements, his civilization, depend upon astral conditions, and these will change, millennium by millennium, as the sun's energies waste away, dissipated in space.

Bertrand Russell quotes Jeans as saying 'with universes as with mortals, the only possible life is progress to the grave', and from such 'depressing conclusions' Russell himself sees no escape. Whitehead also says: 'I certainly think that the universe is running down.'

All this has had a small, but not a wholly negligible effect upon the thought of our time. It may have contributed a little to the tinge of pessimism that has pervaded the intellectual world. In place of the old theology, which had faith in a benevolent Providence, manifested in 'a friendly universe', as Smuts described it, we have now a scientist's cosmogony, self-doomed to an inevitable end, passing through cold and darkness to death and nothingness. It is not enough to say that the end is to be exceedingly remote. We have lately discovered that one of our fellow-creatures, the coelacanth, was not only alive in the seas around Africa fifty million years ago, but is alive there still: and Jeans assures us that we have thousands of millions of years yet to go. But that is not sufficient to reconcile us to the sentence he pronounces: 'Physics predicts that there can be but one end to the universe – a "heat-death" in which the total energy of the universe is uniformly distributed, and all the substance of the universe is at the same temperature. This temperature will be so low as to make life impossible . . . and the end of the journey cannot be other than universal death.' He asks 'whether our destiny is to be nothing more than to strut our tiny hour on our tiny stage with the knowledge that our aspirations are all doomed to final frustration, and that our achievements must perish without trace, leaving the universe as though it had never been'. If that is to be our fate, no doubt it will be some consolation to know that it is to be long postponed; but philosophically that is no satisfaction. Time is not the factor of ultimate importance, any more than size. It is the end, the purpose, that matters.

ii

The Second Law of Thermodynamics is absolute and cannot be gainsaid. [1] Nevertheless, here as in so much else, the recent discoveries in fundamental physics have brought about a change in the situation. It is found that there may be at work countervailing processes. While the sun's radiation certainly causes what is termed a 'loss' of energy, at the same time there may be going on, at the very high temperature of its interior, a synthesis of atoms of hydrogen into atoms of helium;

[1] Dr. G. J. Whitrow, however, draws attention to the fact that 'the legitimacy of applying the Second Law to the *whole universe* has been criticized by E. A. Milne in his *Life of Sir James Jeans* (C.U.P., 1952), pp. 164-6'.

and this would be accompanied by the 'release' of vast amounts of additional energy. We know that such a process is possible, because this is precisely the principle of the hydrogen bomb. We know too that the volume of the sun, as apparently of stellar bodies generally, consists mainly of hydrogen; while, in the sun, helium is also abundant — whence its name.

The bearing of this upon the hitherto unchallenged theory of 'the dying sun' is important. It may be that the loss of energy through radiation is counterbalanced by its increase through this process of synthesis, when atoms of hydrogen fuse into helium. It may be even more than counterbalanced. It is thought that possibly the sun is growing hotter.

And another new feature has come into the picture which, philosophically, may be more valid. During the present century it has been realized that the term 'empty space' is incorrect and misleading. The vast regions of the cosmos contain particles, atoms, molecules and stellar dust, which, although sparsely scattered over the immense distances, constitute in their total an enormous quantity of matter. It is calculated indeed that its mass may be as great as that of all the stars put together — perhaps much greater. From this matter the sun's gravity may be continually adding to the volume of its substance, bringing vast new increments of energy to replenish its wasting assets.

iii

Our ether hypothesis would describe these processes in different terms. It conceives that the primordial given stock of energy of the universe is present eternally and everywhere, able to supply all the heat needs of all the galaxies for all time, and possibly with only a minute call upon its potential powers. But it is true that energy in its active state may appear or increase in one part of the ocean of quiescent ether and may diminish or disappear in another. And it is not denied that particular sequences of activation may come to an end: whether they had produced a transient particle enduring for an instant, or the heat of a star that endures for billions of years. It is evident that the thermal activities of stars and satellites may decrease and come to an end. Our companion, the moon, is there to prove it. The dark stars, or diffused matter discovered by the new science of radio-astronomy, might furnish other examples. In that respect the acceptance of an ether theory would make no difference. But in so far as it would provide inexhaustible possibilities of active energy at call everywhere and always, it would bring in a new factor: also by furnishing a matrix for the continuous creation of new matter in the form of particles and atoms, and a perpetual medium for the transmission of light, heat and gravity. All this would work in with the newly recognized processes of the hydrogen–helium synthesis and the gravitational accretion from matter diffused in space.

If indeed nature has other forces at work to counterbalance her wasting law of thermodynamics, then physics may be able to free us from this nightmare of the dying sun. Perhaps soon Science may come to bear a less formidable aspect altogether — an affair not so markedly of hateful nuclear bombs, a solar system diseased at the heart, a universe of galaxies fleeing from one another at terrific speeds. Without lapsing into wishful thinking, it may even allow some room for cheerfulness; remembering that remark to Dr. Johnson by his friend Oliver Edwards (the word 'philosopher' then including scientist): 'I have tried too in my time to be a philosopher, but, I don't know how, cheerfulness was always breaking in.'

6. The Ether

i

Quiescent energy. To prevent possible misunderstanding, it may be useful to elucidate further our basic conception of quiescent energy.

Orthodox physics has for a long time past accepted the principle that energy exists, imperceptibly, in a state of inactivity, and teaches this to students under the name of 'potential energy'. Examining a number of the textbooks now in use in the elementary and advanced schools under the London County Council, I have found typical passages such as these: 'A brick on the table has more energy than a brick on the floor, though both are stationary; for if the brick is allowed to fall from the table to the floor it can *do work* in doing so. Energy which a body possesses as a result of its position is called "Potential Energy".' 'Energy is the name given to the capacity, or power, of doing work and obviously anything which can produce motion possesses energy, e.g. a wound watch-spring, when released, moves the cog-wheel system of a watch. Stored-up energy of this kind is called potential energy.' 'When we wind any clock, we put into it quickly a quantity of potential energy which afterwards comes out very slowly in working the clock.' The possibility of energy being at one time active and at another time inactive is therefore fully recognized: but the ether theory that we are now submitting is different, and could not accept the principle in that form.

The real universe does not exhibit any difference at all between a brick as it is on the table and the same brick as it is on the floor. If any work has been done through its fall, it was not the brick that did it but the earth's gravity. As proves so often to be the case, we have been led into error by treating as one event a situation that consists of two events. Someone first lifts the brick on to the table: he brings in a muscular effort in order to overcome the earth's gravital force. When the brick is laid upon the table, the structure of the table continues to counteract the pull of gravity: the situation has become stabilized and that event is over and done with. When, at some later time, the brick is pushed off the table it falls at once to the floor. That is the second event, its beginning and its end. The two are quite independent of one another. There is no reason to try to bridge the time-interval between them by imagining that the energy 'put into' the brick by lifting it remains 'stored' inside it indefinitely and is finally 'released' by its fall.

It is true that if we measure the amount of active energy that is engaged in lifting the brick, and afterwards the amount in its fall, we shall find that the two are exactly equal. If the brick weighs a pound and the table is three feet high, it will be three foot-pounds in each case. But it is a mistake to jump to the conclusion that this must be because there is a specific dose of three foot-pounds of energy which remains the same, either active or potential, throughout these proceedings. The reason for the equality is quite simple — and far more credible. The upward movement and the downward movement, although separate from one another, are counterparts. The amount of gravital force that had to be overcome in the first event was three foot-pounds, and that was therefore the measure of the muscular effort required to overcome it. In the second event, the amount of gravital force employed in bringing the brick down was the same as the amount that had to be overcome in order to lift it up — also three foot-pounds.

In the other example of the spring of a watch or clock, there is indeed a difference in the spring itself, when it is wound up and when it is run down. It is not that some phantom potential energy has first been put into it all at once and afterwards allowed to trickle out. The difference arises from the elasticity of the molecules of the steel in the spring; it resides in the forces that bind those molecules together. When the spring is wound up they are put under strain and stretched; the mechanism to which it is attached hinders the return to normal; as the cog-wheels go round, the strain is gradually relaxed and the elastic spring slowly unwinds.

Potential energy, as still taught in the schools, is clearly no more than a myth. When it comes to be discarded, an ether theory would offer an alternative.

ii

Inertia. Relativity also recognizes that energy exists in a state of inaction. In a paper, dated 1948, included in the collection of essays published in 1950 under the title *Out of my Later Years,* Einstein wrote: '. . . The most important result of the special relativity system concerned the inert mass of a material system. It became evident that the inertia of such a system must depend on its energy content so that we were driven to the conception that inert mass was nothing else than latent energy.'

Whether the epithet used is Potential, Latent, Inert, or Quiescent, the idea of energy being manifested in a different state at one time from what it is at another, is the same. But each of the first three of those terms is open to objection. *Potential* has long been identified with the supposititious 'energy of position'. Besides, it has a touch of metaphysics about it: it brings in the teleological idea of purpose: it does not convey the notion of a state or process existing in its own right, but of something that exists only by virtue of something else that is expected to come after. *Latent* is much the same, but has also a suggestion of something concealed, almost surreptitious. The objection to *Inert* is more than verbal: it is philosophic, and needs to be more carefully considered.

Inertia in physics, and particularly in relativity theory, has a specialized meaning. The definition given in the *Oxford English Dictionary* is: 'That property of matter by virtue of which it continues in its existing state, whether of rest or of uniform motion in a straight line, unless that state is altered by an external force. Also called *vis inertiae* (force of inertia).' De Broglie can speak of a body being 'endowed with inertia'. Physicists constantly use the phrase 'subject to inertial forces'. But the realist is always suspicious of such expressions as 'a *tendency* of objects to persist', or ' a *property* of matter which consists in . . .', or 'a body being *endowed* with . . .' — regarding them as scholastic and question-begging. As to '*inertial forces*', he will consider that a contradiction in terms. Inertia is essentially not a force but, on the contrary, the absence of a force. The real universe has no place for nothingness, or for negative quantities on the other side of nothingness.

A state of rest was regarded by Newton, and is still regarded by present-day physicists, as part of the problem of motion. But this may be contested. So long as there is a state of rest the problem of motion has not presented itself. A mountain, or the Great Pyramid, is at rest, but it presents no problem of motion. The only problem it presents is the nature of the mechanism of the earth's gravity. It is the same with a football lying on the ground. A moment later it may be kicked and sent flying through the air, but until that happens it is no more a subject for the science of dynamics than if it were a stone that has been lying on the ground for a hundred years and may continue to lie there for a hundred years more. When we were discussing Impetus we analysed the motion of a ball in flight through the air into four possible stages — the start, the continuance, the acceleration, and the stoppage. We are not called upon to make it six stages, and to include a state of rest at the beginning and another state of rest at the end. These are not stages at all. They are outside the process that we are considering, which is one of motion relative to environment, and nothing else: it begins with the start and ends with the stoppage.

If we are asked once more: What about an object isolated in empty space? — we would answer again that the real universe does not give us any empty space, nor any isolation. But if we are to engage in abstract theory as a kind of intellectual game, we would say that, when there are no relations with other objects or events, there can be no motion. Relativity theory has taught us that absolute motion is an impossibility: that being so, there can be no absolute rest either. Whether actual or theoretical, Inertia, as an element in the universe, disappears.

The word *quiescent* is free from the objections that may be raised against *potential*, *latent*, or *inertial*. A differentiation between active and quiescent is factual, and not mathematical. And it is no more metaphysical than the difference between walking and sitting, or waking and sleeping.

iii

Energy and Matter. Professor Max Born says: 'There is no doubt, matter and energy are the same', but this appears to be an over-simplification. All matter indeed is energy, but not all energy is matter. Radiation waves are energy, but they are not material; similarly with lines of force. Quiescent energy also would not be material. On the other hand, energy in the particle pattern must be counted as matter, for no boundary can be drawn between particles and atoms, which are composed of particles: and so on to molecules, and then to gases, liquids and solids.

Although radiation waves and lines of force on the one hand, and particles on the other, are not the same, they belong to the same order: all of them are active energy, varying only in pattern. And it is known that they can affect one another. Light rays are slowed down when they pass through a medium impregnated with matter: the velocity of light is slightly less in the earth's atmosphere than in outer space, and less still in water: the differences have been calculated with exactitude. Masses of sea water act upon the light that falls upon them as a sieve, with gradations according to wave-lengths. We are told that: 'Light fades out rapidly with descent below the surface. The red rays are gone at the end of the first 200 or 300 feet, and with them all the orange and yellow warmth of the sun. Then the greens fade, and at 1000 feet only a deep, dark, brilliant blue is left. In very clear waters the violet rays of the spectrum may penetrate another thousand feet. Beyond this is only the blackness of the deep sea.'

If a train of light-waves meets a solid opaque object it is stopped altogether. On the other hand when lines of force from a magnet fall upon an iron object — that is to say upon a system of particles constituting such an object — it will be drawn towards the magnet. It is evident that when non-material energy enters a region in which the ether is already patterned into particles cohering as matter, there is some kind of effect between them. De Broglie, writing from the standpoint of present-day physics, speaks of 'energy exchanges between matter and radiation', and of the need 'to study a great number of problems about the interaction of matter and radiation'. Although an ether theory would not speak of 'energy exchanges', it would certainly recognize 'interactions' between matter and radiation, and it seems likely that the study of these will play a large part in the physics of the future.

Subject to minima and maxima, the ether continuum embraces all velocities, all size-levels and all intensities.

In velocities, the minimum is at the threshold where quiescent energy is transformed into active. This, in our measurements, is perhaps the same, or of the same order, as Planck's elementary quantum of action. The maximum is the velocity of light *in vacuo*.

In size-levels, the minimum might be of the same nature: the maximum would be the size of the universe. Theoretical physicists attempt to calculate what that is: but the calculations necessarily depend upon the primary assumptions that may be chosen; these differ from one another, and the validity of any of them is problematical. Apart from the quantum, there is no absolute unit of measurement. Every size-level is relative to other size-levels: each one is large when related to the one below and small when related to the one above.

As to intensities — the temperature of our bodies, a little less than a hundred degrees Fahrenheit, seems very hot compared with the $459°$ below zero of the absolute cold of outer space: but it is not far away from it when compared with the temperature of over a million degrees at the heart of an explosion of an atom bomb. The ether forces stirred into action by such an explosion are colossal judged by the standards of our own experience; but there is no reason to think that they make more than an infinitesimal call upon the powers that lie quiescent in the cosmos.

Philosophically all these comparisons are unimportant. They have no bearing upon our own values, and need not affect our demeanour in face of the universe. It is as absurd to suggest that man should feel humiliated and humble when he thinks how much smaller he is than a galaxy, as it would be that he should be puffed up with pride because he is, and in about the same proportion, bigger than an electron.

7. The Michelson-Morley Experiment

i

We have still to consider the question whether an ether of the kind we are suggesting is not ruled out by the negative result of the critical experiment of Michelson and Morley.

The purpose which those scientists had in view was to discover the velocity of the earth in its movement round the sun, relatively to the quasi-gaseous, or elastic, ether that was at that time supposed to be the universal continuum. The mechanism employed in the experiment was an arrangement of an electric lamp and an interferometer apparatus at the centre, together with two mirrors, each rigidly fixed at the same distance away; one was placed on the line of the earth's movement along its orbit, the other at right angles to it. A flash of light was divided into two by a half-silvered glass plate and the rays were sent simultaneously in the two directions: reflected back by the mirrors, they were recombined at the centre. It was expected that, owing to the earth having travelled an infinitesimal, but calculable, distance during the time that the rays were going and returning, the time taken by one ray would be different from that of the other, which would not have been affected in the same way. This would be shown by the two wave rhythms, when reunited, not coinciding: they would overlap one another, and this interference would at once be detected by the apparatus. No significant effect, however, was found. The test was repeated many times, by many experimenters and under all kinds of conditions; but the original results, although they have been challenged, are regarded by physicists in general as correct.

This negative result contradicted the established laws of mechanics. Whittaker says that 'an object thrown from a carriage window in a moving railway train has a velocity which is obtained by compounding its velocity relative to the carriage with the velocity of the train (the ballistic theory)'; but, he adds: 'Michelson showed experimentally that the velocity of a moving mirror is without influence on the velocity of light reflected at its surface'; and 'it is now known certainly that the velocity of light is independent of the motion of the source'.

In these circumstances, physicists have felt themselves obliged to surrender the belief that any kind of universal continuum exists, with properties expressible by the laws of mechanics. This conclusion also is open, however, to formidable objections. It would throw us back on the doctrine of action at a distance, which, as Newton said, is philosophically impossible. It is contradicted by the experience of mankind, and of all animal and plant life as well, as to the reality of the conveyance of heat, light and gravity — from the sun to the earth for example—since these could not travel without a physical medium to convey them. In the end, physics abandoned the attempt to resolve these contradictions within the framework of the universe given by experience and interpreted by our sense-data. This is the main reason why it now takes its stand within the mathematical framework of a relativist geometry. Realist philosophy, however, remains dissatisfied. Seeking a way of escape, we may ask whether it may not be possible to conceive some different kind of ether that would be compatible with the null result of Michelson and Morley.

ii

I discussed the problem briefly in my previous book, *Essay in Physics*. And I did so on the basis of an ether consisting of energy in either of two states, quiescent and active, all physical phenomena being the result of processes of activation in various patterns. Reading those passages afresh, they seem to me not to have been expressed effectively. I will now attempt it again, with the help of an illustration.

Consider the movement of an ocean liner, travelling on a calm sea. Our hypothesis would regard its momentum as having been caused initially by the work of the engines, making the blades of the propellers revolve and press against the surrounding water. This movement of a massive body sets up a process of activation in each volume of quiescent energy successively reached: the process continues, by a chain reaction, in a straight line: it would correspond to Faraday's idea of a 'line of force'. It is this which, added to the momentum from the engines, gives the ship its impetus. If the engines are stopped, the ship does not stop then and there, as would otherwise have had to be expected. Its impetus carries it on, for half a mile or a mile perhaps, until the process is brought to an end by the effect of the earth's gravity: this tends to make the water remain where it is, resisting the pressure of the prow, as it seeks to push away the surface layer of the sea to either side.

The activation affects, at each successive point-instant, whatever is within the zone of ether that is concerned. It permeates the steel hull of the ship and all its contents — the molecules, atoms and particles of the air in the rooms and passages, and all material objects, including the bodies of the people on board. The whole is being moved together as a unit. If an accident were to happen: if in a fog the ship were to run into a rock or an iceberg, then the hull, and everything fixed to it, would be brought to a sudden stop; while the impetus would continue, for a brief moment, to affect anything that was free to move — chairs or crockery and the like, and the people, who would all be hurled forward violently.

In ordinary circumstances, and in calm weather, a passenger is not conscious of the ship's movement over the sea. As he walks along the corridors, it makes no difference to his sensations, or to the effort of walking, whether he is going in the direction that the ship is travelling, or in the opposite direction, or across from one side to the other. If his pace is, say two miles an hour, and the speed of the ship thirty miles, it would be misleading to say that he is moving at one moment at a rate of thirty-two miles an hour, at the next of twenty-eight, and then of thirty. In other words the two speeds are not in fact being compounded.

This is so because the motion of any object is relative to its own environment, there being no such thing as absolute motion. If we were to suppose an object alone in the universe, it would be impossible to say whether it was moving or at rest: the question would be meaningless. In the case of the passenger, the environment that is significant will be the ship, its hull, rooms and corridors.

If it is asked what is the size and contour of this zone of activation, we can say that our own perceptions give the answer. The zone comprises everything that we see is participating in the momentum and impetus of the ship, and nothing else. This would become quite evident if a passenger were to go up to the sun-deck while the ship was at full speed. Opening a door at the top of the staircase and stepping out, he would find himself instantly exposed to the blast of a wind of thirty miles an hour. He is forced to cling at once to a rail, or take shelter behind some fixed screen, or he would find himself blown back violently along the deck. But this wind exists only in relation to the ship and what is in it. If it is calm weather, a seagull a few yards overhead soaring in any direction would be flying in still air. The case is not, as it seems to the passenger, that of a strong current of air rushing over the sea against his body: that is an illusion; there is no such current. It is his own body that, with the ship, is being strongly pushed against the air, which itself is static. (It is the same kind of illusion as when we think that it is a movement of the sun, and not

of our own bodies, that causes what we call the sunset.) Whatever
the force may be that is causing this, it is affecting only the ship and
its contents. A distant observer watching from the land, or from
another vessel, or from a plane passing over, would not be affected,
and would feel nothing. This therefore is the zone of activation.

iii

Now suppose that some physicist has been able to construct a
Michelson-Morley apparatus so accurate that it would be able to
record by means of light rays even a velocity as small as thirty miles an
hour, and so compact that it could be set up on board a liner, and that
he makes the test. The fact that the ship is actually in motion across
the Atlantic is unquestioned: and the effectiveness of the apparatus
is not challenged: yet, when the experiment is made, it is found that
no movement whatever is indicated. Perhaps he might then erect his
apparatus again on land, in order to set the easier test of the earth's
movement round the sun, at a velocity not quite so minute relatively
as the ship's movement over the sea. But the result is the same. The
physicist concludes that the only possible explanation is that the
existence of an ether, as a medium for the transmission of light, is
disproved. The real universe (if there is any) must be different from
that.

An ether hypothesis of the kind that we are suggesting here would
put forward, however, another explanation. It is that the assumption,
from which Michelson and Morley started, was wrong. They assumed
that the earth — as any other material body — was one thing, while
the ether, if it existed, would be another. Their apparatus, with its
rods, mirrors and lamps, and its interferometer, belonged to the earth,
and moved with it. The trains of light-waves, on the other hand,
would belong to the ether: they were separate and travelled 'in space',
loose and independent. But that assumption has no grounds, either of
observation or of inference, to support it. And an all-pervading
energic ether, such as we are considering, does not need such an
assumption; it is indeed inconsistent with it. For that duality could
not occur. The earth, with the material apparatus, is not *in* the ether
and travelling *through* it. All together — earth, apparatus and light-
waves as well — *are themselves ether*: the solid parts consist of atoms, and
ultimately particles, which are patterns of one kind in — or *of* — ether;
and the waves are also ether — differing only in pattern. The same
applies to the ship's motion relatively to the sea.

The conclusion that we submit is, therefore, that the null result of
the famous experiment has no bearing upon the hypothesis we are
presenting, and offers no obstacle to its acceptance.

iv

I would add a supplementary note on a separate matter.

Radiation waves have been studied for nearly three centuries, and with striking results; particles for the last fifty or sixty years, and again with revolutionary effects on theoretical and practical physics. But we have been driven to a conviction that, if there is an ether, these cannot be its only patterns. Neither spherical waves, nor circling, spinning or vibrating particles, can account for the momentum and impetus of massive objects. We are obliged to conclude that there must exist in the real universe some third kind of mechanism, operating longitudinally. This was foreseen, and designated, by Faraday when he spoke of 'Lines of Force'. Physicists, however, have never taken up this idea. They have been content with Newton's First Law of Motion; not fully appreciating that that is no more than a restatement, in precise terms, of the problem that confronts us; it makes no attempt to discover the nature of the process actually operating. When something more was asked for, it was offered only in terms of mathematics. The consequence is that the idea of Lines of Force has not yet been seriously studied.

The discussion in which we have now been engaged suggests the possibility of fresh avenues waiting to be explored. For it may be that in the Michelson-Morley experiment two kinds of ether activation are proceeding at the same time: one, in the pattern of lines of force, carrying along the earth, and the scientific apparatus with it; the other, in the pattern of radiation waves, conveying the rays of light. If that is so, the question naturally arises of the interrelation between them. Do they interfere with one another or not?

They may possibly be at quite different levels of size and velocity—one of the order of the particle, the other of gross material objects. If, from this or any other cause, the two do not directly affect one another, this would be a further reason why a device, such as that employed in the experiment, could not establish any connection between the movement of the earth and that of the light rays. Perhaps such a question might be as futile as it would be to ask whether the motion of a man walking would affect the motion of the particles in the atoms of the cells that make up his body, and ought to be compounded with it.

But this, with all other questions of the same nature, would need consideration by those who are qualified by knowledge and technical ability to deal with them, if and when the ether becomes a subject of intensive scientific investigation.

8. *Unity of the Cosmos*

Again and again in the course of our inquiry we have been able to strengthen a case in one field of science by citing analogues in other fields: we say that nature often employs in different connections the same mechanical model. This similarity is specially marked in the physics of light and of sound. The propagation of sound-waves is subject to the same general laws as light and other radiation waves. Although sound-waves are longitudinal and light-waves are transverse, both have the wave formation of crest and trough and both are transmitted by a medium. A leading authority on acoustics tells us that, in the period between 1920 and 1939, much effort was devoted in university and industrial laboratories 'to demonstrating the acoustical analogues of practically all the optical experiments which bear on the wave nature of light. Interference, refraction, diffraction, dispersion, transmission and reflection by thin plates, were all demonstrated and shown to follow the same general theory as has already been worked out for light. Interferometers and other instrumental techniques were consciously based on past experience with optical instruments. Ultrasonic lenses, diffraction gratings, concave and convex mirrors were all developed'. There must be some reason why this striking similarity should be possible.

There had to be a reason also why it should be possible for one kind of manifestation of energy — heat, light, electric current, mechanical work, radio, X-rays — to be transformed into others: it was discovered that all of them were either products of electromagnetic forces belonging to different parts of a single wave-band, or else of currents of particles. An ether theory would suggest that the similarity between the mechanisms of light and of sound is of the same order. In fact it is not similarity at all; it is not a question of analogy; it is a case of identity — basically the two mechanisms are one and the same.

Light originates in the oscillation of atoms: sound originates in the vibration of violin strings, piano wires, vocal cords in a larynx, or whatever it may be — we can see a tuning-fork actively vibrating. Both light and sound are propagated by a mechanism of expanding spherical waves, subject to the inverse-square law. We say that the difference between them is that the sound-waves are waves of air and the light-waves are not. But when we examine the matter more closely we must recognize that, while the sound process is affected by the atoms or molecules of air, it is not they that do the work. Each atom or molecule of oxygen or nitrogen or carbonic-acid gas is not self-moving. It may be swung to and fro, but it has no dynamic powers of its own. Like water waves in the sea or radiation waves across space, there must be something else underlying that is dynamic. That something can only be the ether. So we are brought to the conclusion that these processes are not similar because of some mysterious and inexplicable coincidence. They are not analogies at all. They are one and the same process, an ether-process. The difference is that some are affected by the presence of matter; others, at a lower size-level, are not. Particles also are an ether-process, but of another pattern. Impetus is yet another.

Consider a clap of thunder. We have there three different phenomena, perceptible by three different organs of our bodies. There is first an electrical discharge, which the nervous system may feel as a shock; and may be so injured by it that the body instantly dies. There is also the flash of lightning, vividly seen by the eye. There is thirdly the crash of thunder, heard by the ear. The electric current consists presumably of a stream of negatively charged particles. The light consists of a wave-formation of expanding spheres. The sound likewise, but with waves of a different kind, moving at a much lower velocity. All three originate at the same moment and in the same region. Can it be doubted that all three are products of one event, occurring in a single medium?

We have mentioned the fact before that, when a radium atom disintegrates, there are produced, at that moment in that place, three different things — a chemical atom of helium, a stream of electrons, and a beam of gamma rays. Evidently the conclusion to be drawn must be the same.

This book began with the plea that Philosophy, Science and Religion must survey the universe as a whole — one in its past history, one in its present substance. This is not an idea imposed by human minds, with a liking for symmetry and a gift for logic. We may find that it comes to us from a reality underneath, that the unity of the physical world reflects the unity of a basic ether.

A final note must, however, be added. It is always usual in these discussions to speak of '*the* ether', taking for granted that, if there is any ether at all, there is only one. But this is an assumption and nothing more. Theoretically there is no reason to say that, if there is one ether, there cannot be a second, with differences that are outside, not only our knowledge but our conception: perhaps even a third. This may have a bearing on the unresolved problems of the distinctions between Matter and Life and Mind. We shall not pursue this further, as it is, and is likely long to remain, sheer guesswork. Nevertheless it may be well to keep at the back of our minds the possibility that, if we cannot escape dualism with regard to the material and the living, and again perhaps between the living and the mental, these may originate in other dichotomies deeper down.

MIND AND BRAIN

Thomas Henry Huxley — Lay Sermons

What is the cause of this wonderful difference between the dead particle and the living particle of matter appearing in other respects identical, that difference to which we give the name of Life?

I, for one, cannot tell you. It may be that, by and by, philosophers will discover some higher laws of which the facts of life are particular cases — very possibly they will find out some bond between physico-chemical phaenomena on the one hand, and vital phaenomena on the other. At present, however, we assuredly know of none; and I think we shall exercise a wise humility in confessing that, for us at least, this successive assumption of different states — (external conditions remaining the same) — this *spontaneity of action* — if I may use a term which implies more than I would be answerable for — which constitutes so vast and plain a practical distinction between living bodies and those which do not live, is an ultimate fact; indicating, as such, the existence of a broad line of demarcation between the subject-matter of Biological and that of all other sciences. . . .

If scientific language is to possess a definite and constant significa-tion whenever it is employed, it seems to me that we are logically bound to apply to the protoplasm, or physical basis of life, the same conceptions as those which are held to be legitimate elsewhere. If the phaenomena exhibited by water are its properties, so are those pre-sented by protoplasm, living or dead, its properties.

If the properties of water may be properly said to result from the nature and disposition of its component molecules, I can find no intel-ligible ground for refusing to say that the properties of protoplasm result from the nature and disposition of its molecules.

It may seem a small thing to admit that the dull vital actions of a fungus, or a foraminifer, are the properties of their protoplasm, and are the direct results of the nature of the matter of which they are composed. But if, as I have endeavoured to prove to you, their proto-plasm is essentially identical with, and most readily converted into, that of any animal, I can discover no logical halting-place between the admission that such is the case, and the further concession that all vital action may, with equal propriety, be said to be the result of the molecular forces of the protoplasm which displays it. And if so, it must be true, in the same sense and to the same extent, that the thoughts to which I am now giving utterance, and your thoughts regarding them, are the expression of molecular changes in that matter of life which is the source of our other vital phaenomena.

Past experience leads me to be tolerably certain that, when the propositions I have just placed before you are accessible to public comment and criticism, they will be condemned by many zealous persons, and perhaps by some few of the wise and thoughtful. I should not wonder if 'gross and brutal materialism' were the mildest phrase applied to them in certain quarters. And, most undoubtedly, the terms of the propositions are distinctly materialistic. Nevertheless two things are certain; the one, that I hold the statements to be substantially true; the other, that I, individually, am no materialist, but, on the contrary, believe materialism to involve grave philosophical error.

This union of materialistic terminology with the repudiation of materialistic philosophy I share with some of the most thoughtful men with whom I am acquainted. . . .

There can be little doubt, that the farther science advances, the more extensively and consistently will all the phaenomena of nature be represented by materialistic formulae and symbols.

But the man of science, who, forgetting the limits of philosophical inquiry, slides from these formulae and symbols into what is commonly understood by materialism, seems to me to place himself on a level with the mathematician, who should mistake the x's and y's with which he works his problems for real entities — and with this further disadvantage, as compared with the mathematician, that the blunders of the latter are of no practical consequence, while the errors of systematic materialism may paralyse the energies and destroy the beauty of a life.

D'Arcy W. Thompson — Growth and Form

My sole purpose is to correlate with mathematical statement and physical law certain of the simpler outward phenomena of organic growth and structure or form, while all the while regarding the fabric of the organism, *ex hypothesi*, as a material and mechanical configuration. This is my purpose here. But I would not for the world be thought to believe that this is the only story which Life and her Children have to tell. One does not come by studying living things for a lifetime to suppose that physics and chemistry can account for them all. Physical science and philosophy stand side by side, and one upholds the other. Without something of the strength of physics philosophy would be weak; and without something of philosophy's wealth physical science would be poor. . . .

We may readily admit then, that, besides phenomena which are obviously physical in their nature, there are actions visible as well as invisible taking place within living cells which our knowledge does not permit us to ascribe with certainty to any known physical force; and it may or may not be that these phenomena will yield in time to the methods of physaicl investigation. Whether they do or no, it is plain that we have no clear rule or guidance as to what is 'vital' and what is not; the whole assemblage of so-called vital phenomena, or properties of the organism, cannot be clearly classified into those that are physical in origin and those that are *sui generis* and peculiar to living things.

C. Lloyd Morgan — The Emergence of Novelty

In late nineteenth-century discussion much stress was laid by advocates of evolution on the hypothesis that instinctive behaviour is 'no more than compound reflex action'. Is that the interpretation which I still seek to endorse? It is not. What, as a biologist, I accept is that the analysis of instinctive behaviour yields reflex acts *as constituents*. What I reject is the doctrine that the compound is 'no more than' the sum of its constituents. . . .

I am (to say the least of it) doubtful whether mind, as a distinctive kind of relatedness within the cosmos, has arisen by emergence from the supposedly precedent kind of cosmic relatedness which we designate physical. My belief is that the evolution of mind has advanced in co-relation with that of those physical events the outcome of which is the physiological organization of a living body.

E. D. Adrian, O.M. — The Physical Basis of Mind

The part of our picture of the brain which may always be missing is, of course, the part which deals with the mind, the part which ought to explain how a particular pattern of nerve impulses can produce an idea; or the other way round, how a thought can decide which nerve cells are to come into action . . . The physiologist cannot look at it except as a natural scientist and at present that seems almost certain to lead him into trouble. My own feeling is that before the trouble comes to a head it will have been solved by some enlargement in the boundaries of natural science, by the progress of psychology, for instance. In fact, psychology can scarcely get along without coming to terms with the relation of body and mind.

Sir Russell Brain — Mind, Perception and Science

For at least a century the prevailing philosophical attitude has been determined by the belief, variously expressed, that the 'laws' of matter are fundamental, and that mind is at least potentially capable of explanation in terms of those laws. This idea has had profound effects in all spheres of thought. I believe it to be the product of a mistaken view as to the nature of our knowledge of the mind and the brain respectively, and the relationship between them; and that it is possible to accept all the new knowledge which neurophysiology and psychology can provide, and yet preserve the mind's autonomy in its own sphere. That, at any rate, is the thesis of this book.

W. E. Le Gros Clark — The Physical Basis of Mind
In conclusion, I might emphasize — though perhaps it is not really necessary to do so — that the anatomist is primarily concerned with the study of the brain as the material substratum of mental processes. No more than the physiologist is he able even to suggest how the physicochemical phenomena associated with the passage of nervous impulses from one part of the brain to another can be translated into a mental experience. But, by the study of the structural organization of the brain, and by observing the effects of a local disturbance of this structure on the working of the mind, it is becoming possible to define in more and more detail the particular anatomical dispositions which appear to be necessary as a basis for mental activity, or perhaps I should say, for the manifestations of mental activity.

Wilder Penfield (Professor of Neurology and Neurosurgery, McGill University, and Director of the Neurological Institute, Montreal) *— The Physical Basis of Mind*
When a man is conscious, one may conceive that within his brain impulses are passing along a million insulated nerve fibres that compose this complex, impulses that are somehow co-ordinated into the orderly sequences of deliberate thought. What is the real relationship of this mechanism to the mind? Can we visualize a spiritual element of different essence capable of controlling this mechanism? When a patient is asked about the movement which he carries out as the result of cortical stimulation, he never is in any doubt about it. He knows he did not will the action. He knows there is a difference between automatic action and voluntary action. He would agree that something else finds its dwelling-place between the sensory complex and the motor mechanism, that there is a switchboard operator as well as a switchboard.

W. Grey Walter (Department of Physiology, Burden Neurological Institute, Bristol) *— The Living Brain*
Any discussion of mind except as a function — the supreme function — of brain, lies beyond the scope of this work and must always remain

outside the purview of physiology . . . No sane physiologist would look for a mechanism identifiable as Mind; but he may quite reasonably say: 'At one time behaviour was *so*; later it was *thus* — the transformation of one mode into the other I will call *Mentality*.'

J. E. Eccles — The Neurophysiological Basis of Mind
The observations relating to mind, i.e. mental phenomena, are part of the experience that a scientist should recognize as providing problems which are suitable for scientific investigation. It is a purely arbitrary and biased procedure to exclude such experiences from the fields of investigation where science may properly operate. . . .

It may be postulated that any thought pattern in the mind has a counterpart in a specific spatio-temporal pattern of neuronal activity....

There is one partial approach to the key problem of the 'how' of mind-brain liaison that hitherto has not been essayed. It arises from the questions: How does it come about that liaison with mind occurs only in special states of the matter-energy system of the cerebral cortex? Is there any special property of this system that places it in a separate category from all the remainder of the matter-energy, or natural world, and even from its own matter-energy system when it is not in this special state of activity? It is here contended that such a special property in outstanding measure is exhibited by the dynamic patterns of neuronal activity that occur in the cerebral cortex during conscious states, and the hypothesis is developed that the brain by means of this special property enters into liaison with mind, having the function of a 'detector' that has a sensitivity of a different kind and order from that of any physical instrument. . . .

It is not here contended that all action is willed. There can be no doubt that a great part of the skilled activity devolving from the cerebral cortex is stereotyped and automatic, and may be likened to the control of breathing by the respiratory centres. But it is contended that it is possible voluntarily to assume control of such actions, even of the most trivial kind, just as we may within limits exercise a voluntary control over our breathing. . . .

The neurophysiological hypothesis is that the 'will' modifies the spatio-temporal activity of the neuronal network by exerting spatio-temporal 'fields of influence' that become effective through this unique detector function of the active cerebral cortex. It will be noted that this hypothesis assumes that the 'will' or 'mind influence' has itself a spatio-temporal patterned character in order to allow it this operative effectiveness. . . .

The observer will experience a private perceptual world which is an interpretation of specific events in his brain . . . We can regard the perceptual world of each observer as a kind of map built upon the spatial relations between objects of the external world, but also giving us symbolic information in terms of the secondary qualities, as is customary in ordinary maps with their conventions for rivers, towns, railways, etc. For example, colours, sounds, smells, heat add cold as such belong only to the perceptual world of an observer and are merely symbolic of events in the physical world which they are quite unlike....

The task of scientists has been to attempt to build up a progressively more valid or real physical world, i.e. a world more and more purified from the symbolic bias that is necessarily introduced into the perceptual world by the manner in which it is derived from the physical world. This is done by the discovery of rules by which the real physical world may be inferred from the symbolic data of the perceptual world, as for example the correlation of wave frequency in the physical world with colour of light in the perceptual world. . . .

It should be pointed out that, in this discussion of the functioning of the brain, it has initially been regarded as a 'machine' operating according to the laws of physics and chemistry. In conscious states it has been shown to be in a state of extreme sensitivity as a detector of minute spatio-temporal fields of influence. The hypothesis is developed that these spatio-temporal fields of influence are exerted by the mind on the brain in willed action. . . .

The present theme has been to show how recent neurophysiological developments make it possible to give in many respects a fairly adequate functional description of the nervous system that is based on physics and chemistry and that gives some clue as to the manner in which the gulf between mind and matter may ultimately be bridged. For the scientist there should be no doubt that the problem of interaction of mind and matter is a real problem and not a pseudo-problem arising from confusions in the usage of words.

A. S. Ewing — The Relation between Mind and Body as a Problem for the Philosopher

The mental side of our nature is made up of experiences which are intrinsically different from anything that could exist in the physical world or figure in textbooks of physiology as observable phenomena....

The fact is that we are not yet in a position to frame a satisfactory philosophical theory of the relation between body and mind.

NOTES

[To page 44] *Should we use the spelling 'Ether' or 'Aether'?*

Sir Edmund Whittaker and Professor Dirac write 'aether', and Sir Arthur Eddington used to do so. But the *Concise Oxford Dictionary* gives 'ether' only; and Collins's *Author's and Printers' Dictionary* (published by the Oxford University Press) gives 'ether', *not* 'ae—'. Fowler's *Modern English Usage* does not mention the word specifically, but says: 'It seems desirable that in the first place all words in common enough use to have begun to waver between the double letter and the simple e . . . should be written with the "e" alone' (p. 11).

As late as the middle of the nineteenth century, Faraday was still writing 'phaenomena' (e.g. a quotation in Whittaker's *Aether and Electricity*, p. 196); and T. H. Huxley does the same throughout his book *Lay Sermons*, published in 1870. But no one would think of doing so now. Nor would anyone use 'aetherial' as the adjective. It seems desirable that the simpler form should be generally used also for the noun: all the more so if physics were to recognize the validity of some form of ether theory, and the term should come into wider use, both in applied sciences such as radio-engineering and in the vernacular. Nor should the advantage of a uniform practice in Britain and in the United States be overlooked; and there is no doubt which alternative Americans will prefer.

I sent a copy of this note to Dr. Gilbert Murray, the most eminent of our Greek scholars and translators, and ventured to ask him for his opinion. He wrote in reply (November 19th, 1952): 'I should spell "ether" with a simple "e", very much on the ground that Fowler gives. Custom is certainly on the side of the "e", and, as you say, one would hardly write "aetherial".'

For these reasons I am not following the eminent writers who have kept to the diphthong.

[To page 145] *Church attendances*

Mr. Seebohm Rowntree took a census in York in 1899 of attendances by persons over 16 at all places of worship. Under similar conditions as regard weather and time of year, he repeated this census in 1935 and again in 1947. The percentages of the adult population attending were (the figures for 1947 had not been finally tabulated):

1899 — 35.5
1935 — 17.7
1947 — approximately 10

The Protestant Sunday Schools of England and Wales had attendances, approximately, of

1887 — 5,733,000
1920 — 5,008,000
1954 — 2,800,000

The total number of children of school age (5-15) in 1954 was 6,629,000. On the other hand account must be taken of the large audiences that listen to religious broadcasts on the radio. The B.B.C. estimate that 'nearly one-third of the adult population hear at least one of the religious broadcasts on a Sunday, and the majority of these listeners are believed to be men and women who are not regular church-goers'. During the week there are altogether about thirty religious programmes of different kinds in the Home Service and the Light Programme.

[To page 162] *Mau Mau and Religion*
A very different and far more extreme case is reported from another part of Africa, relating to the terrible crimes that have marked the Mau Mau rising in Kenya. Dr. L. S. B. Leakey, who was born and brought up among the Kikuyu and is well acquainted with the whole situation, says: 'Few people, I find, realize that Mau Mau has its own religious creed, based upon our "Apostle's Creed" and a terrible and hideous parody of it. This was issued in printed form and learned by heart by hundreds of thousands of Kikuyu . . . Mau Mau also uses solemn forms of prayer addressed to Almighty God . . . So much, indeed, has Mau Mau become a religion that there is nearly always an act of prayer and worship both before and after the administration of their foul and filthy oath ceremonies, while those taking the oath have to start by repeating the words, "I truly swear by Almighty God and before these assembled witnesses", and then go on and promise to commit murder and even, if called upon to do so, to kill their own mothers and fathers and children.'

REFERENCES

In several lectures, published in recent years, I have dealt with the same subjects as in this book, and I have occasionally repeated here passages which had formed part of them. I have not, however, included specific references in this list as it would not be likely to serve any useful purpose; but I would express my acknowledgements to the publishers of the lectures and the bodies at whose invitation they were delivered.

The titles of those lectures are:

Creative Man (Romanes Lecture, 1947. Oxford University. Also included in *Creative Man and Other Addresses*, Cresset Press, 1949);
What is Happening to Religion Today?;
Does Religion Stand to Reason? (Inaugural Lectures to the London School of Religion, 1951);
The Classical Age and Our Own (Presidential Address, 1953, to the Classical Association);
A Century's Changes of Outlook (Hibbert Centenary Lecture, 1953);
Philosophy and the Life of the Nation (Royal Institute of Philosophy, 1956).

I have also repeated here and there one or two passages from my earlier book *Belief and Action*.

PAGE

Preface, vii
    'Whither the argument may blow . . .' — Plato, *The Republic*, (Jowett, 394).

1   Antiquity of Galilee skull. — Letter of November 18th, 1953, from K. P. Oakley, Department of Geology, British Museum (Natural History).

1   Capernaum, Luke vii.

5   'Like gnats above a stagnant pool . . .' — John Galsworthy, *Fraternity*.

6   Alexander Pope, *An Essay on Man*.

7   *Bulletin of the Ramakrishna Mission*, Institute of Culture, vol. IV, no. 7, July 1953, p. 155. See also Dr. S. Radhakrishnan, *Eastern Religions and Western Thought* (Index — 'Maya') (Oxford, Clarendon Press).

9   'Learn what is true in order to do what is right', is the summing up of the whole duty of man, for all who are unable to satisfy their mental hunger with the east wind of authority. — T. H. Huxley, *Lay Sermons*, p. 280 (Macmillan, 1899).

PAGE

11   Number of species — see Julian Huxley, 'Species and Evolution', *Endeavour*, January 1946.

12   Sun and moon, Genesis i, 16, 17.

12   Eclipses. From *The Times*, February 26th, 1952. 'A million devout Hindu pilgrims from all parts of India bathed today in the sacred lakes at Kurushetna on the occasion of the solar eclipse . . . Excellent arrangements by the East Punjab Government enabled all the devotees to bathe without casualty. When the sun's surface began to darken the great multitude shouted and blew conch shells, because the popular legend has it that a demon is trying to swallow the sun and the devout must help the sun god with their prayers, in return for which they will earn his blessings.'

15   G. Meredith, *The Amazing Marriage*, chap. xxii (Constable & Co.).

20   W. R. Inge, *Science and Ultimate Truth*, The Fison Memorial Lecture, 1926, p. 28 (Longmans, Green & Co. Ltd.).
     W. R. Inge, 'Philosophy and Religion', in *Contemporary British Philosophy*, edited by J. H. Muirhead, vol. I, p. 195 (George Allen & Unwin Ltd.).
     Among others who take the same view are Dr. W. R. Matthews, *The Purpose of God*, p. 117 (James Nisbet & Co. Ltd.); and C. Lloyd Morgan, *Emergent Evolution*, p. 175 (Williams & Norgate Ltd.).
     C. E. M. Joad, *Return to Philosophy*, pp. 67-8 (Faber & Faber).
     Among those who express the opposite opinion (against the reality of Values) are von Ehrenfels, *System der Werttheorie*, vol. I, p. 2, quoted by W. R. Sorley, *Moral Values and the Idea of God*, p. 133 (C.U.P.).
     Bertrand Russell, *Religion and Science*, p. 230 (Thornton Butterworth Ltd.).

21   'Earth was not Earth . . .' — G. Meredith, 'Appreciation', quoted by G. M. Trevelyan, *Selected Poetical Works of George Meredith*, p. 41 (Longmans, Green & Co. Ltd.).

24   Dalton's 12 elements were hydrogen, carbon, zinc, oxygen, phosphorus, iron, azote, sulphur, tin, chlorine, lead, copper. — Lecture in Manchester, 1835.

24   W. Heisenberg, *Philosophic Problems of Nuclear Science*, p. 55 (Faber & Faber Ltd., 1952).

25   L. de Broglie, *The Revolution in Physics*, p. 62 (Routledge & Kegan Paul, 1954).

PAGE

25 H. Dingle, *Proceedings of the Royal Institution*, vol. XXXV, part 1, no. 158, March 2nd, 1951, p. 77.

27 Wilson cloud chamber — see P. M. S. Blackett, 'The Birth of Nuclear Science', *The Listener*, March 4th, 1954, p. 381.

28 Cosmic radiation — W. F. Libby.
Radio-carbon Dating — *Endeavour*, January 1954, p. 7 (Imperial Chemical Industries).

29 F. Hoyle, *The Nature of the Universe*, p. 105 (B. Blackwell, Oxford, 1950).
H. Bondi, *Cosmology*, p. 144 (C.U.P., 1952).
Sir Harold Spencer Jones, the Astronomer Royal, 'The Continuous Creation of Matter', *The Listener*, July 17th, 1952, p. 99.
J. Robert Oppenheimer, *The Listener*, November 26th, 1953, p. 913.

31 Faraday, quoted by J. Bronowski, *The Listener*, March 2nd 1950.

31 Sir A. S. Eddington, *Proceedings of the Royal Society*, vol. CII 1923, p. 281.

31 Sir E. Whittaker, *From Euclid to Eddington*, p. 81 (C.U.P., 1949).

32 Sir E. Whittaker, *op. cit.*, p. 112.
Sir E. Whittaker, *History of the Theories of Aether and Electricity*, vol. II, p. 151 (C.U.P., 1953).
Sir I. Newton, *Opticks*, p. 401 (Bell & Sons).

32 Sir I. Newton, 'For the cause of gravity . . .' Letter to Bentley, dated Trinity College, Jan. 17th. 1692-3, printed in Horsley's *Isaaci Newtoni Opera*, vol. IV, p. 437, and quoted by Dr. Andrade in *An Approach to Modern Physics*. (I am indebted to him for the reference.)

34 Viscount Samuel, *Essay in Physics*, p. 66 (B. Blackwell, Oxford, 1951).

39 Sir I. Newton, from a letter, quoted by Floriun Cajori in *Appendix to Mathematical Principles*, p. 634 (C.U.P.).

39 A. Einstein, *The Theory of Relativity*, p. 63 (Methuen & Co. Ltd.), quoted by M. Born, *Natural Philosophy of Cause and Chance*, p. 123 (Oxford, Clarendon Press).

40 Sir I. Newton, *Opticks*, p. 348 (C.U.P.).

40 Michelson-Morley — see R. W. Wood, *Physical Optics*, pp. 817-827 (The Macmillan Company, New York) — see also Sir E. Whittaker, *From Euclid to Eddington*, p. 96.

41 Sir J. Jeans, *The Astronomical Horizon*, p. 22 (O.U.P., 1945).

42 A. Einstein, 'Relativity and Ether', *The World As I See It*, p. 204 (John Lane: The Bodley Head, 1935).

PAGE

43 Sir A. Eddington, *New Pathways in Science*, pp. 39, 48 (C.U.P., 1935).

43 P. A. M. Dirac, *Nature*, November 24th, 1951, vol. CLXVIII, p. 906.

44 Sir E. Whittaker, *Aether and Electricity*, vol. I, p. 5.

44 Lord Cherwell, Dr. Lee's Professor of Experimental Philosophy, Oxford, *Physics and Philosophy*, Robert Grosseteste Memorial Lecture, May 1955, p. 15.

45 Sir O. Lodge, *Ether and Reality*, pp. 39, 91 (Hodder & Stoughton, 1925).

45 Lord Rayleigh, *Life of J. J. Thomson*, p. 203 (C.U.P.).

45 W. Heisenberg, *Philosophic Problems of Nuclear Science*, p. 103 (Faber & Faber, 1952).

46 Faraday, quoted by Sir E. Whittaker, *From Euclid to Eddington*, p. 121.

47 W. I. B. Beveridge, *The Art of Scientific Investigation*, p. 145 (Heinemann, 1950).

47 Sir O. Lodge, *Ether and Reality*, pp. 173-5.

47 W. Heisenberg, *Philosophic Problems of Nuclear Science*, p. 103.

47 W. I. B. Beveridge, *The Art of Scientific Investigation*, pp. 1-3, 143-6 (W. Heinemann Ltd., 1950).

48 'And Art made tongue-tied by Authority.' —Shakespeare, Sonnet LXVI.

51 Wave-lengths — see E. N. da C. Andrade, *The Atom and its Energy*, p. 58 (G. Bell & Sons, 1947).
    (In metric measurements) see L. de Broglie, *The Revolution in Physics*, pp. 71-2 (Routledge & Kegan Paul, 1954).

53 Sir I. Newton, *Opticks*, p. 374.

59 Sir E. Whittaker, *Aether and Electricity*, vol. I, p. 172.

66 Sir Charles Sherrington, O.M.
    Man on His Nature, p. 312 (C.U.P., 1940).
    The Brain and Its Mechanism, p. 32 (Rede Lecture, C.U.P., 1934).
    The Integrative Action of The Nervous System, p. 24 (C.U.P., 1947).
    The Physical Basis of Mind, p. 4. (Blackwell, 1950).

68 C. Mayhew, *The Observer*, October 24th, 1954.

69 Dr. E. D. Adrian, O.M., *The Advancement of Science*, vol. XI, no. 42, September 1954, p. 124.

70 Dr. E. D. Adrian, O.M., *Recent Developments in the Study of the Sense Organs*, The Trueman Wood Lecture: Royal Society of Arts, March 17th, 1954.

70 R. W. Emerson, *Essays*, On Circles.

PAGE

70 'The mind can measure . . .' — G. MacBeth, *The New Statesman*, December 4th, 1954.

71 Shakespeare, *Midsummer Night's Dream*, Act V, Scene 1.

74 G. Meredith, *The Amazing Marriage*.

74 See L. de Broglie, *The Revolution in Physics*, p. 100.

74 W. Heisenberg, *Philosophic Problems of Nuclear Science*, p. 56 (Faber & Faber).

75 A. N. Whitehead, *Essays in Science and Philosophy*, p. 144.
A. N. Whitehead, *Modes of Thought*, pp. 191, 197.

75 J. Boswell, *Life of Dr. Johnson*, 1774, vol. II, p. 84 (J. M. Dent & Co.).

79 J. Huizinga, *In the Shadow of Tomorrow*, p. 116 (Heinemann).

80 'Lazarus hungry . . .' — William Watson, 'England my Mother', *Poems* (John Lane).

82 Japanese Sun-goddess — see Anesaki, *History of Japanese Religion*, p. 29 (Kegan Paul).

82 'The Right Divine of Kings . . .' — Alexander Pope, *The Dunciad*.

83 Hegel, quoted by W. R. Inge, *Outspoken Essays, Second Series*, p. 128 (Longmans, Green & Co. Ltd.).

84 Fichte, quoted by W. R. Inge, *op. cit.*

84 Treitschke, quoted by A. J. Balfour, *Essays Speculative and Political*, p. 231 (Hodder & Stoughton).

84 A. Hitler, *Mein Kampf*, 24th edition, pp. 148-9.

84 B. Mussolini, *Enciclopedia Italiana*, vol. XIV, p. 849, article on 'Fascism'.

86 *Memoirs of the Crown Prince of Germany*, p. 27.

86 Sir A. Chamberlain, *Politics from Inside*, p. 599 (Cassell).

86 Viscount Grey of Fallodon, *Twenty-five Years*, vol. I, p. 51 (Hodder & Stoughton).

87 B. Mussolini, *The Times*, June 11th, 1940.
Berlin Foreign Office, *The Times*, July 16th, 1940.

87 Goebbels, article in *Das Reich*, quoted in *The Times*, December 24th, 1942.

87 O. Spengler, *The Decline of the West*, vol. I, pp. 39, 104, 107, 129, 418 (Allen & Unwin).

91 H.M. Queen Elizabeth II, *The Times*, April 22nd, 1952.

91 'Institutions are like . . .' — K. R. Popper, *The Open Society and its Enemies* (George Routledge & Sons).

92 Goethe, quoted by O. Spengler, *op. cit.*, vol. I, p. 21.

97 n B. Jowett, quoted by Abbott and Campbell, *Life of Benjamin Jowett*.

PAGE

98 'There are two critical points...' — Prof. L. S. Hearnshaw, President of Psychology Section, Meeting of the British Association for the Advancement of Science, Oxford, 1954, *The Advancement of Science*, vol. XI, no. 42, September 1954, p. 223.

98 A. N. Whitehead, *Modes of Thought*, p. 156 (C.U.P., 1938).

99 An interesting and forcible address, with the title *In Defence of Free Will*, was delivered as an Inaugural Lecture by C. Arthur Campbell, Professor of Logic in the University of Glasgow, and published by Jackson, Son & Company, Glasgow, 1938.

100 Gandhi's assassin — Alan Campbell-Johnson (from a contemporary diary), *Mission with Mountbatten* (Robert Hale, 1951).

100 'Although we hold it to be wrong...' — E. Westermarck, *The Origin and Development of the Moral Ideas*, vol. I, p. 19 (Macmillan & Co., 1924).

100 Spinoza, *Ethic*, part IV, Propositions, 21, 22, trans. by Hale White (O.U.P.).

101 L. Sterne, *Tristram Shandy*, bk. II, chap. XII.

101 Evolution of ideas — This has also been put forward by W. R. Inge, *Outspoken Essays, Second Series*, p. 180 (Longmans, Green & Co. Ltd.).

103 The Golden Rule — Leviticus xix, 18; Matthew vii, 12; Lyall, *The Sayings of Confucius*, p. 75, cf. also pp. 18, 52 (Longmans, Green & Co. Ltd.).

104 S. Radhakrishnan, *The Bhagavadgita*, p. 310 n (George Allen & Unwin.).

106 William Wordsworth, *The Excursion*.

111 The nervous system ... — Dr. Carpenter, quoted by William James, *Principles of Psychology*, vol. I, p. 112.

111 Bertrand Russell (Earl Russell), *The Observer*, February 20th, 1955.

113 n Sir Richard Steele, *The Tatler, Bickerstaff Essays*, 'False Doctoring'.

114 'Your thoughts are making you.' — Bishop Steere, quoted by *The New Statesman*, January 18th, 1919.

114 Matthew Arnold, *Mixed Essays* (Equality), (Smith, Elder & Co.).

115 Viscount Samuel, *House of Lords' Debates*, March 9th, 1955, col. 842.

116 '... loved not wisely ...' — Shakespeare, *Othello*, Act V, Scene 2.

116 E. Gibbon, quoted by Richard Cobden, *Political Writings* (Pamphlet *Russia*).

PAGE

119   *Criminal Statistics*, England and Wales, 1953, pp. vii, viii, 1954, p. viii (pub. 1955), (H.M. Stationery Office).

121   They shall be simple . . . — John Addington Symonds, *These Things Shall Be.*

122   La justice sans force, et la force sans justice: malheur affreux — quoted by *Paris-Soir*, August 21st, 1935.

126   W. B. Yeats, quoted by *The New Statesman*, August 20th, 1955.

127   W. R. Inge, quoted by *Treasury of Humorous Quotations* — Esar and Bentley, p. 106 (Phoenix House Ltd.).

127   '. . . because their thought is so shallow . . .' — G. H. Lewes, *History of Philosophy.*

128   *P.E.N. News*, June 1950.

128   F. Kreisler, reported in the *News Chronicle*, February 3rd, 1955.

128   '. . . of caricaturist proportions . . .' — Charles Wheeler, R.A., 'Modern Sculpture', *The Times*, November 24th, 1954.

130   Maxwell Fry, 'The Architect's Dilemma' (Broadcast), *The Listener*, February 24th, 1955.

131   'The starkness of the new brutalism' — Robert Harding, *The Sunday Times*, July 24th, 1955.

131   American Embassy in Madrid — *The Times*, April 26th, 1955.

134   'Nature not an aggregate . . .' — Thomas Carlyle, *Sartor Resartus.*

134   'a whiff of actual being . . .'—G. Meredith, *The Amazing Marriage*, chap. IX.

136   A. N. Whitehead, *Modes of Thought*, p. 170 (C.U.P.).

137   Egyptian Book of the Dead — J. H. Breasted, *Ancient Times: a History of the Early World*, pp. 74, 91 (Ginn & Company, Boston, 1916).

138   '. . . all systems of Hindu thought . . .' — S. Radhakrishnan, 'Hinduism', *The Legacy of India*, p. 285 (Oxford, Clarendon Press).

142   Antisthenes, quoted by Francis Bacon, *Apophthegms, Essays, etc.*

142   G. Lowes Dickinson, *Religion.*

144   Dr. Cyril Garbett, Archbishop of York, *Physician Heal Thyself*, 1945, *Watchman What of the Night?*, 1948, *The Church of England Today*, 1953 (Hodder & Stoughton). *The Times*, October 13th, 1955.

146   Rev. T. W. Manson, D.D., Rylands Professor of Biblical Criticism and Exegesis, Manchester University, B.B.C. Home Service, *The Listener*, December 1st, 1955.

148   'Lament no more . . .' — Sophocles, *Oedipus at Colonus.*

151   'The noblest movements . . .' — Ramsay Muir, *An Autobiography* (Lund Humphries & Co.).

PAGE

151 'No one can walk backwards . . .' — Joseph Hergesheimer, *The Three Black Pennys* (Heinemann).

151 C. A. Coulson, *The Advancement of Science*, December 1954, p. 331.

152 G. Ryle, B.B.C. broadcast, December 22nd, 1955.

152 n A. N. Whitehead, *Process and Reality*, p. 21 (C.U.P.).

152 William Cowper, *The Task*.

156 'Man builds the soaring spires . . .' — G. Meredith, *Earth and Man*.

156 T. Carlyle, *Sartor Resartus*, bk. II, chap. III.

156 'the swing of a door . . .' — G. Meredith, *The Amazing Marriage*, chap. XIX.

156 'Religion has a nourishing breast . . .' — *ibid.*, chap. XLI.

157 'anything is credible . . .' — Helen Diner, *Emperors, Angels and Eunuchs* (Chatto & Windus, 1938).

160 Jeremiah xxv, 6.

162 S. R. Swart, Minister of Justice in South Africa, quoted by *The Observer*, May 29th, 1955.

168 Expectation of Life — I am indebted for these statistical comparisons to Mr. Ritchie Calder.

References to Appendices

172 E. N. da C. Andrade, 'The Uncertainty Principle', B.B.C broadcast, *The Listener*, January 14th, 1954.

172 L. de Broglie, *The Revolution in Physics*, p. 159.

172 W. Heisenberg, *Philosophic Problems of Nuclear Science*, p. 14.

172 'the new conception . . .' — P. M. S. Blackett, 'Discoveries from the Big Machines', B.B.C. broadcast, *The Listener*, March 18th, 1954.

172 L. de Broglie, quoted by H. Semat, *Introduction to Atomic Physics*, pp. 144, 153, 165 (Rinehart & Co., Inc., New York, and Chapman & Hall Ltd., 1947).

172 'aspects' — e.g. L. de Broglie, *The Revolution in Physics*, pp. 160, 76, 176, 289.

173 L. de Broglie, *ibid.*, p. 217.

175 'And the spat spray . . .' — H. C. Haines, 'The Yield', *The Listener*, January 14th, 1954.

175 Sir John Cockcroft, *The Times*, February 21st, 1951.

178 Cyclotron — *The Times*, May 22nd, 1952, January 13th, 1953.

180 Sir E. Whittaker, *Aether and Electricity*, vol. I, p. 172.

188 E. P. Hubble, *The Observational Approach to Cosmology*, pp. v, 30, 43, 45, 65 (Oxford, Clarendon Press).

PAGE

188   See also a Paper presented to the Royal Astronomical Society, pub. in *The Observatory*, June 1953, p. 99. G. J. Whitrow, *The Structure of the Universe*, pp. 30-8 (Hutchinson's University Library, 1949).

188   M. A. Ellison, *Endeavour*, July 1953, p. 164 (pub. by Imperial Chemical Industries).

189   E. Finlay-Freundlich, 'Red Shifts in the Spectra of Celestial Bodies', *Philosophical Magazine*, ser. 7, vol. XLV, no. 362, p. 303, March 1954.

190   Philipp Frank, *Einstein, His Life and Times*, p. 165 (Jonathan Cape, 1948).

190   The Nature of the Upper Atmosphere — H. S. W. Massey, *Endeavour*, April 1954.

191   Sir J. Jeans, *The Mysterious Universe*, pp. 1, 13 (C.U.P., 1930). Sir J. Jeans, *The Universe Around Us*, p. 336 (C.U.P., 1929).

192   Bertrand Russell, *Religion and Science*, p. 218 (Thornton Butterworth Ltd.).

192   A. N. Whitehead, *Essays in Science and Philosophy*, p. 90.

192   J. C. Smuts, *Holism and Evolution*, p. 352 (Macmillan & Co. Ltd.).

194   J. Boswell, *Life of Samuel Johnson*, April 17th, 1778, vol. II, p. 441 (J. M. Dent & Co., 1901).

194   Textbook definitions of Potential Energy — see the present author's *Essay in Physics*, p. 151.

196   A. Einstein, *Out of My Later Years*, p. 56 (Philosophical Library, New York).

196   *Oxford English Dictionary*, vol. V, p. 243.

196   L. de Broglie, *The Revolution in Physics*, p. 93.

197   M. Born, *Natural Philosophy of Cause and Chance*, p. 75.

198   Light penetration — R. L. Carson, *The Sea Around Us*, p. 49 (Staples).

198   L. de Broglie, *op. cit.*, pp. 107, 197.

198   Atomic explosion temperature — Statement by Prime Minister on Atomic Bomb Test in Australia, *House of Commons' Debates*, October 23rd, 1952, col. 1277.

199   Sir E. Whittaker, *Aether and Electricity*, vol. II, pp. 38, 39.

200   Viscount Samuel, *Essay in Physics*, p. 78.

204   Light and sound — D. O. Sproule, 'Ultrasonic Techniques, Some Effects and Applications', *The Times Science Review*, Autumn 1952, p. 14.

206   Thomas Henry Huxley, *Lay Sermons*, pp. 65, 119, 126 (Macmillan & Co.). First published, 1870.

PAGE

207   D'Arcy W. Thompson, *Growth and Form*, pp. 14, 19 (C.U.P., 1951).

208   C. Lloyd Morgan, *The Emergence of Novelty* (Williams & Norgate).

208   E. D. Adrian, *The Physical Basis of Mind*, p. 5 (Basil Blackwell, Oxford, 1954).

208   Sir W. Russell Brain, *Mind, Perception and Science*, p. 2.

209   W. E. Le Gros Clark, *The Physical Basis of Mind*, p. 24.

209   Wilder Penfield, *The Physical Basis of Mind*, p. 64.

209   W. Grey Walter, *The Living Brain*, p. 180 (Gerald Duckworth & Co. Ltd., 1953).

210   J. E. Eccles, *The Neurophysiological Basis of Mind*, pp. 264-86 (Oxford, Clarendon Press, 1952).

211   A. S. Ewing, *The Relation between Mind and Body as a Problem for the Philosopher*, pp. 112, 119. Lecture to the Royal Institute of Philosophy, pub. in *Philosophy*, April 1954.

INDEX

INDEX